Taxation, Welfare and the Crisis of Unemployment in Europe

The views expressed are purely those of the authors and may not, and in any circumstances, be regarded as stating an official position of the Commission of the European Communities.

Taxation, Welfare and the Crisis of Unemployment in Europe

PUBLISHED ON BEHALF OF THE COMMISSION OF EUROPEAN COMMUNITIES

Edited by

Marco Buti

Head of Unit, Directorate-General for Economic and Financial Affairs, European Commission, Belgium

Paolo Sestito

Ministry of Labour, Italy

Hans Wijkander

Professor of Economics, Stockholm University, Sweden

Edward Elgar

Cheltenham, UK • Northampton, MA, USA

Published by
Edward Elgar Publishing Limited
Glensanda House
Montpellier Parade
Cheltenham
Glos GL50 1UA
UK

Edward Elgar Publishing, Inc.
136 West Street
Suite 202
Northampton
Massachusetts 01060
USA

A catalog record for this book is available from the British Library

Library of Congress Cataloging in Publication Data
Taxation, welfare, and the crisis of unemployment in Europe / edited by Marco Buti,
Paolo Sestito, Hans Wijkander.
    Includes bibliographical references and index.
    1. Labor supply—Effect of taxation on—European Union countries. 2. Welfare
recipients—Employment—European Union countries. 3. Unemployment—European
Union countries. 4. Public welfare—European Union countries. 5. Income tax—
European Union countries. I. Buti, Marco. II. Sestito, Paolo. III. Wijkander, Hans.

HD5764.A6 T39 2001
331.13'794—dc21

00–060973

ISBN 1 84064 511 3
Printed and bound in Great Britain by MPG Books Ltd, Bodmin, Cornwall

Contents

PART IV   GENERAL EQUILIBRIUM EFFECTS

Figures

Tables

The editors

Marco Buti is responsible for public finances at the Directorate-General for Economic and Financial Affairs, European Commission and visiting professor at the European University Institute (Italy). He is editor and co-author of *Economic Policy in EMU – A Study by the European Commission Services*, (Oxford University Press, 1998), and *The Welfare State in Europe – Challenges and Reforms*, (Edward Elgar, 1999).

Paolo Sestito has studied at the universities of Naples, Ancona and at the London School of Economics. He has worked at the Research Department of the Bank of Italy and as an economic adviser in the Directorate-General for Economic and Financial Affairs of the European Commission. He has published extensively on labour market issues.

Hans Wijkander is Professor of Economics at Stockholm University. From 1996–9, he was Economic Adviser at the Directorate-General for Economic and Financial Affairs, European Commission. His main research field is Public Economics with some work also in Contract Economics and Labour Market Analysis.

Other contributors

Sören Blomquist, Uppsala University, Sweden
Richard Blundell, University College and Institute for Fiscal Studies, London, UK
François Bourguignon, Delta and Ehess, Paris, France
Lans Bovenberg, CPB Netherlands and Bureau for Economic Policy Analysis, The Hague, The Netherlands
Michele Ca'Zorzi, European Central Bank, Frankfurt, Germany
Ruud de Mooij, CPB Netherlands and Bureau for Economic Policy Analysis, The Hague, The Netherlands
Matias Eklöf, Uppsala University, Sweden
Ricardo Fernández Bayón, Directorate-General for Economic and Financial Affairs, European Commission, Belgium
Johan Graafland, CPB Netherlands and Bureau for Economic Policy Analysis, The Hague, The Netherlands
Carlos Martínez Mongay, Directorate-General for Economic and Financial Affairs, European Commission, Belgium
Aino Salomäki, Directorate-General for Economic and Financial Affairs, European Commission, Belgium
Werner Roeger, Directorate-General for Economic and Financial Affairs, European Commission, Belgium

1. Overview

Marco Buti, Paolo Sestito and Hans Wijkander

1 TAX AND BENEFIT SYSTEMS AND THE EUROPEAN EMPLOYMENT CRISIS

Article 2 of the Treaty establishing the European Community stipulates that the Community should promote a high level of employment. The mix of structural and macroeconomic policies recommended to tackle the European unemployment problem has been outlined since the early 1990s in the *Broad Economic Policy Guidelines*. More recently, the *Employment Guidelines* have laid out the labour market elements of a co-ordinated European employment strategy. Both policy recommendations have emphasized the need to reform tax and welfare systems in Europe.

Lately, the special European Council in Lisbon in March 2000 reiterated the importance of assessing whether concrete measures are being implemented by EU countries 'to alleviate the tax pressure on labour and especially on the relatively unskilled and low-paid, improve the employment and training incentive effects of tax and benefit systems'. The European Commission has also contributed extensively to the intellectual debate on the reform of tax and welfare systems in Europe.[1]

The grave European unemployment problem dates back to the beginning of the 1970s and the deep recession caused by the first oil crisis. This led to significantly increased unemployment, from a pre-crisis level of 3–4 per cent, in both the EU countries and the US. Since then unemployment in the EU countries has increased gradually to the current, painful, double-digit level in several Member States, including Germany, France, Italy and Spain, the four largest in the euro area. During the 1970s, US unemployment was higher than that in the EU countries but it has since fallen and now hovers around 5 per cent.

The labour market problem in Europe is worrying, not only because of the level of unemployment, but also because of its features. Unemployment is very unevenly distributed, with 'fringe' workers (youngsters, elderly, women and ethnic minorities) bearing the brunt of it. In many countries, the employment rate of prime-aged men is comparable to that of the US (86 per cent on average in the 1990s in EU-15, compared with 87 per cent in the US). This holds true even in some of those EU countries with high overall unemployment. Another worrying feature is that unemployment is significantly more persistent in Europe than in the US. Half of those out of work in Europe have been so for over a year. Individuals who command lower wages are more likely to be unemployed and to remain so. Low-skilled unemployment is, in fact, double that of the high skilled (14 per cent compared with 7 per cent, in 1997). It must also be stressed that Europe's economic performance is hampered not only by low employment rates, but also by working-time patterns, though the situation varies across countries. The average number of hours worked per year in Europe is markedly lower than in the US (according to OECD data, 1952 in the latter country compared with 1559 in Germany, 1631 in France and 1544 in Sweden).

Although the causes of Europe's unemployment crisis have been much debated in both political and academic circles, no entirely conclusive results have emerged. Quite naturally, since the problem first appeared in a deep downturn, explanations were initially sought in terms of macroeconomic disturbances. Nowadays there seems to be a near consensus that structural factors play a significant role in aggravating the problem and, more generally, in thwarting Europe's work potential (see for example, Bean, 1994; IMF, 1999; and OECD, 1994). However, many structural factors can potentially contribute to the problem and here there is much less of a consensus about which factors are the more important. Nevertheless, tax and benefit systems have been singled out by many, including the EU, as potentially important and there is indeed scientific evidence that the working of tax and benefit systems can aggravate the above-mentioned negative features of the EU labour markets.[2]

That is not to say that higher tax and a larger public sector is unambiguously negative for employment. The net effect of taxation on employment may very well be positive if tax revenue is used to finance relative employment-intensive public production. The high-tax Scandinavian countries, where employment rates are also high, might well constitute examples. Some benefits (for example, removal subsidies) may also increase labour market flexibility and, through that, contribute to high employment. This means that the relation between tax and benefit systems and unemployment is complex; the share of aggregate income allocated through public sectors is far from being the only factor that matters. Microeconomic aspects of tax and benefit systems need to be considered as well.

However, there are some basic features of tax and benefit systems that undisputedly create negative incentives. A first observation: since taxes reduce the private return from working and unemployment benefits and as other public support programmes for unemployed or the poor reduce income losses during unemployment, incentives to take up or even search for a job are reduced when a worker is unemployed. These disincentives are probably stronger for unskilled workers since the levels of unemployment benefit and other social welfare safety nets are closer to their net incomes than to those of skilled workers. Although the debate on work disincentives at the low end of the productivity scale usually emphasizes workers' behaviour, firms' unwillingness to post wage offers too close to unemployment benefits because of efficiency wage considerations, as well as the existence of statutory or *de facto* minimum wages, may produce similar effects. Low-productivity workers are more frequently unemployed and for longer periods of time than are highly skilled workers. This means that the employment outcome for low-productivity workers is not necessarily only the result of opportunistic worker behaviour. This might motivate minimum wages upheld by labour market organizations being given some attention.

Second, the rather long period of time during which, in most countries, an unemployed worker can collect benefits, may contribute to the persistence of unemployment over time. Third, the interaction of tax and benefit rules often creates disincentives among low-skilled workers to increase hours of work. This may also hold true for those upper income workers facing the top income tax rates, but the compounded marginal effect of tax and transfers is, in many countries, higher at the low end of the income scale than in the middle or at the top of it.

Even institutional factors, such as differences in vacation time – either prescribed by law or by collective bargaining – may be shaped by the way taxes operate. A tax structure where many voters face high marginal income tax rates may lead to strong political pressure to increase statutory vacation time which, to an individual voter, would appear rather inexpensive.

Similar considerations to those concerning work effort and working time apply for incentives to acquire skills as a means to improve future job and income prospects. While the US ranks very high, with an enrolment rate to college and tertiary education of 21.5 per cent of persons between 22 and 25 years old in 1996, in the EU only Finland (28.8 per cent) and Denmark (23.5 per cent) show a higher enrolment rate. All the other member countries have lower enrolment rates (OECD, 1998). Although there may be a variety of other potential explanations for this observation – such as availability of college places and family education tradition – it is noteworthy that the US, where tuition fees are more common and where family support is more important than in European countries, ranks so highly. This may partly be the result of relatively low marginal income taxes that increase the private returns to education.[3]

Besides these negative effects, the tax and welfare system may contribute to aggravating the unemployment problem once we take into account its interplay with other labour market features (Buti *et al.*, 1998). It is, for example, plausible that generous unemployment benefits strengthen insider power on the labour market. This may make wages unresponsive to unemployment and sustain real-wage levels that, in turn, lead to extensive capital–labour substitution (see Daveri and Tabellini, 1997).

2   OPTIMAL TAXATION AND LABOUR SUPPLY

Early thinking on income taxation was mainly developed around the concept of 'ability to pay' or 'equal sacrifice', which indicate that equity was a dominant concern. Individual income was essentially viewed as unaffected by taxation and the most preferred tax schedule was therefore greatly affected by the particular interpretation of ability to pay or equal sacrifice. In more modern thinking on income taxation, the links between income tax schedules, labour supply and disposable income have come to play important roles. The shifts in focus probably, at least partly, depend on the fact that taxes are higher nowadays and have potentially larger distortive effects.

The most prominent theoretical contribution to the literature on optimal income taxation is Mirrlees (1971).[4] The analysis is based on a fundamental informational asymmetry: the individual worker but not the government is assumed to know his own individual ability to earn income. That is, government does not know individual productivity, and government cannot overcome this information disadvantage. However, government is assumed to know the statistical distribution of workers' productivity and to be able to observe individual income actually earned. This would follow from government inability to observe the working time or the effort required to earn the income, important determinants for individual utility. In such a framework of asymmetric and imperfect information, a tax system aimed at reducing income – or welfare – inequality would, not surprisingly, lead to distorted labour supply. The reason is that tax payments are contingent on income and not on ability to earn income, which drives a wedge between the before-tax and after-tax wage for the last hour worked. Under some circumstances the disutility of a low-productivity worker of taking up a job exceeds the net income increase when tax and transfer reductions are taken into account. That may induce low-productivity workers to choose inactivity.[5]

The basic trade-off in the income taxation problem can be illustrated in the framework of a linear income tax, that is, basic transfer to all workers financed through a proportional tax on income. Clearly, the more generous the basic transfer, the higher the tax rate has to be. The relation between the basic income and the non-active part of the labour force is clear, namely the greater the basic income the larger the number of workers who choose not to work.[6] Hence, more ambitious income redistribution comes with a larger number of inactive workers and it will be the least productive workers who will not consider it worthwhile to take up a job or to actively search for new employment when they have become unemployed. At higher productivity and wage levels the result is not as clear for, while increases in the marginal tax rate unambiguously tend to reduce labour supply through a substitution effect, the income effect normally works in the opposite direction. With a fully flexible tax schedule that allows for different marginal tax rates, in different income intervals, the distortions will be less pronounced, but will not disappear entirely. It is noteworthy that, in practice, tax systems are not fully flexible, owing to administrative costs. In most countries the tax schedule consists of several tax brackets. That is, it is piece-wise linear, which implies that the trade-off between generosity to the non-working low marginal income taxes is indeed present (see Lundholm *et al.*, 1994).

3   TRADE-OFFS FACING TAX–BENEFIT DESIGN AND REFORM

Designing and reforming a tax and benefit system involves a number of trade-offs such as between equity and efficiency, and between efficiency and stabilization. In the previous section we stressed how *equity and efficiency goals* may collide. As indicated, a tax and benefit system that is generous to the non-working may encourage some workers to choose inactivity, *the unemployment trap*. The effect concerning decisions on work effort and work hours is known as the *poverty trap*. In general, there is no radical 'way out' capable of fully circumventing this initial trade-off. For instance, relying uniquely on in-work benefits – so that the income support scheme is provided only to those individuals who are working – would certainly increase the incentives to take up a low paid job and reduce the effects of the unemployment trap. However, it might leave the unlucky ones who do not find a job in extreme poverty. Neither would the implementation of a universal benefit not conditional on the work status – the so-called negative income tax – serve as a radical 'way-out'. While it would allow provision of a minimum income to the socially excluded, it would dilute available resources, as the transfer would also finance individuals otherwise ready to take up a job.[7] Hence the policy-maker would still face the dilemma of either having to enact high enough marginal tax rates across the whole income range in order to raise enough resources for the very poor, or of re-introducing a steeper phasing-out of benefits, thereby reverting to the poverty trap situation created by the presence of a first income range with very high tax rates.

A second, potentially important trade-off is that between *efficiency and stabilization*. As noted above, reducing the distortions associated with the working of tax and benefit systems may require reducing marginal effective tax rates and limiting welfare generosity. More generally, it may entail trimming the size of government. However, these reforms – to the extent that they reduce tax progressivity and redistribute income towards individuals with a higher propensity to save – may lead to lower cyclical stabilization, since reduced taxes that follow on reduced income may not affect consumption significantly. A lower progressivity of the tax system may therefore reduce the stabilizing effects of the tax system. This trade-off has a dynamic dimension too. For instance, long duration or open-ended benefits may be stabilization-friendly but, by hindering structural adjustment, may harm efficiency and growth in the longer term. This is a potentially important problem especially when long-lasting shocks, rather than temporary cyclical fluctuations, hit the economy. In such a case, as noticed by Mélitz (1997), 'too much' stabilization would be particularly undesirable in Europe, where structural adjustment is already very slow.

As mentioned later in section 7, the efficiency–stabilization trade-off may become increasingly important in the future. Indeed, flexibility of tax and benefit systems to macroeconomic conditions is important in EMU where the participating countries have lost the monetary and exchange rate policies as national instruments of stabilizing the cycle and responding to country-specific shocks or compensating for different responses to monetary policy. A major challenge to tax and benefit reform is to make the tax and benefit system efficient in stabilizing the economy while limiting the size of the public sector and maintaining an essentially market economy.

Tax and welfare reform also involves other trade-offs somewhat outside the Musgravian tradition. A trade-off rarely addressed in the literature is that between *horizontal equity* and *administrative simplicity*. Horizontal equity means that individuals regarded as identical in all relevant respects should be treated equally. In principle, this is a very natural property requirement of a tax and welfare system, but its implementation is far from simple. A tax and welfare system that aspires to levying taxes and granting support in accordance with very 'fine tuned' equity judgements may be costly to administer in advanced economies. Should very large administrative resources be devoted to ensuring that identical individuals get identical treatment by the tax and welfare system? If not, one would need to accept a degree of randomness in the tax and welfare system which may still be regarded as horizontally equitable provided there is no systematic favouring or disfavouring or apparently identical individuals.[8] Hence, administrative simplicity may be achieved through sacrifices in terms of *ex post* horizontal equity.

4   COMMON FORCES PUSHING TOWARDS REFORM

What is the empirical relevance of these trade-offs? Do they impinge in the same way across all countries? Have they become more important over time?

While many factors are at work, a number of trends point to a rising importance of the disincentive problems generated by the tax and benefit system. A first factor is the increasing heterogeneity of production and working patterns linked to technological and organizational innovation. For instance, the poverty trap does not have much relevance if individuals face take-it-or-leave-it job opportunities, undifferentiated in terms of duration, hours worked and effort level. However, the current trend may very well be towards a 'customization' of working patterns. The spread of flexible work organizations implies that individuals now have wider work effort and work hours choices, which seems to indicate that the work incentive distortions are becoming more important.

A second element is the rise of non-breadwinner groups, in particular women, as a share of the total work-force. Such a rise may have increased average labour supply elasticity, particularly as far as the lowest segments of the labour market are concerned, and increased the room for tax arbitrage behaviour.

A third trend is the significant change in the distribution of worker productivity, which, on the basis of the evidence on increased wage differences in the US, and to some extent the UK, has taken place since the late 1970s or the early 1980s.[9] Without adjustment of the tax and welfare system such a change may result in several problems. It may be, for example, that the number of inactive workers increases as the number of low productive workers increases, resulting in increased welfare payments and other transfers at the same time as tax revenue falls from workers in the lower end of the income distribution.[10]

While the above trends play an increasingly important role, probably the most relevant factor acting towards a sharpening of the trade-offs previously described comes from the increased ambitions of social insurance. The all-encompassing nature of the system gives rise to many possibilities for opportunistic behaviour to exploit the system in unintended ways, for example, by allowing frequent changes from unemployment benefits to other welfare schemes. That makes the task of piecemeal reform largely ineffective.

5 BUT CROSS-COUNTRY DIFFERENCES REMAIN

While all industrialized countries seem to face a set of common problems and trends, many differences arise in the concrete shape taken by policy trade-offs and in their empirical relevance.

A first factor concerns prevailing social preferences about the equity–efficiency trade-off. Not only do countries' tastes over the relative importance of the two objectives differ, but there are also historical differences among countries with regard to implementation of equity policies. In some countries, the welfare system is targeted to the relief of the poorest while, in others transfers are widespread across the board. These choices hinge on ethical judgements as well as on economic considerations and traditions. For instance, supporting the least favoured individuals by bringing them back into the labour market has ethical implications, which differ greatly from those of supporting their income through transfers.

A second element concerns the way the tax and benefit system interacts with the various features of the labour market such as wage-setting institutions, active labour market policies and job-security provisions. It is not surprising that Anglo-Saxon countries – where wages are largely market determined – are those which have tended to resort to in-work benefit schemes. In those countries, wages can be expected to adjust to such schemes, while they might prove to be a less adequate means of raising incomes, reducing wage costs and promoting employment in countries characterized by strong unions, a relatively centralized bargaining system and a minimum wage – be it statutory or fixed through collective bargaining.[11] Hence, a number of continental countries (for example, France, Italy and Germany, though with different details and coverage) have opted for social security rebates and regulatory reforms which, at least at the market fringes, have lowered labour costs without requiring wages to be reduced and allowed the creation of low-productivity jobs.[12] Whether wage costs will, at a later stage, be restored is of course still an open question.

Tax and benefits are to be viewed also in relation to active labour market policies (hereafter, ALMPs). Well designed ALMPs may, by improving skills and qualifications, increase employment opportunities and long-run earning ability, lessen the risk that the most disfavoured people remain trapped in long-term unemployment or low-wage jobs. Hence, ALMPs may ease the equity–efficiency trade-off since being temporarily in a low wage job represents less of an equity problem than being in such a job for a long time or permanently.[13] However, in order for ALMPs to successfully reintegrate the least favoured people into the market, a flexible enough labour market with sufficiently many job openings and a benefit system that does not unnecessarily distort incentives is required. That said, ALMPs are usually rather costly, require an efficient administration and may therefore be difficult to implement on a very large scale, given a large pool of unemployed.[14] All these elements suggest the need for a prudent and experimental approach, with a careful evaluation of both the design and implementation of ALMPs, taking into account their interplay with tax and benefit systems at large.

Finally, tax and benefit systems interact with employment protection legislation (EPL) since the aim of EPL, as well as the benefit system, is to provide income stability to employees. (Another aim of EPL could be to limit excessive firing and loss of human capital in downturns.) Hence, to the extent that they respond to the same type of market failure (lack of private insurance against unemployment risk), they can be seen as substitutes, implying that they need to be considered together.

An aspect of income security not frequently discussed is labour market 'liquidity', that is, sufficiently many job openings.[15] With a high degree of labour market liquidity the loss of a job need not necessarily imply large income losses and therefore the need for unemployment insurance and EPL may be less pronounced. Paradoxically, with less generous unemployment benefits and given suitable macroeconomic conditions, the labour market might be more liquid, as evidenced/demonstrated by the current situation in the US. This may reduce the need for EPL and unemployment insurance.

An interesting feature of US unemployment is the very low levels of long-term unemployment. However, empirical evidence shows that this high flexibility is achieved through a high degree of willingness among American workers to accept sizable wage reductions to get a new job when, for one reason or another they have become unemployed.[16] In continental Europe, the overall level of income security is higher than in Anglo-Saxon countries, although the situation differs substantially between European countries. *Ceteris paribus* this lowers European workers' willingness to accept downward wage adjustment and may therefore contribute to long-term unemployment. Although the American solution seems more efficient in making use of (scarce) labour, it seems that something has to be sacrificed on the efficiency altar.

Well developed ALMPs represent a way to reduce the efficiency losses that well developed income security and EPL create and can therefore be seen as sensible complements to such policies. This may reduce, but probably not eliminate, the efficiency disadvantage of the highly protective European type of institutions. Some European countries have indeed opted for such a combination of security and adjustment stimulating policy. Hence, liberal labour market regulations, coupled with generous unemployment compensation and extensive ALMPs, are found in Denmark, Finland, Sweden and the Netherlands. Such a combination of benefits and job protection may favour mobility and resource reallocation. Italy and Greece are at the opposite end of the spectrum, with under-developed benefit and training systems and high job-security provisions, especially for permanent workers: such a combination is bound to become increasingly inefficient since accelerated integration, globalization and higher competition require high mobility and smooth factor reallocation.

6 REFORMS ARE UNDER WAY BUT ARE THEY SUFFICIENT?

By and large, the principles of the tax and welfare systems in most EU countries were laid down in the first decades after the Second World War and have not undergone fundamental changes since. After a period of expansion up to the beginning of the 1980s, changes have been of a gradual type, mostly motivated by expenditure-trimming objectives, particularly in recent years.[17]

Although fundamental reforms are scarce, many piecemeal, partial measures spanning all aspects of tax and welfare systems are now being taken in EU countries. Reform measures include:[18]

1. Simplification of the tax system, broadening the tax base, reducing taxes on labour and reducing the shadow economy. Sweden, Denmark, Spain, Italy, Portugal and the Netherlands have made important reforms in their tax systems along these lines.
2. Tightening of eligibility criteria, with stricter definitions of work availability requirements and tougher sanctions on those refusing to take up a job or a training course – Denmark, Finland, Germany, Sweden and the UK. Administration of benefits has been improved. In some cases, the duration of benefits and/or replacement ratios has been reduced in an attempt to curb work disincentives – Denmark, Ireland, the Netherlands, Spain and Sweden. So far, however, the effects of these measures on expenditure levels and number of beneficiaries are unclear.
3. In the UK, introducing income disregards and allowing for a gradual withdrawal of benefits has modified in-work benefits aimed at topping up low wages.
4. A number of targeted measures to reduce labour costs for the low skilled have been put in place to increase the demand for low-skilled labour. Action to curb high marginal effective tax rates has been taken in several countries, for example, Denmark, France, Ireland, the Netherlands, Sweden and the UK. In some cases such as the Netherlands, overall tax wedges on labour have been reduced.

Do the on-going changes move in the right direction? Is the pace of reform sufficient to tackle the challenges outlined above? While a complete answer to these questions goes well beyond the scope of this introduction, a few general remarks can be offered.

Given the differences in traditional social policy orientations and labour market institutions, it is not surprising that the many interventions carried out in countries in the EU, and more generally in the OECD, have not been following a common blueprint. The fragmented approach and piecemeal nature of these interventions (documented also in this volume) are not worrying *per se*, since technical complexity of the reforms and the interplay of several features and institutions 'naturally' call for a cautious experimental approach. Under this interpretation, partial reforms might form part of a sequential strategy eventually leading to efficiency-enhancing changes.

However, less optimistic scholars stress a number of 'political economy' mechanisms that work as obstacles to a bolder approach to welfare reform. Pierson (1996) and Saint-Paul (1995a and 1995b) suggest that when welfare systems are large and complex, uncertainties about overall advantages of reform, as well as a clear identification of winners and losers, make it difficult to establish a political constituency supporting a complete overhaul of the system. Social and political resistance to change in social protection systems may also be a reaction to the increasing openness of economies. As pointed out by Bean *et al.* (1998), trade with developing countries – which specialize in low-skill intensive products – tends to exert a downward pressure on wages of low-income workers, a category of individuals who benefit most from resource redistribution provided by tax and benefit systems. Hence, they are likely to resist welfare reforms, which tilt the equity–efficiency trade-off to their disadvantage.

7 EMU ENHANCES THE EU ROLE

The rising EU attention on the reform of tax and benefit systems derives not only from the worsening of the employment situation, but also from the acceleration of economic and monetary integration. On the one hand, increased factor and consumer mobility tends to reduce national governments' freedom to tax available resources for redistributive purposes. Revenue losses may arise from the movement of tax bases towards countries applying lower tax rates; the role of benefit-taxation and user charges, etc. is bound to increase, while that of ability-to-pay taxation is likely to be restrained.

On the other hand, the need to use the tax and benefits system as a shock absorber is enhanced by the absence of national monetary independence. Tax and welfare systems will have to provide adequate built-in macroeconomic stabilization but they must also facilitate adjustment at the microeconomic level. The latter function will also gain in importance in the future since higher trade integration will increase competition and spur organizational and technological innovation, thereby increasing the relevance of the micro and structural shocks *vis-à-vis* the macroeconomic and aggregate disturbances. Accommodating these two tasks within the tax and benefit system is indeed a challenge to tax and benefit reform.

The EMU institutional arrangement – multiple fiscal authorities *cum* one monetary authority – has implications for the reform strategy. With national monetary independence, countries adopting efficiency-enhancing reforms might count on a supportive monetary stance since the reforms reduce inflationary bottlenecks by improving labour flexibility. In EMU, since the concern of the European Central Bank is the average inflation in the euro area, an accompanying monetary response would not be forthcoming in the event of isolated reforms in individual countries. This lack of response may possibly lower the incentives to an individual country to reform and may therefore call for a co-ordinated strategy.[19]

For political economy reasons, supranational co-ordination may also ease the social acceptance of reforms domestically. Such spillovers provide a further rationale for the call in the 1999 *Employment Guidelines to Member States* to 'review and, where appropriate, re-focus its benefit and tax system and provide incentives for unemployed or inactive people to seek and take up work or measures to enhance their employability and for employers to create new jobs'.[20]

8   THIS VOLUME

The papers collected in this volume analyse the role of European tax and benefit systems in incentives to create and take up jobs.

The first chapter by Bourguignon, provides an overview of some basic issues relating to the trade-off between equity and efficiency. The discussion is based on the nowadays standard framework of optimum income taxation. The issues are, first, to what extent taxes and transfers actually redistribute net income among different income classes. He concludes that there is considerable redistribution through the tax and benefit systems and, in countries where the average tax rate is high, most of the redistribution comes from the benefit system. The intuition for the latter conclusion is that, where average tax rates are high, taxes are usually broad-based and close to proportional. A second issue is how marginal tax rates vary according to gross income, were they the optimum rates. This issue is highly relevant since it can be questioned whether the marginal tax rates we observe in many countries are warranted from an optimality point of view, that is, relatively high effective marginal tax rates at very low income levels and also rather high levels at the top. Optimum marginal income tax rates, of course, depend on many factors such as social preferences over income distribution; the responses of labour supply to marginal net income, income elasticity of labour supply, government non-transfer expenditure, and so on. The discussion is carried out in the simplest possible framework and it is shown that, under quite reasonable assumptions, optimum tax schemes involve high marginal income taxes at low income levels. The reason is that the large distortionary effects at low income levels – in many cases involving (voluntary) unemployment – are balanced against the negative labour supply effects of high marginal income taxes at higher income and productivity levels. The lesson to be learned from this is that, within the informational setting of the Mirrlees' type of optimum taxation model, one should, in fact, expect quite high marginal tax rates in the lower end of the income distribution when the average tax pressure is high. If that were a highly undesirable outcome, one would have to question the setting or the level of the average tax pressure.

The next four papers describe the burden of taxation and the generosity of the welfare systems in Europe.

The optimum taxation framework indicates that unemployment among low productive workers may be a consequence of high effective marginal tax at low income levels which, in turn, seems to be related to a high average tax pressure. The chapter by Martínez Mongay and Fernández Bayón (Ch. 3) adds to the analysis of the first by outlining average tax pressure development over time in EU Member States and its interplay with government spending behaviour. It also covers a number of issues dealt with in the first chapter and in recent literature on the relation between taxation and unemployment in Europe. The paper starts by analysing the evolution of the tax wedge – the difference between the gross wage and the wage net of taxes – across EU Member States, the US and Japan over the period 1970–98. The analysis focuses on the effective taxation on labour, which is given by total compensation to labour in the national account, divided by total non-wage labour costs and personal income taxes. The comparison between the EU as a whole and the US reveals that the effective taxation on labour is higher and has increased much more on the European side of the Atlantic. In parallel, the size of the public sector in European economies is larger than in the US, and employment performance has, overall, been poorer. While these correlations are suggestive, by themselves they do not necessarily imply causality. In order to provide answers, the chapter explores the causal relationships linking taxes, expenditure and labour market outcomes and concludes that there seems to be a strong causal relationship running from expenditure to the level of labour taxation and from the level of labour taxation to unemployment.

The chapter by Aino Salomäki (Ch. 4) deals with the disincentives associated with unemployment insurance and other benefits. European unemployment benefit system is a cause of concern because, as discussed above, the gains from provision of unemployment insurance are accompanied by potentially serious efficiency losses. The need for reform is clear, but the critical question is how to provide a necessary safety net for the unemployed without unduly reducing work incentives.

The chapter reviews and examines various approaches to comparing the living standard of the unemployed with those in work. A new indicator is developed from data obtained from the European Community Household Panel.

There are two important findings with regard to labour market policy in this study. First, it confirms that, regardless of the approach applied, net replacement rates for low-paid workers are higher than for the rest of wage distribution. Hence, work incentives for this group are weaker and a larger number of low-productivity workers are more likely to be found trapped in unemployment. Second, unemployment benefits are often complemented or substituted by other benefits. In many countries, benefits such as housing allowance or social assistance keep the net replacement rate high for a long period if unemployment continues. As the take-up rate of benefits in general among the unemployed is higher than that of unemployment benefit alone, the study concludes that the whole range of benefits needs to be taken into account in order to gain a full picture of the working of benefit systems.

Sestito and Ca'Zorzi (Ch. 5) provide a preliminary assessment of the impact of reforms on the GDP share of social protection expenditure across EU countries, taking account of the responsiveness of social protection expenditure to employment fluctuations. The chapter does not support the notion of a general reduction of social protection expenditure. In qualitative terms, marginal changes to the welfare system have been more frequent but have tended to offset one another. Cuts in some welfare components have simply been matched by expansions in others. The results also show that several categories of expenditure have reacted strongly to the employment cycle, although formally not targeted at the relief of joblessness. EU countries differ considerably, not only in their total and internal composition of social protection expenditure, but also in the way expenditure responds to the employment cycle. Broadly speaking, welfare expenditures are found to be less reactive in the Mediterranean countries than in the Nordic and Anglo-Saxon countries, with the remaining continental countries in a mid-way position.

Part III addresses the topic of how to evaluate the effects of tax and welfare reforms. Blundell (Ch. 6) deals with methods for evaluating labour supply responses to income support to low-income workers who actually take up jobs. Interest in such a programme has increased in the US and the UK given the increased wage differences between skilled and unskilled workers and a fall in the absolute level of real wages of unskilled workers since the late 1970s. These developments threaten to reduce labour supply among low-income workers and give rise to increased unemployment. In such a context, tax and benefit reforms that make work pay become increasingly interesting and so also do methods to evaluate labour supply responses to reforms. However, since the question of taking up a job or not usually involves large changes in labour supply – switching between unemployment and a full-time job for example – evaluation cannot be based on too simplistic a labour supply view.

An additional problem with such reform is that while a given scheme may provide a sufficiently strong economic incentive for an inactive worker to take up a job, it may at the same time give rise to incentives among already active workers to reduce labour supply. The reason is that the economic incentives to take up a job must at some income levels be phased out, which increases the effective marginal income tax for workers in this income interval. Such a scheme might increase income for one worker in a family, but render the family ineligible for the support should the spouse also take up employment. This implies that the effective marginal income tax becomes very high and that the spouse is therefore strongly discouraged from working. Which of these effects dominate is a purely empirical question and the answer to it may give hints for the appropriate design of in-work benefit reforms.

Three evaluation methods are discussed in the chapter. The first, the Quasi-Experimental Approach, is discussed in relation to the Canadian Self-Sufficiency Programme. The method is similar to that used in experiments in natural sciences in that a group of individuals is subjected to the reform while another group serves as a control group. The second method, the Natural Experiment Approach, is applied to the US Earned Income Tax Credit. Again a group of individuals is affected by the reform and is compared with a control group. A feature of this method is that it aims to eliminate effects on labour supply from the cycle by comparing differences before and after the experiment between the two groups. The third is the Discrete Choice Structural Approach. This method uses microeconometrics to estimate parameters by governing individual choice. These parameters are then used to simulate labour supply responses to reforms. Ordinary labour supply elasticities are not sufficient for doing this as workers face non-convex budget constraints which implies that small policy changes can lead to 'jumps' in behaviour.

The chapter by Blomquist and Ekelöf (Ch. 7) deals with labour supply effects of tax reforms in Sweden in the 1980s and 1990s, which were not primarily concerned with low-productive worker labour market participation as it was not a political issue in Sweden at that time. It describes a series of tax reforms that took place from the beginning of the 1980s to 1991, culminating in a major reform in 1991. The starting point of the reforms was a situation with a complicated tax system with many deductions and special rules that opened up possibilities for tax planning which reduced the tax burden for some taxpayers in non-intended ways. Another feature was the extremely high statutory marginal income tax for people with normal income. The reforms aimed to bring down marginal tax rates for most taxpayers by broadening the tax base and simplifying tax rules. Distributional neutrality over income groups was a constraint on the reforms. Thus, changes occurred in income tax schedules, commodity taxation, real estate taxation, government transfers, and so on.

Blomquist and Ekelöf decompose the effects on labour supply of the various major reforms for taxpayers with different wage rates and summarize that information in 'mongrel functions', that is, functions that map gross wage rates on preferred hours of work. They find that the changes in marginal income taxes increase labour supply for all gross wage levels while the changes in capital income taxation, VAT and transfers all go in the other direction. The net effect on labour supply is that the reductions in marginal income taxes dominate the other effects, and more so the higher the income. Unfortunately, this major reform coincided with the deepest business downturn for several decades in Sweden, which affected both participation and hours worked and thus hampered the acquisition of knowledge as to its effects.

The chapter by Bovenberg, Graafland and de Mooij (Ch. 8) describes policy changes in the Netherlands that have taken place since the beginning of the 1980s. These changes were aimed at curing the 'Dutch disease' characterized by the combination of aggressive trade union policies, low employment rate, high unemployment and a high fiscal burden, which form a vicious circle when the factors sustain each other. To find the cure, discussions took place between trade unions, employers federations and government to establish a near consensus view on the nature of the problems and then to formulate a strategy to tackle them. Providing each of the parties involved with an overview of the complete package of required changes probably facilitated getting all parties aboard and the successful implementation of changes. A key feature of the package was wage moderation whereby nominal wage increases were small in exchange for tax reductions partly financed by reductions in transfers. That component led to increased profits, investment, and made it possible for Dutch firms to increase exports.

The package also involved changes aimed, in particular, at increasing labour supply. Hence, the social security system was reformed with tighter eligibility criteria and lower replacement rates. Marginal income taxes were also lowered. It seems likely that these reforms affect labour supply of low-productivity workers and second income earners in particular. The reforms appear to have been successful and Dutch economic performance during the last fifteen years or so is sometimes referred to as 'the Dutch miracle'. The chapter also presents an evaluation tool. Changes of the type described above have significant effects on both production and consumption. As it is difficult for policy makers to examine each channel through which reforms work and also to account for interactions among different effects, the authors suggest a computable general equilibrium model. Their model, MIMIC, is used for policy experiments in the Netherlands.

Finally, the chapter by Roeger and Wijkander (Ch. 9) deals with tax solutions to one presumed cause of European unemployment, namely, skill-biased technical progress in combination with rigid relative wages. The recent development on the US, and to some extent UK, labour markets whereby wage differences between skilled and unskilled workers have increased is the starting point of the chapter. This development has been followed by reductions in unemployment. In continental European countries, wage differences have not changed significantly, but there have been increases in unemployment levels. Economists have argued that these developments are one another's mirror images. An underlying skill-biased technical progress is a potential cause of the developments since, in combination with flexible relative wages, it would cause increased wage differences and, together with rigid relative wages, unemployment.

The chapter develops a computable two-sector, two skills-type, two-commodity model – the two sectors, manufacturing and services; the two skill-types, skilled and unskilled workers; and the two commodities, manufacturing and services. The model is calibrated for France, not only to reflect the outcome at a given moment in time, but also to replicate growth trends. The calibration shows that skill-biased technical progress is indeed necessary to explain the development in certain crucial variables. A number of policy experiments aimed at reducing the unemployment rate are carried out within the calibrated model. The first experiment seeks to abolish relative wage rigidity, the second to tax the more skill-intensive commodity and subsidize the less skill-intensive commodity; the third experiment is to increase progressivity in income tax. Although not completely unexpected, the experiments point to a variety of welfare effects on different types of workers of different policies. This suggests that it may be politically difficult to implement some of the policies. The authors show that general equilibrium effects through commodity prices may outweigh direct effects from increased income taxes.

The contributions in this volume are theoretically and empirically rigorous and are careful to re-trace the microeconomic foundations of claims (or allegations) about the impact of tax and benefit systems on labour market performance. The analyses are rooted in the concrete experience of European countries, which makes the policy conclusions all the more relevant.

Re-designing tax and benefit systems in Europe is a difficult task. However, the unemployment emergency, the increasing relevance of spillovers of 'bad' domestic policies on partner countries in EMU and peer pressure from closer policy co-operation, are all gradually eroding resistance to change. Tax and welfare systems are being reformed throughout the EU. Nevertheless, fear of undermining the equity foundations of the European social model and difficulty in attaining political support for change hinder radical reforms and may also diminish possibilities to change several interdependent systems, either simultaneously or in sequence.

As corroborated by these analyses, European policy makers now face tough choices. Reforms are costly and 'win–win' moves are scarce. Recognizing and understanding the complex trade-offs – a precondition to pushing the reform process forward – is the aim of this volume.

NOTES

1. See, for example, the companion volume Buti *et al.* (1999).
2. See Ljungqvist and Sargent (1998).

3. Furthermore, relatively high college premiums on gross wages also contribute to high private returns to college education.
4. James Mirrlees was awarded the 1997 Nobel Prize in economics for that contribution.
5. Bunching at the bottom is a well-known phenomenon in the literature on income taxation, see for example, Atkinson and Stiglitz (1980).
6. This result holds under the reasonable assumption that marginal utility of income decreases when labour supply increases from zero.
7. A negative income tax conditional on effective job search, as proposed by Snower (1995), may contribute to alleviate such a problem.
8. If one is prepared to accept a degree of randomness in the treatment of identical individuals, the question can be raised if one could also deliberately introduce some elements of randomness in the tax and welfare system provided identical individuals are *ex ante* treated equally. In theoretical models it has been shown that such deliberate randomness can lead to *ex ante* Pareto improvements (see Brito *et al.*, 1995).
9. See Juhn *et al.* (1993). The factors underpinning the changes in wage dispersion in the US often mentioned in the literature are technology changes, trade with developing countries, immigration of low-skilled workers and decreased unionization. Evidence of a skill-biased technical progress is found in Roeger and Wijkander, Ch. 9 this volume.
10. This implies that the tax and welfare system may have to be adjusted so that it becomes less generous to inactive or needy workers or tax revenue from workers at higher income levels can be increased, or some combination of the two adjustments. Although it is not entirely clear, the rather large tax reform in the US in the mid-1980s seems to be rather close to the combination of the two adjustments. Welfare systems became less generous while tax loopholes were closed and tax bases widened. The latter adjustments probably increased tax revenue from middle-income earners.
11. Note, however, that a relatively low minimum wage may be justified in countries with in-work benefits to the extent that monopsony exists in the labour market. In such a case, a wage floor, by preventing the firm from setting wages too low (that is, below marginal productivity of labour), would be beneficial for employment.
12. The two alternative routes are also characterized by different administrative aspects and presuppose a different worker–firm relationship. In one case the firm is cashing the rebate (not necessarily well known to the worker), while in the other case the worker is claiming for a tax allowance (and sometimes for a more favourable earnings-disregard) with the individual firm not necessarily informed.
13. In the recent US welfare reform experience, they have been very often instrumental in cutting open-ended benefits without abandoning the neediest people. For an analysis of how financial incentives (in-work benefits and the expansion in the federal EITC) have interacted with activation measures in the recent US experience, see Blank *et al.* (1999).
14. The dramatic increase in the number of unemployed following the external shock at the beginning of the 1990s may be at the roots of the strain of Sweden's ALMP-based welfare system.
15. One usually brands a market for a particular financial security as liquid if there are many transactions taking place in the security in question. The idea is that if this is the case there is an established market price of the security and the security can easily be sold and bought.
16. Such loss of income is, however, much lower in the US than in highly regulated economies. Indeed, while the likelihood of losing one's job is considerably lower in continental Europe, the loss of income a worker is confronted with when firing actually occurs is high. Focusing on prime-age men, Cohen (1999) finds that such loss of income is twice as large in France than in the US.
17. Although there are some examples of rather large changes, such as the reduction in the generosity of the welfare state in the UK in the 1980s and the discrete drastic cut in marginal income tax rates in Sweden in 1991.
18. The following list of measures and countries is only for illustrative purposes and does not pretend to be exhaustive.
19. These arguments are similar to those concerning the incentives for labour market reform in EMU. For a discussion of the various mechanisms at work, see Calmfors (1998).

20. In this context, co-ordination does not mean harmonization such as the imposition of common 'social standards' which, by reducing the flexibility of wages across countries and regions still characterized by very differentiated productivity levels, would be likely to have harmful consequences.

REFERENCES

Atkinson, A. and J. Stiglitz (1980), *Lectures on Public Economics*, New York: McGraw-Hill.
Bean, C. (1994), 'European Unemployment: A Survey', *Journal of Economic Literature*, **XXXII**: 573–619.
Bean, C., S. Bentolila, G. Bertola and J. Dolado (1998), *Social Europe: One for All?*, CEPR Monitoring European Integration, 8.
Blank, R.M., D. Card and P.K. Robins (1999), 'Financial Incentives for Increasing Work and Income Among Low-Income Families', mimeo.
Brito, D.L., J.H. Hamilton, S.M. Slutsky, and LP. Stiglitz, (1995), 'Randomization in Optimal Income Tax Schedules', *Journal of Public Economics*, **56**(2): 189–223.
Buti, M., D. Franco and L.R. Pench (eds) (1999), *The Welfare State in Europe – Challenges and Reforms*, Cheltenham, UK and Northampton, MA: Edward Elgar.
Buti, M., L.R. Pench and P. Sestito (1998), European Unemployment: Contending Theories and Institutional Complexities', *EIB Economic and Financial Reports*, 1.
Calmfors, L. (1998), 'Macroeconomic Policy, Wage Setting, and Employment – What Difference Does EMU Make?', *Oxford Review of Economic Policy*, **14**(3): 125–51.
Cohen, D. (1999), 'Welfare Differentials Across French and US Labor Markets', *CEPR Discussion Paper*, 2114.
Daveri, F. and G. Tabellini (1997), 'Unemployment, Growth and Taxation in Industrial Countries', *CEPR Discussion Paper*, 1681.
IMF (1999), *World Economic Outlook*, Washington.
Juhn, C., K.M. Murphy and B. Pierce (1993), 'Wage Inequality and the Rise in Returns to Skill', *Journal of Political Economy*, **101**(3): 410–42.
Ljungqvist, L. and T. Sargent, (1998), 'The European Unemployment Dilemma', *Journal of Political Economy*, **106**: 514–50.
Lundholm, M., J. Slemrod, S. Yitzhaki and J. Mayshar (1994), 'The Optimal Two-Bracket Linear Income Tax', *Journal of Public Economics*, **53**: 269–90.
Mélitz, J. (1997), 'The Evidence About Costs and Benefits of EMU', *Swedish Economic Policy Review*, Autumn: 359–410.
Mirrlees, J. (1971), 'An Exploration in the Theory of Optimum Income Taxation', *Review of Economic Studies*, **38**: 175–208.
OECD (1994), *The Jobs Study*, Paris.
OECD (1998), *Employment Outlook*, Paris.
Pierson, P. (1996), 'The New Politics of the Welfare State', *World Politics*, **48**: 143–79.
Saint-Paul, G. (1995a), 'Labour Market Institutions and the Cohesion of the Middle Class', *CEPR Discussion Paper*, 1298.
Saint-Paul, G. (1995b), 'Reforming Europe's Labour Market: Political Issues', *CEPR Discussion Paper*, 1223.
Snower, D.J. (1995), 'Unemployment Benefit versus Conditional Negative Income Tax', *IMF Working Paper*, 96.

PART I

The Issues

2. Redistribution and labour-supply incentives[1]

François Bourguignon[2]

INTRODUCTION

A growing concern in many developed countries during the last ten years or so has been that generous redistribution systems might be detrimental to those they are intended to help. By guaranteeing a minimum income or an income supplement to those whose purchasing power falls below a given limit, these systems would be responsible for strong labour-supply disincentives, the cost of which may be very high. In particular, recipients of such benefits may find themselves progressively marginalized from the labour market. What was once found a major social conquest is thus increasingly seen as the source of social problems and in particular as a possible cause for social exclusion. The rolling back of the Welfare State began some years ago in the US with the limitation of the duration of eligibility for welfare benefits. In the UK, a debate is currently taking place about ways of re-establishing work incentives while maintaining redistribution principles.[3] Similar concerns exist in continental European countries where strong income guarantee programmes have been developed over the last two or three decades.

The major difficulty in dealing with these issues is that our current knowledge of the labour-supply behaviour of low-skill or low-ability persons is limited. The development of labour-supply econometrics since the 1970s has not delivered what was hoped for. Without some explicit large-scale social experimentation it is unlikely that we will be able to measure with desired accuracy the elasticity of labour income or labour supply with respect to after tax wage rates, especially at the two extremes of the distribution of abilities which are the most important from a social welfare point of view. But the implementation of such controlled experiments would raise serious ethical and social problems and, to date, the so-called 'natural experiments' that economists are eager to follow have proved to be of limited use. Although all must be done to improve our empirical knowledge of labour-supply behaviour, we must admit that we do not know enough to come up with satisfactory applications of existing theoretical models of optimal redistribution. Decisions about keeping existing redistribution systems as they are, or reforming them, must therefore be made with a rather large degree of ignorance.

In this chapter, I intend briefly to review the various basic elements on which policy analysis and policy-making in this field should be grounded. I consider successively the following questions. a) *Where do we stand* in the field of redistribution? How do existing redistribution systems in European countries work and perform in the equity/efficiency space? b) *Where would we like to go?* Are there general lessons to be learned from optimal taxation theory? Or is that framework essentially inconclusive because it is based on too simple a model of labour-supply or on parameters of which empirical knowledge is too imprecise? c) *What can we practically do?* Are there reforms of existing systems that may be deemed desirable even with our imperfect knowledge of labour-supply behaviour? In particular, would some version of the basic income–linear income tax scheme, for which there seems to be some renewal of interest, be such?

Before attempting to answer this ambitious set of questions, I must point to some obvious limitations of this presentation. First, because of space restrictions, I make no attempt at exhaustivity in the way this chapter covers the (huge) existing empirical and theoretical literature on redistribution and labour-supply incentives. Second, very much of the material I shall be reviewing is taken from various recent projects in which I have been involved and also sometimes from others, not yet fully completed.[4] Third, the focus of this chapter is on the low income part of the distribution scale. While labour-supply response is equally if not more important elsewhere in the distribution scale and, in particular, at the top, I shall say comparatively little on the various attempts made to identify labour-supply behaviour in that part of the distribution.

1   EQUITY AND EFFICIENCY IN PRESENT REDISTRIBUTION SYSTEMS: SELECTED CASES IN EUROPE

The size of taxes and social security contributions, that is, all 'mandatory contributions' relative to GDP is often taken as a measure of the importance of redistribution in a given country.[5] A simple international comparison shows that this may be quite misleading, however. Table 2.1 shows, for instance, that total mandatory contributions in the mid-1990s amounted to approximately 45 per cent in France and Germany but only to 35 per cent in the UK, although this does not mean that redistribution is much less important in the latter country. The difference simply reflects the fact that part of the UK pension system is privately funded, whereas publicly managed pay-as-you-go systems are in operation in France and Germany. Once these insurance-like premia, or at least that part which closely corresponds to actuarially neutral insurance mechanisms, are taken away from the various national systems, the size of redistribution becomes more comparable. Even so, however, it is important to recognize that only part of the remaining taxes are meant to be truly redistributive, the remaining being practically neutral.

*Table 2.1   The extent of redistribution in some European countries (1994)
(per cent of GDP)*

	France	Germany	UK
Households' gross factor income	73.5	77.4	77.0
Social security contributions	*22.7*	*20.4*	*6.3*
Social security benefits	*22.1*	*16.0*	*6.1*
Households' net factor income and replacement income	73.0	73.0	76.8
Direct taxes	*7.1*	*9.8*	*9.9*
Non-contributory benefits	*3.7*	*4.4*	*6.5*
Household disposable income	69.5	67.5	73.4
Other taxes	16.4	14.6	18.2
Total mandatory contributions	**44.7**	**43.3**	**34.8**

Source: Bourguignon (1998).

Redistribution occurs by taking away income from individuals in a non-neutral way, that is, not proportionally to their income, but also through giving to households and individuals in a non-neutral way. In other words, redistribution occurs both through the financing and the spending sides of the public sector budget. Not all public expenditures are to be taken into account, however. Benefits which are the actuarially fair counterpart of contributions for pensions, health or unemployment insurance must be taken away since they do not have any redistribution role. Public expenditures which may be considered as neutral from a distribution point of view may also be ignored. This seems a reasonable assumption for most expenditures but the debate continues on various sensitive items like education and health expenditures. Practically, however, it has become customary to include in the redistribution system only expenditure with no direct tax or contribution counterpart, explicitly and directly aimed at modifying individual disposable income ('non-contributory benefits' in Table 2.1).

With such a definition, it is interesting that the importance of redistribution is comparable across the three OECD countries shown in Table 2.1. The sum

of direct income taxes and non-contributory benefits represents 10 to 15 per
cent of GDP in France, Germany and the UK, or 15 to 20 per cent of the net
factor and replacement income of households. Similar orders of magnitude
would be obtained in several other OECD countries. Based on such figures, the
potential for redistribution thus seems truly considerable.

Table 2.2 shows the redistribution operated by the income tax and non-contributory benefits in selected European countries. Redistribution is measured
here as the difference in the income shares of the bottom or top half of the
population before and after taxes and transfers. It is thus expressed in net terms.
The fact that the income tax redistributes 2.5 per cent of the total household
income from the top to the bottom half of the population in Germany does not
mean that there is some negative income tax in operation in Germany. Rather,
the share of the top half of the distribution is lower by 2.5 percentage points
when shares are evaluated before or after the income tax. Equivalently, one
could say that the bottom half of the distribution gained 2.5 per cent of the total
household income when compared with the hypothetical case with proportional
income tax.

*Table 2.2   Comparative redistributive performances of redistribution systems
in some European countries (1994) (per cent)*

		Net redistribution from 50% richest to 50% poorest	Average tax or benefit rate
Belgium	Benefits	1.2	4
	Taxes	4.2	22.6
France	Benefits	3.1	5.9
	Taxes	1.8	10.5
Germany	Benefits	4.4	6.5
	Taxes	2.5	14.4
Ireland	Benefits	4.1	8.8
	Taxes	3.1	22.4
Italy	Benefits	0.4	0.7
	Taxes	0.9	12.7
UK	Benefits	3.7	5.9
	Taxes	2.1	16.2

Source: Bourguignon (1998), calculations made with Euromod (Prototype Euro6).

With this definition, the redistribution actually achieved is indeed substantial although less than what would be potentially feasible in view of the

aggregate tax and benefit rates. So, the redistribution operated by the income tax and non-contributory benefits in France is equivalent to transferring more than 5 per cent of the total household income from the top to the bottom half. However, as this transfer practically takes place between the top quintile and the bottom quintile of the distribution, percentages expressed in terms of initial household incomes are more impressive. Overall, redistribution in France involves a net tax rate equal to 16 per cent on the richest 20 per cent of the population and a net benefit rate equal to 60 per cent on the poorest 20 per cent.[6]

Table 2.2 shows some diversity in the performances of the redistribution systems across the countries appearing there. Yet several features are readily apparent. a) In general, countries where redistribution is important are also countries where non-contributory benefits are important. b) For the same proportion of total household income, the redistribution achieved with non-contributory benefits is much more important than with income tax. c) It is generally the case that the redistribution achieved with income tax increases with the aggregate income tax rate. Thus, there is more redistribution through income tax in Belgium or in Ireland – with an average income tax rate above 20 per cent – than in Germany or in the UK where the tax rate is around 15 per cent. There are, however, exceptions to this rule. The income tax achieves less redistribution in Italy than in France, despite a comparable tax rate, and that obtained in the UK is only a little more pronounced than in France despite a much higher tax rate.

The explanation for the relatively lower redistribution power of income tax is easy to understand. In countries where the tax rate is high, a large part of the tax is, in fact, close to being proportional because the tax base is very broad. Where the aggregate tax rate is lower, there is more potential for very progressive taxation. This is the case for instance in France where less than 50 per cent of households are taxable through what is formally known as 'income tax'.[7] In most cases, however, non-contributory benefits appear to be much more efficiently targeted and progressive than is income tax.

As it is well known, the economic cost of redistribution lies in the distortions that it induces in the price structure and, in particular, the disincentives it creates for labour supply by lowering the net price of labour. It is difficult to evaluate the cost of these distortions without the help of a full structural labour supply model. However, one may indirectly get some idea of these distortions by considering the wedge that redistribution systems introduce between the economic and the actual price of labour for workers. The relevant concept from that point of view is that of the 'effective marginal tax rate' (EMTR) which measures the share of the marginal gain from labour that is confiscated by the redistribution system. 'Effective' means here that we consider simultaneously both standard income taxation and benefit means-testing. At the upper end of the income distribution, the EMTR is high because of the progressivity of income tax. At the lower end, it is still higher in cases where additional income from work may imply that a household will no longer qualify for some means-tested benefit, or will lose part of what it receives. In both cases, the EMTR thus measures the relative difference between the economic and the actual return to labour or efforts.

EMTRs are not directly observed. They must be computed on the basis of all existing rules that determine the income tax paid by and the non-contributory benefits received by a household. The EMTR shown in Figures 2.1 and Table 2.3 have been obtained from the prototype of Euromod, an integrated European micro-simulation tax-benefit model. This prototype relies on representative samples of households for selected European countries and on computer programs that compute the taxes to be paid and the benefits to be received for each sample household according to the redistribution system rules in the corresponding country.[8] EMTRs are obtained by repeating this calculation after incrementing the (gross) labour income of the member of the household with the highest earnings by some arbitrary amount.[9] Figure 2.1 has then been obtained by averaging the EMTR for all households belonging to a particular decile or vintile of the distribution of equivalized household incomes. Because the EMTR depends on variables other than income per adult equivalent – household or family composition, labour-force status, and so on – this procedure conceals some heterogeneity of EMTRs, but is consistent with the idea of focusing on redistribution along the income scale rather than in some other dimension.

Figure 2.1 for France is rather typical of the way the EMTR depends on the level of income in most European countries where non-contributory benefits are an important part of the redistribution system. The EMTR curve has a U-shape with high marginal rates in the lower end of the distribution and at the top. Because the curve is defined in vintiles, the right-hand side of the U is less pronounced in Figure 2.1 than it would be were the EMTR of the top centile represented.[10] At the top, the EMTR essentially reflects the increasing marginal income tax rate, whereas at the bottom it corresponds to a high proportion of households who benefit from the minimum income guarantee, RMI. After some transition period, any additional income for a household qualifying for the RMI is taken out of the benefit received, so that the corresponding EMTR is 100 per cent.[11] However, all households in the first vintile of equivalized income are not RMI recipients. On average, therefore, the EMTR is smaller than 100 per cent. The peaks observed around the seventh vintile and then at the tenth vintile correspond respectively to the ceiling of means-tests for various benefits (housing benefit in particular) and to a peculiarity of the French income tax for households who are liable for it but whose income is below some threshold.[12]

The situation is comparable in all countries where non-contributory benefits represent an important part of the redistribution system. In all these countries

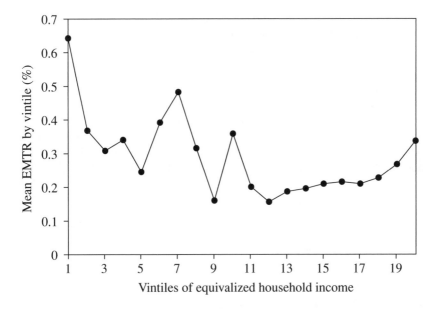

Figure 2.1 EMTR as a function of equivalized household income: France (1994)

the marginal tax rate curve has the same U-shape observed in the case of France.[13] In most cases, moreover, the proportion of households facing extremely high marginal tax rates is quite substantial. As shown in Table 2.3, the proportion of households facing EMTR above 60 per cent varies from 7 per cent in Belgium and France to 16 per cent in the UK.

It is precisely at that stage that the question of the equity/efficiency trade-off of redistribution systems arises. Most European countries have developed a sizable redistribution potential, even when redistribution is defined in the restricted sense discussed above. In all countries, this system is undoubtedly effective in that it achieves substantial transfers of income from the top to the bottom of the distribution scale and sizable increases in the income of the bottom deciles. Some countries fare better than others on that account. However, in all countries, this is obtained at the cost of important distortions of labour-supply incentives with an important proportion of households facing effective marginal tax rates significantly above 50 per cent, some actually close to 100 per cent. Very poor or very rich households are concerned with these high marginal tax rates and the problem is to know whether these distortions do not generate economic costs that may drastically reduce the social benefit of redistribution. Most of the present debate on the reform of the redistribution systems in

Table 2.3   Statistical distribution of EMTRs in selected European countries (proportion of total household population) (per cent)

Effective marginal tax rate (%)	Belgium	France	Germany	Ireland	UK
Less than 10	16.1	11.5	0.1	15.2	2.8
10–20	1.9	20.0	24.0	1.1	6.3
20–30	3.4	45.4	9.6	11.5	25.3
30–40	12.2	9.7	22.6	16.9	43.7
40–50	51.4	3.2	26.2	15.7	3.1
50–60	8.2	2.4	7.3	27.7	3.0
60–70	4.0	1.1	2.1	1.3	1.0
More than 70	2.8	6.7	8.1	10.6	14.8
Total	**100.0**	**100.0**	**100.0**	**100.0**	**100.0**

Source: Bourguignon (1998) on the basis of Euro6, Euromod prototype.

European countries is about this issue, the main difficulty being precisely to evaluate the actual cost arising from high EMTR distortions.

2   LESSONS FROM THE OPTIMAL TAXATION LITERATURE

This trade-off between equity and efficiency in redistribution is at the centre of the optimal taxation literature that began almost 30 years ago with the well-known work of Mirrlees. From the point of view of policy-making, this literature raised great hopes. Assuming some satisfactory empirical knowledge of labour-supply, the basic optimal taxation model would simply permit judgements on interpersonal comparisons of welfare or social welfare functions to be mapped into an optimal income tax schedule or, more generally, an optimal redistribution system. Overall, however, the implementation of this model, under one form or another, turned out to be disappointing. Our empirical knowledge of labour-supply behaviour proved to be too limited to be of very much use in an optimal taxation framework. Also, that framework itself may have proved to be based on too simple a representation of labour-supply and income-generating behaviour to be of very much use. Yet, this theoretical framework may still provide some guidance on some general desirable properties of redistribution systems. There has been some debate, for instance, on whether the marginal tax rate curve of Figure 2.1 should be horizontal, increasing or U-shaped and, in the latter case, how high the branches of the U should go. These points we briefly review below.

The Basic Model of Optimal Taxation

Under its canonical form the optimal taxation model may be formally stated as follows.

$$Max_{T0} \int_{w_0}^{A} G\{U(C^*, L^*)\}.f(w).dw \tag{2.1.1}$$

under the constraint that:

$$\int_{w_0}^{A} T(wL^*).f(w).dw \geq B \tag{2.1.2}$$

and (C^*, L^*) being the solution of:

$$Max_{C,L} \; U(C,L) \text{ subject to } C = wL - T(wL), L \geq 0 \tag{2.1.3}$$

In this expression, $U(\;)$ represents the preferences of an agent among all possible combinations of consumption expenditures (C) or labour time and efforts (L). (C^*, L^*) is his/her preferred combination given the budget constraint he/she faces. In that constraint, $T(\;)$ stands for the net tax schedule which is assumed to be a function of the gross income from labour. The level of utility actually achieved by the agent is $U(C^*, L^*)$. Through (2.1.3), it depends on his/her ability or productivity, w, and the income tax schedule. The distribution of productivity in the population is defined on (w_0, A) and is represented by the density function, $f(\;)$. Finally, B is the revenue that the government has to raise. Thus, the government is assumed to maximize the sum of socially-valued individual utilities, $G(\;)$, with respect to the tax schedule under the constraint that agents choose their labour-supply optimally. The social utility function $G(\;)$ and the individual utility function $U(\;)$ are assumed to satisfy standard properties of utility functions – they are increasing and respectively concave and quasi-concave.

The concavity of $G(\;)$ implies that the government would like to redistribute from people with high levels of indirect utility and therefore high productivity and gross income to people with low utility, productivity and income. The way of doing this is to have tax payment, $T(\;)$, increasing with income. However, if it increases too rapidly, labour-supply, L^*, will fall and there will be little to redistribute after meeting the government budget constraint (1.2). The trade-off between efficiency – high level of labour-supply and gross income – and equity or redistribution is thus the core of the model. Under this very general form, it can be seen that the optimal tax schedule $T(\ )$ will essentially be a function of the labour-supply behaviour of agents, as represented here by the utility function $U(\ )$, the distribution of abilities in the population summarized by $f(\ )$, and finally, the social welfare function defined by the function $G(\ )$.

The general solution of this problem is rather intricate and we shall not enter such technicalities here.[14] A special case which has recently received very much attention is when the individual utility function is additively separable and quasi-linear with respect to consumption, C. In that case, the supply of labour depends only on the productivity term, w, after correction by the marginal tax rate, T'. The corresponding function writes as:

$$U(C,L) = C - k \cdot L^{1+\frac{1}{\varepsilon}} \qquad (2.2)$$

where k and ε are positive constants. ε is simply the elasticity of labour-supply with respect to the productivity term, w. With no taxes, it may indeed be seen that the maximization of (2.2) under the budget constraint $C = w.L$ implies that labour-supply is proportional to w^{ε}. With this specification of preferences, it may then be shown that the optimal tax schedule is such that an individual with productivity w, faces a marginal tax rate, T', given by:

$$\frac{T'}{1-T'} = \left(1 + \frac{1}{\varepsilon}\right) \cdot \frac{1 - F(w)}{w \cdot f(w)} \cdot \left[1 - S(w)/S(w_0)\right] \qquad (2.3)^{15}$$

where $F(\ )$ is the cumulative function associated with $f(\ )$ and $S(w)$ stands for the average marginal social value of the income of all individuals with pro-ductivity higher than w.

The interpretation of that expression is rather simple. By increasing the marginal tax rate at w, the government loses some revenue because people at that level of productivity will reduce their labour supply. This loss would be obtained by multiplying the left-hand side of (2.3) by the term $f(w)$, i.e., how many people are there at w, and the term $w/(1 + 1/\varepsilon)$, i.e., by how much gross income falls. An increase in the marginal tax rate at w would also increase the tax revenue from all individuals above w since the whole tax schedule would be lifted from the corresponding level of income on. The other terms remaining on the right-hand side of (2.3) describe that effect. The additional revenue that the government obtains is proportional to the number of people above w, i.e., $1 - F(w)$. But this revenue must be corrected by the marginal social value of the corresponding individual incomes relative to the marginal social value of an additional unit of government revenue, the latter being simply the average marginal social value of income in all the population.

Problems in Implementing Empirically the Optimal Taxation Model

Within this simplified framework, the computation of the optimal tax rate schedule thus requires the knowledge of the elasticity of labour-supply with respect to productivity, the distribution of productivity in the population, and some social welfare function. Paradoxically, the last of these three elements is probably the one which raises least problems since it is essentially normative. For instance, a practice leading to very simple calculations consists of imputing a constant marginal social value of income for the proportion q of agents at the bottom of the distribution and a lower constant value for the remaining $1 - q$. Social value judgements are thus represented by two parameters: q and the ratio of the social marginal values of income. The corresponding social welfare function $G(\ )$ is represented in Figure 2.2. However, using a standard iso-elastic form for the function $G(\ )$ where the elasticity parameter may be interpreted as some measure of the aversion of policy makers towards inequality does not lead to intractable calculations.

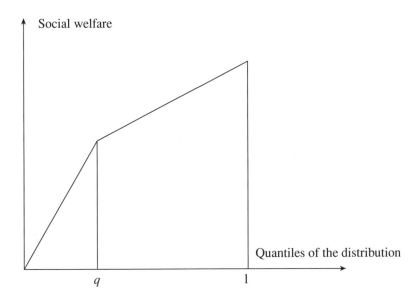

Figure 2.2   Shape of the social welfare function in optimal taxation model

Selecting a value for the labour-supply elasticity and a distribution of individual productivity raises more difficulties. Listed here are the major ones. First comes the issue of how to interpret the 'labour-supply' variable, L, and the associated 'productivity', w. Common practice consists of associating the former with hours of work and the latter with the gross hourly wage rate. But the interpretation of the basic model (2.1) may be more general than that. L may include other important dimensions of labour supply which are not observable, efforts in particular or, in a dynamic framework, on the job accumulation of human capital.

Second, even if one restricts the model to L being the number of hours of work and w the wage rate, then comes the problem of getting a reasonable and reliable wage elasticity of labour-supply. A considerable literature has been accumulated on this subject over the last 20 years or so. Yet, it is not clear that our knowledge of the elasticity of labour-supply is more precise today. Of course, databases have become more numerous and of better quality. The range of estimation techniques has also considerably broadened from simple OLS regressions to sophisticated structural models of labour-supply. When the time comes for imputing a value for ε, however, a considerable range of uncertainty remains. Elasticities are different whether the estimation is made on men or women, whether hours of work or participation is considered, whether structural restrictions consistent with model (2.1.1) above are imposed, whether the non-linearity of the tax system is taken into account or not, whether the dynamic aspect of labour-supply is accounted for, and so on. Surveys of what may be one of the most lively fields of applied microeconomics are available – see in particular Blundell (1992), Blundell *et al.* (1998), Pencavel (1986). If there is a consensus to recognize that labour-supply, under one form or another, reacts positively to changes in net wages and negatively to unearned income, elasticity estimates vary considerably. However, we shall see that this may not be the most serious problem for the implementation of the optimal taxation model.

Third, if one considers that the hourly wage rate is indeed the appropriate measure of the productivity term w of the theoretical model above, estimating the distribution $f(\ )$ of individual productivities would seem relatively easy. It would simply be a matter of direct observation. But this would be true, of course, if all individuals were actually working and if the only source of variation in labour-supply was non-zero hours of work. Practically, many individuals in the population do not work. Moreover, given a generous redistribution system, it may be optimal for them not to work. This is precisely the kind of issue on which an optimal taxation model should focus. But how would it be possible to design an optimal benefit system at the bottom of the distribution of productivities, if no information is available on the proportion of people standing at the various ladders of the productivity scale in that range of the distribution?

The fourth and last difficulty that we would like to stress is the difficulty arising from having to deal simultaneously with individuals and households. Wage rates and labour-supply are concepts that refer to individuals. The consistency of the optimal taxation model would thus require that it relied on individuals. Practically, however, the evaluation of social welfare is based on the concept of households. This is, on the one hand, because the allocation of goods among household members is not known and, on the other, because there are obvious externalities and economies of scale in living together. Clearly, *n* persons living together fare better with a given budget than *n* persons living separately with the same total budget. Indeed, most studies of income distribution or redistribution take the household as the basic statistical unit. But in the optimal taxation framework, this would require either defining labour-supply and 'productivity' at the household level, a rather artificial construct which we actually use below, or to account explicitly for the simultaneous and interactive individual labour-supply decisions taken by the various household members. The model would then become multi-dimensional, each household being characterized by, say, two wage rates and two labour-supplies. But this seems to make the model totally intractable.[16]

Where do we stand? Does this long list of difficulties in implementing empirically the optimal taxation model mean that it is useless? Not really. It would certainly be illusory to try to implement it rigorously by introducing in it some refined structural model of labour-supply based on debatable identifying assumptions. But there is still the possibility that the marginal tax rate curve given by (2.3) exhibits some property of regularity when applied to situations not unreasonably far from the 'real world'. Hence the question of the general shape of the optimal marginal tax rate curve analysed in some recent contributions. Is there enough regularity in the $f(\ )$ distribution so that, under reasonable assumptions on the social welfare function $G(\ )$, the optimal EMTR curve is U-shaped, horizontal, increasing or decreasing? Diamond (1998) gives some sufficient conditions for this curve to be U-shaped but finds a flattened right branch in a simple application to the distribution of hourly wage rates in the US. Saez (1998) finds a more pronounced U-shape using the observed distribution of annual household incomes in the US. Atkinson (1995) analyses the shape obtained with Log-normal and Pareto distributions for $f(w)$, an interesting property of the Pareto distribution being that the middle term in the right-hand side of (2.3) is constant. Salanié (1998) finds a decreasing curve in the case of France when using the observed distribution of household wage income.

Looking for Some Regularity of the Optimal Tax Schedule

The following results are inspired by the preceding literature. However, they rely on a slightly different methodology to estimate the distribution of abilities. They also refer to several EU countries.

The main departure from previous attempts at figuring out the general shape of the optimal EMTR consists of avoiding some of the problems mentioned above due to interpreting too closely the optimal taxation model in terms of hours of work and hourly wage rate. Instead of focusing on these variables, we *infer* them from the observation of gross labour incomes, the existing tax-benefit system and preferences consistent with the assumption of a constant wage elasticity of labour-supply. We also work with observed aggregate household incomes and derive for each household a single ability parameter, w, which summarizes the earning capacity of the household that is consistent with preferences given by (2.2) and the existing tax-benefit system. However, in what . follows we disregard differences among households arising from their size. In other words, we consider that household size enters additively the preferences represented by (2.2).[17]

Formally, we do the following. We assume that the observed net income or consumption expenditures, C^*, and unobserved labour-supply are derived from the model above. In other words they are the solution of:

$$Max\, U(C,L) = C - k \cdot L^{1+\frac{1}{\varepsilon}} \quad s.t. \quad C = w \cdot L - T_0(w \cdot L) \qquad (2.4)$$

where $T_0(w \cdot L)$ stands for the existing tax-benefit system. This model can be inverted so that the unobserved productivity term, w, can be expressed as a function of the observed consumption expenditures or disposable income, C^*, conditionally on preferences, summarized by ε, and the current tax-benefit system:

$$w = \Phi[C^*; T_0(\ ); \varepsilon] \qquad (2.5)$$

In effect, it may be shown that this inversion needs to know only the marginal tax rate rather than the full tax schedule faced by a household.

The interest of this method is to be fully consistent with the model being used and with the available data. It also permits dealing with households rather than with individuals. However, it does not solve the problem of unobserved abilities. Some households in the sample have zero-observed gross labour income, a rational decision in view of the fact that actual tax-benefit systems often guarantee a minimum income to households. The way we handle this case is simply by computing the 'reservation productivity' below which households optimally choose not to work and then by drawing randomly a value for w in a Log-normal distribution truncated from above by this 'reservation productivity'. The parameters of this Log-normal distribution are such that it pastes smoothly with the distribution of abilities computed for values above the reservation level and smoothened through Kernel techniques. At the other end the distribution $f(w)$ cannot be estimated reliably either. This is because of fewer and fewer observations for increasingly high incomes. Smooth pasting of the Kernel estimate of the density with a Pareto distribution was done for the upper two centiles of the distribution.

This methodology was applied to three samples of households taken from household surveys in France, Italy and the UK. The inversion method (2.4)–(2.5) was applied to present tax-benefit systems in these three countries as simulated by the Euromod prototype model using two values for the wage elasticity of the labour-supply: a) $\varepsilon = 0.1$, which may be thought as close to the bottom end of the range of existing estimates, and b) $\varepsilon = 0.5$, which should be around the middle of that range. As may be seen on the left-hand side of Figures 2.3, the resulting Kernel estimate of the density of abilities is indeed substantially different for the two values of that elasticity.

Overall this methodology implies that the way in which the optimal taxation schedule depends on the wage elasticity of the labour-supply is more complex than suggested by formula (2.3). For a given distribution of observed labour income in the population a change in ε not only shifts the whole optimal marginal rate curve up or down in accordance with the first terms on the right-hand side of (2.3) but also modifies the imputed distribution of abilities, $f(w)$.

For the two values of ε being used the right-hand side of Figures 2.3 shows the optimal effective marginal tax rate schedule derived from (2.3) under simple assumptions concerning the social welfare function, $G(\ )$. The marginal social value of consumption is assumed to be constant for all individuals but at a higher level for the bottom $q = 20\%$ of households ranked by level of ability. It is simple to prove that, with such a social utility function, the last term in the right-hand side of (2.3) is constant for the top $(1-q)$ of the population, so that the optimal marginal tax rate is then proportional to the curve $(1-F)/wf(w)$. The optimal marginal tax rate curve is different for the q poorest households, which explains the angulous point observed in all optimal marginal tax rate curves at 20 per cent.

Of course, it is necessary to select some value for the ratio between the marginal social value of consumption in the bottom 20 per cent and in the rest of the population. The higher this ratio, the closer the social utility function to the Rawlsian objective where only the welfare of the bottom 20 per cent matters. On the contrary, the lower the ratio the closer is society to a pure efficiency objective where only total output matters. The results in Figures 2.3 are based on a calibration of the social utility function, $G(\ )$, such that, in all countries, it would be optimal not to have anybody below a limit between 40 and 50 per cent the mean disposable income in the country under analysis if the elasticity of labour supply were equal to 0.1. In other words, the social welfare function that is postulated is such that it would be optimal to *eliminate poverty*, defined

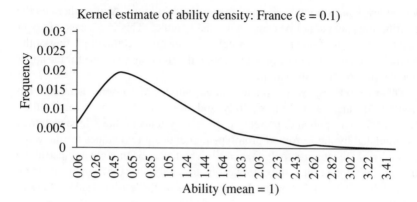

Kernel estimate of ability density: France (ε = 0.1)

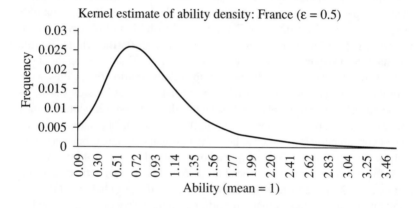

Kernel estimate of ability density: France (ε = 0.5)

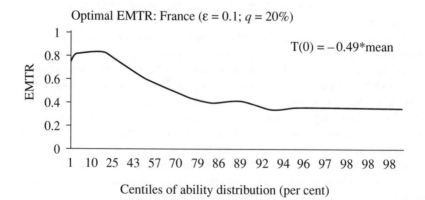

Optimal EMTR: France (ε = 0.1; q = 20%)

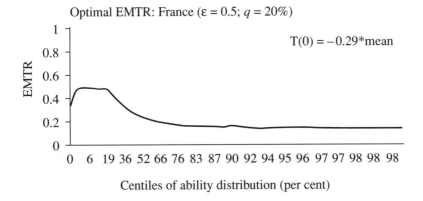

Figure 2.3a   Estimation of distribution of 'household abilities' and optimal marginal tax rate: France, 1994

in accordance with the criteria used by the EC, *if the elasticity of labour supply was very low*, and therefore if no big output losses should be expected from taxation.

To be complete the description of the optimal redistribution schedule must include not only the EMTR at all levels of income or ability[18] but also how much is paid or received by households with some arbitrary level of ability. With this information and knowing how much is being paid on each additional bit of labour income starting from this level – that is, the marginal tax rates – it is then possible to compute the actual amount paid or received by a household as a function of its gross labour income or ability. The value of $T(0)$ which appears in the bottom panels of Figures 2.3 is the information necessary to perform that calculation. It corresponds to the disposable income that would be received by a household with zero ability and therefore with zero gross labour income. In the present case this value is determined under the assumption that B in the government's budget constraint is zero. In other words, we are considering a tax-benefit system that is purely redistributive. In that system all households in society pay a negative income tax $T(0)$ – or receive the corresponding absolute value as a universal benefit – and pay the tax generated by the marginal rate schedule determined by (2.3).

The assumptions made on the social marginal values of consumption for the bottom q and top $(1 - q)$ households in the population is such that the universal benefit $T(0)$ is between 40 and 50 per cent of the mean gross labour income in the various countries when labour-supply is very little elastic ($\varepsilon = 0.1$). Not surprisingly the amount of that transfer falls when redistribution is assumed to be

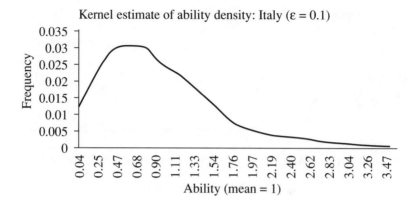

Kernel estimate of ability density: Italy (ε = 0.1)

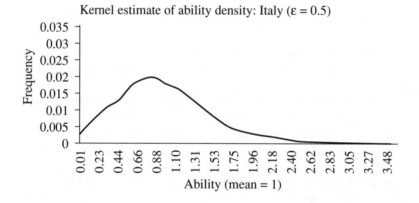

Kernel estimate of ability density: Italy (ε = 0.5)

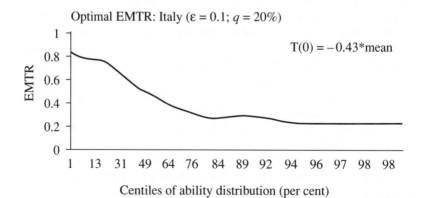

Optimal EMTR: Italy (ε = 0.1; q = 20%)

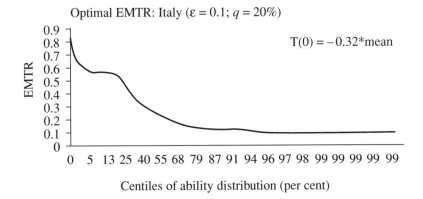

Figure 2.3b *Estimation of distribution of 'household abilities' and optimal marginal tax rate: Italy, 1994*

more costly, that is, when going from $\varepsilon = 0.1$ to $\varepsilon = 0.5$ or from the North-east to the South-east panel of Figures 2.3. Interestingly enough, the social welfare that is being used leads also to comparable optimal universal transfers across countries when the highest elasticity figure is used. The drop in the universal transfer seems to be more pronounced for France, but the distribution of abilities in that country also seems significantly different from that in the two other countries.

The structure of optimal redistribution rather than its overall size is what we are really interested in. From that point of view, it can be seen that in the three countries being analysed the shape of the optimal marginal tax rate schedule is the same. It starts at a rather high level for low productivity households, it then decreases continuously and flattens out at the top of the distribution. The main difference among the three cases appearing in Figure 2.2 lies in the starting level of the marginal tax rate. It is substantially lower for France than for Italy or the UK.

Of course, the problem is to know whether this similarity across countries is genuine or whether it is artificially due to using the same social welfare parameters and labour-supply elasticity in the three countries. To answer this question, it is necessary to handle separately the two tails of the imputed distribution of abilities. For the upper tail, it was assumed that the distribution could be approximated by a Pareto distribution, which we have seen was leading to constant optimal marginal tax rates. With much more detail on the distribution the optimal EMTR curve might turn out not being horizontal and different across countries. This is not very likely though. The Pareto is known to be a rather good approximation of the distribution of high incomes. Thus a non-horizontal optimal EMTR curve for high incomes is more likely to be justified

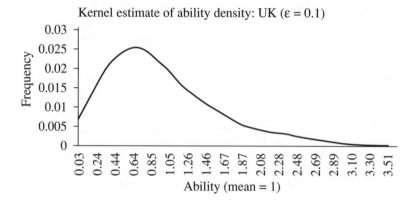

Kernel estimate of ability density: UK ($\varepsilon = 0.1$)

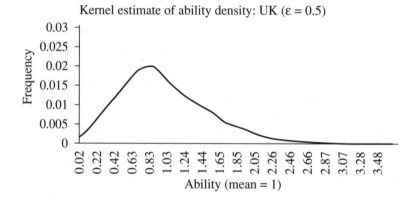

Kernel estimate of ability density: UK ($\varepsilon = 0.5$)

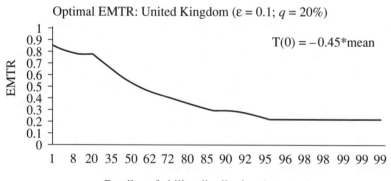

Optimal EMTR: United Kingdom ($\varepsilon = 0.1$; $q = 20\%$)

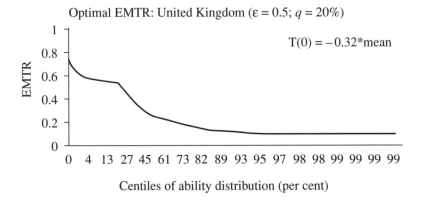

Figure 2.3c Estimation of distribution of 'household abilities' and optimal marginal tax rate: UK, 1994

by social welfare considerations or by non-constant labour-supply elasticity. In particular, it is possible to generate the upward sloping branch of the U-shaped curve observed in the real world by assuming that the marginal social value of consumption is decreasing very quickly at the upper end of the distribution rather than remaining constant as in the present exercise. The same result may be obtained by assuming that the elasticity of labour-supply is decreasing in the upper tail of the distribution. However, there is no strong reason to expect that this is indeed the case.

At the other end of the distribution, one could also suspect that replacing the unobserved distribution of abilities by a truncated. Log-normal distribution could also be responsible for a high marginal rate of taxation there. There are other reasons to explain that result, though. First, the Log-normal approximation is done on a very short interval in Italy because of the absence of guaranteed income schemes in the present redistribution system. Yet, the shape of the optimal EMTR curve at the bottom of the distribution is practically the same as in the UK. Second, the optimal EMTR is high and decreasing, or at least non-increasing, much beyond the interval on which the Log-normal approximation is taken. Third, there is some variability across countries. The optimal EMTR curve is flat in the case of France – and, in fact, increasing for the very first centiles of the distribution. Except perhaps for this limited exception, the fact that the optimal EMTR is higher toward the bottom of the distribution seems rather robust.

This does not mean that the optimal EMTR should be close to unity for households with very low ability, unlike what seemed to be the case with some of the real world situations reviewed above. In the particular case under analysis it can even be shown that as long as the density $f(w)$ is increasing – a rather natural property at the bottom of the distribution – then the optimal EMTR is necessarily below unity provided that the wage elasticity of labour-supply is strictly positive.[19] In other words, a 100 per cent EMTR can be optimal only if it is assumed that labour is totally inelastic with respect to productivity and the marginal tax rate for low productivity households. This is not unlikely for households whose productivity is so low that they can barely survive working all the time that is available with maximum effort. In some sense they could be considered as 'disabled' and thus qualify for benefits associated with that condition. But such cases are not considered here.

The last robust conclusion to be derived from this simple analysis is that the optimal EMTR curve is decreasing in all the middle range of incomes. This simply reflects the fact that the middle term $(1 - F(w))/wf(w)$ is undoubtedly decreasing throughout the range that comprises the most frequent values of the ability variable. This is true in the three countries and the curve is rather steep, going from 50 per cent or more for the third decile to less than 20 per cent for the eighth decile in the case of $\varepsilon = 0.5$. As mentioned above, however, the social welfare function also has a role to play in this downward slope. In particular, a larger value of q, the proportion of the poorest households being given some priority in the social welfare function, would lead to both a higher and a flatter optimal EMTR curve.

On the basis of a simple labour/consumption model, the optimal taxation framework thus seems to lead to some general properties of the redistribution system. The optimal EMTR curve should be decreasing and flattening out for high income, unless the marginal social value of consumption is assumed to decrease very rapidly at the top of the distribution. In the latter case, the optimal EMTR curve should be U-shaped. As optimal EMTRs are strictly positive, the optimal redistribution system also includes a universal benefit which may be taken as a measure of the importance of the redistribution being undertaken. The size of that universal benefit, or equivalently the average EMTR, depends essentially on the labour-supply elasticity and the assumptions behind the social welfare function. An important conclusion of the preceding analysis is that, when the social utility function is calibrated so as for this universal transfer to take reasonable values, that is, 30 to 50 per cent of mean income depending on the labour-supply elasticity, the optimal EMTR is significantly below unity, unlike that which is implied by most income guarantee schemes in place in several EU countries.

3   ISSUES IN TAX–BENEFIT REFORMS

Except for the abnormally high marginal tax rates observed at the median or just below it, the actual EMTR curve evaluated in the case of France in Figure

2.1 is not dissimilar to the shape that was just described for the optimal curve. One would obtain the same kind of conclusion in other European countries with a sizeable redistribution system. Unfortunately, this does not mean that present redistribution systems are optimal however. On the one hand, it must be stressed that EMTR curves of the type shown in Figure 2.1 correspond to average marginal tax rates taken over different types of households. This heterogeneity is simply ignored in the derivation of optimal tax schedules. In particular observed EMTRs are 100 per cent for some households in the bottom of the distribution scale enrolled in minimum income guarantee programmes, whereas the optimal tax model does not lead to this kind of prediction. On the other, the assumptions behind the theoretical model of optimal taxation may themselves be called into question.

The ongoing debate on the necessary reform of the Welfare State bears essentially on these issues. Two questions are particularly prominent. Is it really optimal to have close to 100 per cent EMTR for a significant proportion of households at the bottom of the distribution? Although lower, is it not the case that actual EMTRs are also too high at the other end of the distribution?

The empirical implementation of the theoretical optimal taxation model may partially answer these questions. The critique made to too high EMTRs at both the bottom and the top of the distribution may simply reveal a disagreement about the value of the elasticity of labour-supply, which would be higher, overall or in some specific part of the distribution, than implicitly assumed in actual redistribution systems or may be constant rather than falling in the upper tail of the distribution of abilities. It may also reflect a fundamental disagreement about the social welfare function implicit in that model. Social values may have changed since present redistribution systems were designed. In particular, there may now be less emphasis on quickly declining social marginal values at the top of the distribution.

Such changes in social values or in intuitive estimates of labour-supply response to incentives may indeed justify criticizing the present redistribution system for giving too much weight to equity rather than to efficiency considerations, in the optimal taxation framework. But the theoretical model itself may be found to be inappropriate to represent the effect of redistribution on households' gross labour incomes. For instance, in the special case considered in the preceding section, assuming away income effects on labour-supply may be seen as a severe restriction. Ignoring obvious sources of heterogeneity across households is also a serious problem. In particular, accounting for different demographic compositions of households and for the presence of sources of income other than labour would seem necessary, especially, for the latter, in connection with the upper part of the distribution scale. More fundamentally, however, the labour-supply model on which the whole optimal taxation framework relies may be seen as too simple a view at actual behaviour, even when considered under the restrictive perspective of homogeneous households in terms of demographic composition and unearned income.

Of particular concern is the purely static nature of the model, and implicitly, of the empirical estimates that feed it. Means-testing devices leading to high marginal tax rates at the bottom of the distribution and a high lump-sum transfer are often seen as potentially responsible for *poverty traps*. A person benefiting from minimum income guarantees has little incentive to get a job unless it pays a sufficiently high wage. But precisely because that person is not working he/she will not increase his/her human capital as if he/she were working, that is, through on-the-job training or learning by doing. This will reduce his/her future wage and will make subsidized inactivity[20] more likely in the future. So those unfortunate enough to find themselves temporarily, but still for a while, in need of some income guarantee programme may then find it difficult to get out of it. They may find themselves progressively excluded from the labour market and socially. Paradoxically, minimum income guarantees may thus transform themselves into instruments for social exclusion.[21]

At the other extreme of the distribution, some concern has also been expressed that too high marginal tax rates might reduce returns to all types of investments in human capital and also that too high average tax rates might encourage emigration, another form of a dynamic linkage between redistribution today and labour-supply tomorrow. Clearly, the basic optimal taxation framework reviewed above is not fully equipped to deal with these dynamic issues. Given its analytical complexity it is, in fact, rather unlikely that it will ever be able to do so. On the empirical side, there is also considerable uncertainty about the exact importance of these various dynamic labour-supply incentives.

The hypothesis that strict means-testing of benefits may create inactivity and poverty traps, and also that international mobility may be a behavioural response to excessively high marginal and average tax rates, are arguments that should logically flatten out the optimal EMTR curve. Optimal redistribution would then be close to the 'linear income tax' or the 'basic income/flat tax rate' scheme. This scheme is indeed often justified by the preceding dynamic labour-supply arguments.[22] It may be represented by the following simple equation:

$$y = (1 - t) \cdot Y + A$$

where y is disposable income, Y is gross labour income, t is the unique and constant marginal tax rate and A is the universal benefit or 'basic income'. In terms of the optimal EMTR curves analysed in the preceding section, this redistribution scheme corresponds to a horizontal EMTR curve at the level t and a universal lump-sum transfer $T(0) = -A$.

The problem of switching from existing redistribution systems to this linear (negative) income tax is that it is likely to modify quite drastically the distribution of disposable income in the population. This switch is illustrated in Figure 2.4 in the case of France. In this figure, the curve T represents very approximately the net tax payments of households ranked by increasing incomes in the present redistribution system. $T(0)$ corresponds to the basic income guaranteed to households with no income. The tax schedule L1 corresponds to a linear income tax with the same intercept, $T(0)$, at the origin, thus guaranteeing the same level of disposable income at the bottom of the distribution and revenue neutral from the government point of view. Given the shape of the present net tax curve, it can be seen that this switch corresponds to quite a sizable net redistribution from the middle toward the two extremes of the distribution. Redistribution thus increases at the bottom of the distribution but the EMTR faced by the middle range of the distribution increases quite substantially, here from 0 to $A = -T(0)/\bar{Y}$ where $\bar{Y}$ is the mean gross labour income in the population. Given the parameters of the French redistribution system, this could correspond to an increase of approximate 20 percentage points of the EMTR in the middle range of the distribution, a huge number. An alternative (L2) that would reduce the redistribution from the middle class and its EMTR would consist of having the basic income A in the linear income tax system smaller than the present guaranteed income $T(0)$. Clearly, this would reduce the distribution from the middle class but would also reduce the disposable income of the poorest households. Because of the size of the redistribution involved in the first case from the middle class and because of the difficulty of reducing the level of guaranteed income, these reforms are likely to be politically uneasy.

Another scheme that is presently gaining popularity is the subsidizing of labour at low levels of gross labour income. Since its generalization to all low-income households, a scheme like the Earned Income Tax Credit (EITC) in the US is doing precisely this. In the absence of any other tax, this would actually correspond to negative EMTRs.[23] Practically, however, the EITC is equivalent to a drop of the EMTR for low earnings at a level which is below the EMTR faced by people who benefit from higher earnings. In effect, this is equivalent to making the EMTR curve *increasing* at the lower end of the distribution, rather than decreasing as in most present redistribution systems in Europe or in the optimal schedule analysed above. This clearly cannot be optimal in an optimal redistribution framework. Within the conventional optimal redistribution framework, low-productivity people are pushed out of the labour market through high EMTR and overcompensated through the transfer $-T(0)$. This does not cost very much because their productivity is low, whereas it is possible to raise the revenue necessary to cover the universal transfer on the infra-marginal supply of labour by higher-productivity workers. EITC-like schemes, on the contrary, transfer income to low-productivity workers by increasing the return from their labour. The risk of a poverty trap is thus reduced.

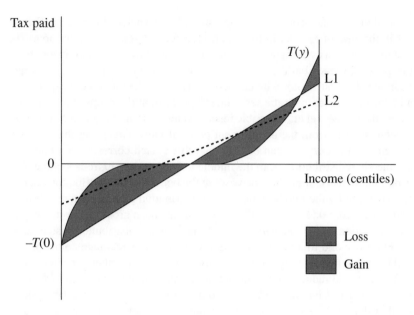

Figure 2.4   Switching to a linear income tax schedule (French case)

CONCLUSION

Redistribution systems in Europe share some common features. After correcting for the public/private nature of social insurance, they tend to represent a high share of GDP but, at the same time, they achieve a substantial redistribution, at least in countries where non-contributory benefits are substantial. However, this is obtained at a cost on labour-supply incentives. Effective marginal tax rates (EMTRs) are generally extremely high at the bottom of the distribution scale because of the importance of means-tested benefits, in particular minimum income guarantee schemes. They are also high, though not as much, at the other end of the scale because of the progressivity of income tax.

Using a simple application of optimal taxation theory calibrated so as to fit the observed distribution of household gross labour incomes, while taking into account the effects of the present redistribution systems on labour-supply, we have investigated the features of optimal redistribution systems in various countries. In view of this analysis, high EMTRs at the very bottom of the distribution scale turn out not to be necessarily sub-optimal whereas optimal EMTR curves appeared definitely much flatter than actual curves at the top of the distribution. Yet, optimal marginal tax rates for the lower centiles of the distribution scale prove to be significantly lower than the 100 per cent rate implied by existing income guarantee programmes. In the middle range of income, optimal EMTR curves were shown to be more regular than actual ones in the case of France.

On that basis, it would thus seem that the major reform required to existing redistribution systems in European countries would be to make actual EMTR curves smoother and flatter in their upper part. However, this is only true with the static view at labour-supply behaviour that is behind the optimal taxation framework. Recent concerns about high EMTRs at the bottom of the distribution in many European countries arose largely because they were seen as being potentially responsible for dynamic poverty traps and a cause for progressive marginalization from the labour-market and social exclusion. Much work is needed on the dynamics of labour-supply in the low-income range and the way it may be modified by reforms of the redistribution system. But the risk that present systems may be responsible for poverty traps would suggest that marginal tax rates should be lowered in the bottom part of the distribution.

Switching to a linear income tax system with a flat marginal tax rate across the whole income range, while maintaining present minimum income guarantees, was shown to be probably infeasible in the case of France. Such a reform was considered too drastic a redistribution away from the middle class and would also increase considerably the EMTR it faces. Introducing features resembling the EITC to reduce EMTRs for households with modest potential income, essentially subsidizing labour at low levels of gross labour income, is probably more easily implementable.

NOTES

1. This paper was presented at a meeting in the European Commission in Brussels in November 1998. A modified version was given as an invited lecture at the congress of the Applied Econometrics Association in Pau, May 1999. Section 3 relies on recent work with Amedeo Spadaro (Bourguignon and Spadaro, 2000). Several tables in the chapter make use of prototype versions of the Euromod model (see Immervoll *et al.*, 1999).
2. Delta and Ehess, Paris (Delta is a joint CNRS, Ehess and Ens research unit).
3. See Department of Social Security (1998).
4. I thank the co-authors of the various pieces on which I will rely, and in particular the team who worked on the first prototypes of the Euromod model. See Bourguignon *et al.* (1997, 1998).
5. See for instance OECD (1998).
6. See Bourguignon (1998, Table 3) .
7. However, all households pay the CSG which essentially is a proportional tax on incomes.
8. For a description of the full Euromod model see Immervoll, O'Donoghue and Sutherland (1999). First applications of prototypes include Bourguignon *et al.* (1997), and Atkinson *et al.* (1999).
9. 1500 euros per year in the present case.
10. It is estimated to be above 70 per cent, see Bourguignon and Bureau (1999).
11. It is actually more because of some peculiarity in the computation of housing benefits, see Laroque and Salanié (1999).

12. This system, known as the 'decote', multiplies the marginal tax rate of small taxpayers by two.
13. Such curves are shown in Bourguignon (1998) for a few EU countries.
14. See Mirrlees (1971), Atkinson and Stiglitz (1980) or Tuomala (1990).
15. Recent work based on this expression include Atkinson (1995), Diamond (1998), Piketty (1997), Salanié (1998). After some change of variable from w to gross income wL^*, (2.3) appears as a differential equation, the integration of which yields the tax schedule. The budget constraint of the government then permits identifying the integration constant, that is $T(0)$ which is to be interpreted as a universal transfer.
16. On the intractability of a multi-dimensional version of the optimal taxation model, see Mirrlees (1986).
17. Household size is explicitly taken into account in Bourguignon and Spadaro (2000). We abstract from it here.
18. Note that under the assumptions used here these are ordinally equivalent.
19. Solving (2.3) under the conditions considered here leads to the result that $\Gamma'/(1 - \Gamma')$ is proportional to $F(w)/wf(w)$. But it is easy to show that this ratio is necessarily less than unity if $f'(\ ) > 0$ between 0 and w.
20. Plus possibly some moonlighting.
21. On this see Atkinson (1998).
22. See, for instance, Atkinson (1995). An additional argument not mentioned here is that of the lack of fairness of benefits given to people who are voluntarily inactive.
23. This possibility is considered in Trannoy (1998).

REFERENCES

Atkinson A.B. (1995), *Public Economics in Action: Basic Income-Flat Tax Proposal*, Clarendon Press: Oxford.
Atkinson, A.B. (1998), *Poverty in Europe*, Oxford: Blackwell.
Atkinson A.B. and J.E. Stiglitz (1980), *Lectures on Public Economics*, McGraw Hill International Editions.
Atkinson, A.B., F. Bourguignon, C. O'Donoghue, H. Sutherland and F. Utili (1999), 'Microsimulation and the Formulation of Policy: A Case Study of Targeting in the European Union', Microsimulation Unit, Department of Applied Economics, Cambridge.
Blundell R.W. (1992), 'Labour Supply and Taxation', *Fiscal Studies*, **13**(3).
Blundell R.W., A. Duncan and C. Meghir (1998), 'Estimating Labour Supply Responses to Tax Reform', *Econometrica*, **66**: 827–61.
Bourguignon, F. (1998), *Fiscalité et redistribution: la France dans une perspective internationale*, Rapport au Conseil d'Analyse Economique, La Documentation Française, Paris.
Bourguignon, F. and D. Bureau (1999), *L'architecture des prélèvements en France: état des lieux et voies de réforme*, Rapport au Conseil d'Analyse Economique, La Documentation Française, Paris.
Bourguignon, F. and A. Spadaro (2000), 'Redistribution et incitations au travail: une application simple de la fiscalité optimale', *Revue Economique*.
Bourguignon F., C. O'Donoghue, J. Sastre, A. Spadaro and F. Utili (1997) 'Eur3: A Prototype European Tax Benefits Model', DAE Working Paper N. 9723 Microsimulation Unit, Cambridge University.
Bourguignon F., C. O'Donoghue, J. Sastre, A. Spadaro and F. Utili (1998), Technical description of Eur3: A Prototype European Tax-Benefits Model', DAE Research Note N.9801 Microsimulation Unit, Cambridge University.

Department of Social Security (1998), 'A New Contract for Welfare', Secretary of State for Social Security, UK.

Diamond P. (1998), 'Optimal Income Taxation: An Example with U-Shaped Pattern of Optimal Marginal Tax Rate', *American Economic Review*, **88**(1).

Immervoll, H., C. O'Donoghue and H. Sutherland (1999), 'An Introduction to Euromod', Microsimulation Unit, Department of Applied Economics, Cambridge.

Laroque, G. and B. Salanié (1999), 'Prélèvements et transferts sociaux: une analyse descriptive des effets incitatifs', mimeo, INSEE.

Mirrlees J.A. (1971), 'An Exploration in the Theory of Optimum Income Taxation', *Review of Economic Studies*, 39.

Mirrlees J.A. (1986), 'The Theory of Optimum Income Taxation', *Handbook of Mathematical Economics*, North Holland, Amsterdam.

OECD (1998), *Economic Outlook*, June.

Pencavel J. (1986), 'Labour Supply of Men: a Survey', in Ashenfelter and Layard (eds), *Handbook of Labour Economics*, North Holland, Amsterdam.

Piketty, T. (1997), 'La redistribution fiscale face au chômage', *Revue Française d'Economie*, **XII**.

Saez, E. (1998), 'Using Elasticities to Derive Optimal Income Tax Rates', mimeo, MIT.

Salanié, B. (1998), 'Note sur la Taxation Optimale', Rapport au Conseil d'Analyse Economique, La Documentation Française, Paris.

Trannoy, A. (1998), 'Fiscalité et redistribution: commentaire', *Revue Française d'Economie*.

Tuomala M. (1990), *Optimal Income Tax and Redistribution*, Oxford University Press.

PART II

The Facts

3. Effective taxation, spending and employment performance

C. Martínez Mongay and R. Fernández Bayón[1]

1 INTRODUCTION

Taxes affect the functioning of the economy by changing the incentive system. The distortionary effects of taxes arise because, by modifying agents' behaviour, they drive a wedge between the price paid by the buyer and the price received by the seller.[2] In particular, taxes on labour drive a wedge between the real wage paid by firms – the producer wage – and that received by workers – the consumer wage. This wedge arises because labour income is taxed three-fold. First, through social security contributions and taxes on payroll and workforce; secondly, the remaining income is subject to the personal income tax; finally, the rest is taxed again when the income is consumed through indirect taxes. The final impact of such a wedge on labour market outcomes depends on the tax incidence or, in other words, on the elasticities of the demand and supply for labour. Taxes on labour are expected to have perverse effects in terms of employment and unemployment when coupled with rigid labour market regulations. Unless labour taxes are fully borne by workers, an increase in the tax wedge induces wage pressure, which results in lower profitability and loss of competitiveness and may lead to higher unemployment.

Such theoretical relationships are well known and will not be the subject of further discussion in this chapter, which deals mainly with the empirical aspects of taxation and its links with employment performance at the macroeconomic level. First of all, this involves the calculation of the tax wedge for the whole economy. In principle, the calculation of the tax wedge could be accomplished through detailed analyses of the evolution of tax laws. Unfortunately, their complexity and the level of detail make it difficult, almost infeasible, to calculate the kind of synthetic indicators needed for macroeconomic analyses. In order to avoid such difficulties, until recently, most analyses of taxation were carried out on the basis of tax/GDP ratios. Although of valuable illustrative potential of the relative weight of taxes in an economy, and a useful tool to make comparisons across countries, they do not have immediate translation into microeconomic concepts in taxation models. Instead, as explained in the Appendix, the methodology of effective taxation, proposed by Mendoza, Razin and Tesar (1994) hereafter MRT, which basically consists of associating particular tax revenues with their corresponding tax bases obtained from national accounts, constitutes a simple but powerful way to estimate the aggregate wedges driven by taxes. Namely, the average effective tax wedges driven by taxes on production factors' incomes, as well as the tax wedge driven by indirect taxes between the consumer aggregate price index and the producer aggregate price index. In this chapter we analyse the evolution of the tax wedge on labour and its components across EU Member States, the US and Japan between 1970 and 1998.

The analysis of such tax wedges reveals that taxation on labour is higher and has increased much more in the EU than in the US. In parallel, the EU's employment performance has been poorer overall, while unemployment shows a steady increasing trend. A number of recent empirical works (*viz.*, Daveri and Tabellini, 1997; Elmeskov *et al.*, 1998, and Blanchard and Wolfers, 1999) have found, by using different specifications and panel data techniques, quite robust relationships between indicators of effective taxation on labour, on the one hand, and employment performance, on the other. This suggests that tax reform, namely cutting taxes on labour, could be an efficient tool for improving, partially at least, employment performance in the EU. This kind of policy recommendation implicitly assumes that taxes are exogenous, so that policy makers can set their levels without consideration of knock-on effects. Although this can be true where changes in tax laws are concerned, such an independence is surely questionable in the long run, and likely, in shorter periods of time. The distortionary effects of taxes by themselves as well as the agents' capacity to avoid taxes, may sterilize any impact of tax reform on the effective tax wedge. Furthermore, the causal relationship between taxes and employment performance could be more apparent than real.

As shown below, taxes, in particular labour taxes, follow the same paths as spending. Indeed, it could well be that increases in expenditures of any kind cause taxes to increase. In this case, any tax reform, unless accompanied by adequate measures on the expenditure side, could have unexpected effects in the long run. Additionally, potential causal links between employment and expenditures could explain the apparent relationship between taxes and employment performance. Consequently, from a policy point of view, the existence of causal relationships linking taxation, spending and employment performance is a relevant issue.

Within this framework, the chapter is organized as follows. Section 2 summarizes the evolution of the structure of the tax burden, distinguishing between taxes on factor incomes – capital and labour – and consumption. Section 3, following the methodology explained in the Appendix, analyses the effective tax rates for the three components of the tax wedge. Some indicators of taxation on low-paid labour are also considered. Section 4 carries out causality analyses to determine the link between expenditures and taxes, on the one hand, and between taxes and employment performance, on the other. Finally, section 5 presents conclusions.

2 TOTAL TAX REVENUES AND TAX REVENUES FROM LABOUR INCOME

The tax burden – the ratio of total tax revenues to GDP – in the EU stood at about 42 per cent in 1998, almost 9 percentage points higher than in 1970 (Table 3.1). The bulk of the increase took place in the 1970s and early 1980s, whereas, from the second half of the 1980s until now, the trend has decelerated significantly. These facts compare sturdily with the US and Japan, where the tax burden accounted for less than one-third of GDP in 1998. Tax revenues in the US went up by over 2 percentage points during 1970–98 (two-thirds of it raised in the 1990s). Furthermore, although the change in the EU and Japan is of the same magnitude, the tax burden in the latter was just 20 per cent in 1970 (34 per cent in the EU). Only in Denmark, Ireland, the Netherlands, and Finland was the tax burden in 1998 lower than at the end of the early 1990s' economic shock. The tax burdens of Sweden (54 per cent of GDP) and Denmark (50 per cent) were the highest among EU Member States in 1998, with Belgium, France, Finland and Austria just 3–4 percentage points down from the 50 per cent baseline. Conversely, Spain, Portugal, Greece, the UK and Ireland have burdens below 40 per cent of GDP, the latter with a rate somewhat comparable to that of the US.

The increase in the tax burden has been accompanied by a similar upsurge in public expenditure. Total expenditures in the EU accounted for 37 per cent of GDP in 1970 – 32 per cent in the US. Almost thirty years later the ratios were 49 per cent in the EU, but still only 33 per cent in the US. It is worth pointing out, however, that the budgetary consolidation process brought about by stage 2 of EMU and the Stability and Growth Pact, coupled with the end of the recession, have induced significant spending cuts in the EU. In the longer run, the possible link between expenditure and taxation is twofold: first, because of financing through social security contributions, in many countries, a rise in welfare spending 'directly' corresponds to rises in taxation; secondly, rises in overall spending may have forced governments to 'pull up' taxes to finance it, especially when the weight of public debt and, more recently, the Maastricht criteria have set a ceiling to the levels of public deficit. Section 4 presents empirical evidence for the EU and the US on these links between tax and spending ratios.

Table 3.1   Total revenues and expenditures (% GDP)

	Tax burden			Total expenditure		
	1998–70	1998–94	1998	1998–70	1998–94	1998
B	11.3	1.0	47.2	10.3	–3.7	52.3
DK	7.7	–0.6	49.9	15.1	–5.4	56.9
D	5.7	1.0	42.3	9.5	–0.5	48.1
EL	12.2	3.1	36.0	24.9	–1.9	54.6
E	16.4	0.2	34.6	21.0	–3.9	42.7
F	11.2	1.6	45.8	16.4	–1.2	53.3
IRL	6.0	–3.8	33.0	–3.4	–8.6	35.6
I	16.3	0.9	42.8	17.9	–5.9	50.6
L	N/A	N/A	N/A	N/A	N/A	N/A
NL	5.6	–1.2	40.2	6.2	–5.5	47.1
A	10.5	2.9	45.9	14.3	–2.2	52.5
P	16.6	3.3	37.9	25.8	1.4	47.2
FIN	14.2	–1.7	46.0	21.3	–8.9	51.9
S	13.6	5.6	53.7	17.2	–9.1	59.3
UK	0.7	2.7	37.7	0.3	–4.9	41.7
US	**2.4**	**1.3**	**29.8**	**0.9**	**–2.5**	**32.6**
JP	9.0	0.6	28.5	19.5	3.4	38.6
EUR-11	10.1	0.8	42.5	13.5	–2.6	49.4
EU-15	**8.5**	**1.1**	**42.1**	**11.6**	**–3.3**	**48.6**

Note: A: Austria; B: Belgium; DK: Denmark; D: Germany; EL: Greece; E: Spain; F: France; FIN: Finland; I: Italy; IRL: Ireland; JP: Japan; L: Luxembourg; NL: Netherlands; P: Portugal; S: Sweden; UK: United Kingdom; US: United States.

Source: AMECO, DG ECFIN, European Commission.

On both sides of the Atlantic, social security contributions (SSC) went up by about 40 per cent or more between 1970 and 1998, although the actual ratio is much lower in the US than in the EU (Table 2.2, first panel). The trend seems to be reversing after the early 1990s' economic crisis, although more intensively in the EU, particularly from 1996, than in the US, where the SSC/GDP ratio has somehow stagnated. Nevertheless, and despite the latest developments, the relative importance of SSC as a source of public revenues has not ceased to increase in most OECD economies over the past 28 years. In 1998, they accounted for 35 per cent of the total tax burden in the EU (31 per cent in 1970) and for 30 per cent in the US (22 per cent in 1970).

Table 3.2 Structure of the tax burden (% GDP)

	SSC			Indirect taxes			Direct taxes		
	1998–70	1998–94	1998	1998–70	1998–94	1998	1998–70	1998–94	1998
B	4.6	–0.5	16.6	–0.4	0.2	12.9	7.1	1.3	17.7
DK	0.4	–0.2	2.6	0.1	0.9	17.9	7.2	–1.3	29.4
D	6.6	0.6	19.2	–1.6	–0.2	11.6	0.7	0.6	11.5
EL	5.1	0.6	12.9	1.7	0.9	14.6	5.4	1.6	8.5
E	5.7	–0.7	13.2	3.5	0.7	11.1	7.2	0.2	10.3
F	4.7	–2.2	18.3	1.4	0.8	16.0	5.1	3.0	11.5
IRL	2.6	–1.6	5.8	–2.5	–0.6	13.4	5.9	–1.6	13.8
I	1.8	–1.9	13.0	5.3	3.4	15.4	9.2	–0.6	14.4
L	N/A	N/A	NIA	N/A	N/A	NIA	N/A	N/A	N/A
NL	3.9	–0.8	16.4	2.0	0.8	11.6	–0.3	–1.2	12.2
A	6.6	–0.2	17.1	0.6	0.6	15.0	3.3	2.5	13.8
P	7.6	1.5	12.5	3.9	0.4	15.0	5.1	1.4	10.4
FIN	7.5	–2.8	13.1	0.6	–0.5	14.0	6.1	1.6	18.9
S	6.4	1.2	15.0	3.4	1.3	15.7	3.8	3.1	23.0
UK	1.5	0.1	7.7	0.4	0.5	13.6	–1.2	2.1	16.4
US	**2.8**	**–0.2**	**8.8**	**–1.8**	**–0.6**	**6.6**	**1.4**	**2.1**	**14.4**
JP	6.8	1.6	11.1	1.2	0.4	8.3	1.0	–1.4	9.1
EUR-11	4.7	–1.0	16.6	1.1	0.9	13.5	4.3	0.9	12.4
EU-15	**4.2**	**–1.0**	**14.8**	**1.0**	**0.8**	**13.7**	**3.3**	**1.2**	**13.7**

Note: Key as for Table 3.1

Source: AMECO, DG ECFIN, European Commission.

Particularly high SSC/GDP ratios are found in Germany, France, the Netherlands, Belgium and Austria, while in Denmark, Ireland or the UK SSC represented a comparatively small GDP share in 1998. In the most recent past, many Member States have reduced SSC. In Italy, France and, to a much lesser extent, in Germany, SSC have been reduced sharply in the last year, while in Finland contributions have gone down by almost three percentage points since 1994.

SSC form one of the components of the tax wedge on labour. Another component is that of indirect taxes paid by labour incomes when these are consumed (Table 3.2, second panel). Unlike SSC, the share of indirect tax revenues to GDP in the EU has remained broadly stable since 1970. In Spain and Portugal the share of indirect taxes to GDP rose significantly following the adoption of the VAT regime after accession, while a large part of the increase in Denmark, Italy, Sweden or Greece has taken place in the most recent past.

The third component of the total wedge is the share of taxes on income and wealth (direct taxes), namely that corresponding to personal income taxes on labour income. The ratio of direct taxes is shown in the third panel of Table 3.2. Unlike the other two broad components of the total tax burden, direct taxes represent a higher GDP weight in the US than in the EU. However, the latter has been in a catching-up process with the US. Between 1970 and 1998, the EU ratio rose by over three percentage points, more than twice the change observed in the US.

Overall, we can conclude that in the EU the total tax burden is distributed almost equally among the three broad categories of taxes, while in the US direct taxes account for almost 50 per cent of total tax revenues. Furthermore, while consumption taxes have not changed very much in the EU, the increase in the tax burden has been mainly financed by revenues from non-wage labour costs (50 per cent) and direct taxes (almost 40 per cent). In the US, the fall in indirect taxes has offset the increase in direct taxes, and the change in the tax burden is fully accounted for by the increase in SSC. This could, in principle, suggest a much less employment-friendly taxation of labour in the US than in the EU. However, this conclusion would not be taking into consideration two facts. First, the tax ratios are higher in the EU than in the US, which would be indicating that the burden on labour is also much higher. Secondly, there is an unobservable component of the tax wedge, namely the part of personal income taxes paid by labour income.

Unfortunately, the decomposition of total direct taxes into those paid by labour income and those paid by capital income is not directly available from AMECO. However, the OECD Economic Outlook databank decomposes direct taxes between taxes on income and wealth paid by businesses and those paid by individuals. The latter are direct taxes on personal income from labour and from capital, which also include taxes on property – a tax on capital income – paid by individuals. As it will be shown in the next section, direct taxes paid by individuals can be decomposed further into taxes on labour and taxes on capital by calculating the effective personal income tax rate, as shown in the Appendix. Table 3.3 shows the share of tax revenues from direct taxes paid by individuals to total direct tax revenues in 1998 as well as the change recorded between 1970 and 1998. Indeed, complements of such figures would refer to the 1998 share – and to the corresponding 1970–98 change – of direct taxes paid by businesses to total direct tax revenues. Table 3.3 seems therefore to suggest that the increase in the ratio of direct taxes to GDP has been accompanied by an increase in the relative weight of direct taxes paid by individuals, which could be indicating a shift in the tax burden from capital to labour in both the EU and the US. Yet, in some Member States (Greece, Italy, the Netherlands, Finland and Sweden) the relative weight of direct taxes paid by individuals to total direct tax revenues has actually fallen. Nevertheless, before drawing conclusions on the basis of such ratios, one should bear in mind that a component of direct taxes paid by individuals are actually taxes on property and capital income. Furthermore, the variation in the share does not forcefully signal at a structural change. The relative increase in direct taxes paid by individuals could be due to changes in tax bases rather than to changes in tax rates. To analyse this issue it is necessary to link each tax category with its corresponding tax base. This is, in a nutshell, the concept of effective taxation, which will be developed in the coming section. Additional details are given in the Appendix.

Table 3.3   Share of direct taxes paid by households to total direct taxes

	1998–70	1998–94	1998
B	2.1	–3.5	80.6
DK	N/A	–3.2	90.2
D	24.2	1.8	74.1
EL	–19.9	–0.2	59.8
E	34.8	–9.7	71.6
F	9.4	–0.2	76.1
IRL	N/A	–5.4	73.9
I	–4.7	–5.4	73.3
L	N/A	N/A	N/A
NL	–16.7	–12.1	63.3
A	3.4	–3.5	85.4
P	11.1	–3.7	70.3
FIN	–6.0	–15.2	81.0
S	–7.4	– 3.1	85.2
UK	N/A	–9.9	73.7
US	**6.1**	**2.3**	**82.2**
JP	10.1	–4.2	60.9
EUR-11*	N/A	–2.5	74.1
EU-15*	**N/A**	**–3.5**	**74.5**
EUR-11**	10.9	–2.4	74.3
EU-15**	**9.1**	**–2.4**	**74.4**

Notes: *Excluding L; **Excluding L, IRL, DK and the UK from EU-15. Excluding L and IRL from EUR-11.

Source: OECD Economic Outlook Database.

3   THE EFFECTIVE TAXATION ON LABOUR

Tax revenues expressed in terms of the GDP represent the average tax burden per unit of total income for each tax category included in the National Accounts. Although of valuable illustrative potential on the relative weight of taxes in an economy, and a useful tool to make comparisons across countries, they do not have an immediate translation into microeconomic concepts in taxation models. If there was only a category of tax and a unique production factor, the total tax burden expressed as a percentage of GDP would give the tax wedge – the difference between the price paid by firms employing the factor and the price received by their owners as a percentage of the former. However, in an economy with several factors of production and with taxes of different kinds, the tax wedge varies across factors and types of taxes. At aggregate level there exist two production factors: labour and capital. Some taxes fall directly on specific production factor-incomes (*viz.* SSC is a tax on wages). Others fall directly on both production-factor incomes (direct taxes), or occur when income is consumed (indirect taxes). Although recognizing the importance of simplifying assumptions, the MRT method described in the Appendix allows for calculations of the average effective tax wedges driven by taxes on production factors, as well as of the tax wedge driven by indirect taxes between the consumer aggregate price index and the producer aggregate price index.

3.1   The Tax Wedge on Labour

Taxes drive a wedge between what firms pay per unit of labour and what this unit actually receives, both measured in terms of units of the output produced by the firm. Such a wedge is the difference between the gross wage deflated by the producer's price (real producer wage w_p) and the wage net of taxes deflated by the consumer's price (the real consumer wage w_c). It arises because labour income is first taxed through social security contributions; then, workers have to pay income taxes on the remaining income which, in turn, once direct taxes have been deducted, will be subject to indirect taxes when the net income is consumed.

The tax wedge can be defined as

$$wedge = (w_p - w_c)/w_p$$

If P_p and P_c are respectively the producer price and the consumer price, and t_c is the consumption tax rate,[3] the following relationships are obtained:

$$w_p = W_p/P_p$$

$$W_c = W_c/P_c$$

and

$$1 - t_c = P_p/P_c$$

where t_c is the difference between the consumer price and the producer price expressed in terms of the former. The relationship between the nominal gross (producer) wage (W_p) and the nominal net (consumer) wage (W_c) is

$$W_c = (1 - t_i)(W_p - ssc)$$

t_i being the personal income tax, and *ssc* being the total of social security contributions paid per unit of labour. Since *ssc* can be expressed in terms of the nominal gross wage

$$nwlc = ssc/W_p$$

the tax wedge can be calculated as

$$wedge = 1 - (1 - nwlc)(1 - t_i)(1 - t_c)$$

The rest of this section is devoted mainly to the analysis of the effective tax rates on labour. The Appendix gives information on the effective tax rates on personal income and consumption.

3.2 Effective Non-wage Labour Costs (NWLC)

The effective NWLC-rate is the ratio of total social security contributions to total labour costs.[4] The fact that a part of total SSC is paid by the self-employed suggests that at least a part of their revenue is treated, from a fiscal point of view, as labour income. The issue at stake is that the total income of the self-employed is also capital income (an income obtained by them as owners of capital) and there is no data singling it out. However, the labour income of the self-employed can be estimated by considering that self-employment activities have an opportunity cost, namely the wage the self-employed could earn should they work as employees. At the macroeconomic level, such a wage equals the average gross wage earned by the employees (wage and salary earners) and, therefore, the total cost of labour can be calculated as the total compensation of employees multiplied by the ratio of occupied population to wage and salary earners.[5]

Table 3.4 reports the evolution of NWLC (in percentage) over the 1970–1998 time-period. The long-run trend is unambiguously positive since the early 1970s. Since the labour-share during the last thirty years has been declining, the rise in the SSC/GDP ratio must have been induced by an increase in the rate leading to a widening of the tax burden on labour. The trend seems to be reversing after the early 1990s' crisis. Such a recent evolution is very much in line with successive recommendations of the Commission's *Broad Economic Policy Guidelines* (see European Commission, 1999). Furthermore, since statutory NWLC rates are overall proportional,[6] the observed fall could be related to efforts to reduce taxation on labour through cuts in SSC. Despite this however, the effective NWLC rate still remains much higher in the EU than in the US or Japan. The exceptions to this rule are the UK, Ireland and Denmark. However, in the latter, as it will be shown below, there is a clear compensation through very high personal income taxes on labour income. It is also worth noting that NWLC have recently declined (notably in France and Finland) and/or practically stagnated in most Member States except Portugal and Germany, where the shares have increased by three and two percentage points respectively over 1994–98. NWLC also went up significantly in Sweden and Austria. In Japan they surged by more than two percentage points in the 4-year period. Conversely, Italy and France curbed NWLC by over three percentage points in the last year.

Table 3.4   Non-wage labour costs

	1998–70	1998–94	1995	1996	1997	1998
B	7.5	0.5	26.2	26.5	26.9	26.9
DK	1.2	–0.4	4.5	4.5	4.5	4.5
D	12.5	2.0	30.5	31.6	32.5	32.2
EL	10.1	0.5	21.1	22.0	21.4	21.5
E	11.1	–0.3	21.0	21.4	21.6	21.6
F	9.6	–3.1	34.8	35.2	34.7	31.6
IRL	6.6	–1.0	11.9	11.4	11.3	11.3
I	5.7	–1.3	25.4	25.9	26.4	23.4
L	N/A	N/A	N/A	19.2	19.0	N/A
NL	9.1	–0.6	28.3	27.4	27.6	27.4
A	9.9	1.0	25.7	26.4	26.7	26.3
P	13.1	3.0	17.9	18.4	19.7	20.4
FIN	14.7	–3.3	25.8	24.5	24.0	23.6
S	11.0	1.7	23.8	24.6	24.3	24.0
UK	2.6	0.2	12.1	12.1	12.0	12.2
US	**5.0**	**–0.3**	**14.3**	**14.3**	**14.2**	**14.0**
JP	9.7	2.2	15.2	15.3	15.6	16.2
EUR-11	9.6	–0.5	28.9	29.3	29.6	28.2
EU-15	**8.4**	**–0.8**	**26.0**	**26.3**	**26.0**	**24.9**

Source: AMECO, DG ECFIN, European Commission.

If one just considers the effective NWLC rate on employed labour, thus excluding the self-employed (see Appendix), the only remarkable difference is a generalized increase of the rate compared with that including the self-employed. The difference is larger for the EU average than for the US or Japan and is obviously due to the fact that imputed gross wages of the self-employed are less taxed than the average wage of the employees. Apart from this, considering either rate does not change the conclusions regarding their evolution, even the most recent one, or the comparisons across countries.

Non-wage labour costs for employed labour have in general two components, namely SSC paid by the employers (SSCER) and that paid by the employees (SSCEE). In a few countries (France, Denmark, Ireland, Greece, Austria and Sweden) gross wages are also directly taxed through taxes on payroll and workforce, but they account for a rather marginal share compared with the two other main components.[7] There is some conventional wisdom that such components have not an equal potential impact on employment performance. In particular, it is argued that SSCER may have a direct negative impact on the demand for labour (Liebfritz, Thornton and Bibbee, 1997, Hamermesh, 1993) and defendants of tax cuts to boost employment as, for instance, Dreze and Sneessens (1996) put strong emphasis on the reduction of SSCER. Table A3.1 from the Appendix shows the evolution and differences across countries of the ratio of SSCER revenues to total labour costs on employed labour. The ratio in the EU in 1998 more than doubled that of the US, although in Ireland, the Netherlands, the UK and, indeed, in Denmark the figure is of the same magnitude or even lower. Overall, the ratio has followed the same positive path as NWLC, and, in most countries, SSCER account for more than 50 per cent of NWLC. The most outstanding exception is the Netherlands where SSCER in terms of the gross wage more than halved, while the share of NWLC actually increased.

3.3 Effective Personal Income Tax Rates and Effective Taxes on Labour

Once non-wage labour costs have been deducted from gross wages, workers pay personal taxes on the remaining labour income. As explained in the Appendix, owing to the lack of comparable data across countries, we follow the MRT methodology and assume that the tax wedge driven by the income tax does not depend on the amount of the labour income but on the total personal income subject to the tax. In this case, the personal labour income effective tax rate equals the total personal income effective tax rate, calculated as the ratio of tax revenues from income taxes paid by individuals to the total income received by them, a part of which being revenues from capital.

The direct tax wedge on labour income arises because gross wages are taxed twice – through SSC and other payroll taxes and through the personal income tax. The labour effective tax rate (LETR) comprises both taxes and, as shown in the Appendix, can be calculated as the ratio of NWLC plus personal taxes on labour income to gross wages, which gives

$$LETR = t_i (1 - NWLC) + NWLC$$

As shown in Table 3.5 the direct tax burden on labour in the EU was 37 per cent in 1998, compared with 26 per cent in the US. Particularly high above average shares are found in the Nordic countries (Sweden, Denmark and Finland), Belgium and Germany, while the UK and Ireland recorded rates lower than that of the US. Interestingly, labour taxes in Greece represented 28 per cent of total labour costs; however, when the self-employed are not included the effective taxation on employed labour goes up to well over 40 per cent. In addition, only in Luxembourg and the Netherlands are effective taxes lower on employed labour than when including the self-employed. While in most Member States the bulk of direct taxes on labour consists of SSC, in Denmark,

Table 3.5   Effective tax rates on labour

	1998–70	1998–94	1995	1996	1997	1998
B	14.8	1.1	42.7	42.9	43.5	43.9
DK	12.5	–1.6	43.7	44.2	43.7	42.7
D	14.0	1.9	42.4	43.1	43.6	43.6
EL	14.6	2.2	26.2	26.9	27.1	27.7
E	17.4	–0.9	29.6	29.9	29.7	29.6
F	13.9	–0.6	41.0	42.0	41.8	40.5
IRL	13.8	–3.2	24.3	23.9	23.9	23.5
I	15.8	–1.3	38.3	39.0	40.5	36.5
L	N/A	N/A	N/A	28.8	27.2	N/A
NL	6.1	–3.5	38.8	37.4	36.4	36.1
A	14.6	3.4	38.8	40.2	41.2	41.2
P	15.8	3.0	25.2	26.1	27.0	27.8
FIN	20.5	–5.2	46.2	46.3	43.9	43.8
S	14.1	5.7	46.4	47.8	47.9	49.9
UK	0.4	0.8	24.3	23.7	23.3	24.7
US	**7.4**	**1.9**	**24.6**	**25.3**	**25.7**	**26.0**
JP	11.2	1.0	21.3	21.1	21.8	21.8
EUR-11	13.9	–0.1	39.7	40.2	40.4	39.3
EU-15	**11.5**	**–0.2**	**37.7**	**38.1**	**37.8**	**37.1**

Source: AMECO, DG ECFIN, European Commission.

the personal income effective tax rate, the highest in the EU at 40 per cent, is the main way for taxing labour income. The long-run evolution is clearly positive (rising by 12 percentage points since 1970) and quite similar across countries, although LETR increased less in the Netherlands and the US and remained broadly stable in the UK. In the most recent past, as with NWLC, the direct tax burden on labour is decreasing slightly in the EU, namely in Ireland, the Netherlands, Finland and Denmark.

3.4 Consumption Taxes and the Tax Wedge

In the EU, almost half of the producer's real wage is gone away in taxes. Significantly high wedges are those of the three Nordic Member States, Belgium, Germany, France and Austria, (Table 3.6). At the opposite extreme, in the US and Japan taxes only represent less than one-third of the gross wage, whereas the lowest tax wedges in the EU are those of Ireland, the UK, Spain, Greece and Portugal. During the last three decades, the tax wedge has increased in the

Table 3.6   The tax wedge

	1998–70	1998–94	1995	1996	1997	1998
B	11.3	1.2	52.0	52.5	53.2	53.6
DK	9.3	–0.5	56.2	56.9	56.7	56.1
D	9.3	1.4	51.0	51.5	51.9	52.1
EL	12.0	2.8	37.4	38.5	39.0	40.0
E	18.4	0.1	38.8	39.2	39.3	39.8
F	11.3	0.3	52.5	53.7	53.7	52.6
IRL	13.2	–1.0	38.7	38.8	39.2	39.3
I	17.1	1.8	48.0	48.4	50.0	49.1
L	N/A	N/A	N/A	46.2	45.0	N/A
NL	7.1	–2.2	47.7	47.0	46.4	46.3
A	11.0	3.3	50.1	51.4	52.7	52.8
P	16.4	2.9	38.7	39.5	40.4	41.0
FIN	16.7	–3.8	55.6	56.1	54.6	54.8
S	13.5	5.8	56.0	57.5	57.9	60.0
UK	0.0	1.3	36.3	35.8	35.9	37.0
US	**5.1**	**1.3**	**31.0**	**31.5**	**31.8**	**32.0**
JP	9.6	1.0	30.5	30.4	30.9	30.9
EUR-11	11.8	0.7	49.4	49.9	50.3	50.0
EU-15	**9.7**	**0.6**	**47.8**	**48.2**	**48.2**	**48.1**

Source: AMECO, DG ECFIN, European Commission.

EU by almost 10 percentage points. While in Spain, Italy, Portugal and Finland the change observed is 15 percentage points or higher, the tax wedge in the US only rose by 5 percentage points.

The surge in consumption effective taxes seems to be common among most Member States (except Germany) and explains largely why the total tax wedge in 1998 was slightly higher than in 1994 (0.6 percentage point rise). On average, NWLC went down by 0.8 percentage points in the EU between 1994 and 1998 and personal income effective tax rates (PIETR) rose by 0.6 percentage points. However, consumption effective tax rates (CETR) went up by 1.2 percentage points between 1998 and 1994.

Only the Netherlands, Finland, Ireland and, to a lesser extent, Denmark have curbed the total tax wedge during 1994–8. In Finland the main components of the reduction were both NWLC and personal income taxes whereas in the Netherlands, Ireland and Denmark the bulk of the fall in the tax wedge is due to a sharp reduction of personal taxes (PIETR). In the four countries NWLC fell – although not as much as they did in Finland. In addition, in all four of them consumption taxes (CETR) increased, but without offsetting the reductions achieved in NWLC and in personal income taxes.

In Spain and France the tax wedge remained broadly stable during the 4-year period. In both Member States consumption taxes rose equally. However, while in Spain NWLC fell marginally and personal taxes followed suit, France recorded the second highest fall in NWLC and still arrived at a tax wedge marginally higher at the end of 1998. This was the result of a strong surge in personal taxes – third highest rise after Sweden and Austria.

In another group of countries (Belgium, Germany and the UK) the tax wedge increased by around 1 percentage point since 1994. In Belgium and the UK, the three components of the tax wedge recorded similar rises, particularly in personal and consumption taxes. However, in Germany, NWLC went up by over 2 percentage points, second highest rise after Portugal, being as well the only European country in which consumption taxes actually fell, although very marginally. Thus, the rise in Germany's tax wedge was fully accounted for by rises in NWLC.

In the remaining Member States (Greece, Portugal, Italy, Sweden and Austria) the tax wedge exhibited significant increases during 1994–98, going from 2–3 percentage points in Italy, Portugal, Greece and Austria to 6 percentage points in Sweden. In Greece, both personal and consumption taxes are responsible for the upsurge in the tax wedge, whereas in Portugal the increase in the wedge was almost fully borne by rises in NWLC, the highest rise in the EU. The most exceptional case is Italy which, despite reducing NWLC, witnessed a very significant rise in its tax wedge, the reason being the striking upsurge in consumption taxes, the highest rise among EU Member States. In Sweden, all three components of the tax wedge went up very signif-

Table 3.7   Summary total economy (1998–94)

	NWLC	PIETR	CETR	Tax Wedge
B	0.5	0.9	0.6	1.2
DK	−0.4	−1.5	1.4	−0.5
D	2.0	0.3	−0.3	1.4
EL	0.5	2.2	1.3	2.8
E	−0.3	−0.8	1.3	0.1
F	−3.1	3.2	1.3	0.3
IRL	−1.0	−2.6	2.0	−1.0
I	−1.3	−0.3	4.5	1.8
L	N/A	N/A	N/A	N/A
NL	−0.6	−4.2	1.3	−2.2
A	1.0	3.5	0.9	3.3
P	3.0	0.4	0.7	2.9
FIN	−3.3	−3.8	0.7	−3.8
S	1.7	5.9	2.2	5.8
UK	0.2	0.7	0.9	1.3
US	**−0.3**	**2.5**	**−0.6**	**1.3**
JP	2.2	−1.2	0.2	1.0
EUR-11	−0.5	0.5	1.3	0.7
EU-15	**−0.8**	**0.6**	**1.2**	**0.6**

Source: From Tables 3.4, 3.6, A3.2 and A3.3.

icantly, with personal and consumption taxes soaring stunningly. Consequently, the Swedish tax wedge rose by 6 percentage points in only four years. Finally, the strong increase in the tax wedge in Austria was due to combined rises in all of its three components, although the bulk of it can be attributed to a very strong increase in personal taxes over the 1994–98 time-period.

3.5   Taxation of Labour at the Lower End of the Wage Scale

We take as the representative of low-skilled workers a single person with no children earning 67 per cent of the average production worker wage (APW). According to the OECD (1998a) statutory direct taxes on labour (including SSC) accounted for more than 40 per cent of the gross wage for low-skilled workers in several Member States (Table 3.8). The rate is in the region of 50 per cent in Belgium, Italy, Sweden and Germany. Only in Ireland, Luxembourg, Portugal and the UK is the rate comparable to or lower than that of the US. In

Table 3.8   Taxation of labour at the lower end of the wage scale, 1997

	Total direct taxes on labour				Of which								
					Personal income tax rate		NWLC				SSC paid by employers		SSC paid by employees
	%	97–96 pps	% APW	97–96 pps	%	% APW	%	97–96 pps	% APW	97–96 pps	%	% APW	%	% APW
B	49.5	−1.0	87.5	−2.0	20.5	74.3	29.0	−1.3	100.0	−4.5	15.9	105.3	13.1	94.2
DK	41.7	0.4	92.5	0.3	30.7	87.5	11.0	1.3	110.0	−0.2	0.3	150.0	10.7	109.2
D	47.7	1.2	91.2	0.4	15.6	73.6	32.1	1.0	103.2	0.2	11.0	110.0	21.1	100.0
EL	35.0	0.1	97.8	0.3	0.9	45.0	34.1	−0.1	100.9	0.0	18.2	101.7	15.9	100.0
E	34.8	0.4	89.2	0.5	8.3	60.1	26.5	0.0	105.2	0.5	20.1	106.9	6.4	100.0
F	41.6	−2.7	85.4	−3.7	6.3	60.0	35.3	−4.7	92.4	−5.6	17.6	85.9	17.7	100.0
IRL	24.9	−1.6	73.5	0.1	16.0	78.0	8.9	−0.5	66.4	−1.7	6.3	79.7	2.6	47.3
I	48.8	0.5	94.8	−0.3	14.9	79.3	33.9	0.0	103.7	0.0	23.7	105.3	10.2	100.0
L	29.7	0.6	84.4	0.1	7.7	55.8	22.0	0.2	102.8	0.2	9.4	106.8	12.6	100.0
NL	38.8	−0.5	89.0	−0.7	3.8	58.5	35.0	0.5	94.3	−0.5	4.1	95.3	30.9	94.2
A	41.1	3.7	90.1	0.0	4.3	42.2	36.8	3.5	104.0	3.5	18.7	108.1	18.1	100.0
P	30.8	0.2	90.9	0.4	3.3	45.8	27.5	0.0	103.0	0.0	16.5	105.1	11.0	100.0
FIN	44.2	−1.1	90.4	0.3	22.2	79.3	22.0	0.3	105.3	1.0	14.3	110.0	7.7	97.5

S	49.2	0.6	97.0	0.2	26.5	93.0	22.7	0.7	102.3	-0.5	16.7	103.1	6.0	100.0
UK	28.4	1.6	88.8	6.6	13.6	81.4	14.8	2.0	96.7	12.5	7.1	104.4	7.7	90.6
US	**29.2**	**0.0**	**93.9**	**0.0**	**16.1**	**88.5**	**13.1**	**0.0**	**101.6**	**0.0**	**5.4**	**103.8**	**7.7**	**100.0**
JP	19.4	1.0	93.7	-1.1	6.6	82.5	12.8	0.0	100.8	0.0	5.8	101.8	7.0	100.0
EU-11	44.2	0.0	90.0	-0.8	11.8	70.9	32.3	-0.7	99.8	-1.1	15.6	100.7	16.7	99.0
EU-15	**42.0**	**0.2**	**90.2**	**-0.1**	**12.7**	**74.0**	**29.3**	**-0.2**	**99.7**	**-0.2**	**14.2**	**101.0**	**15.1**	**98.5**

Source: *The Tax Benefit Position of Employees*, OECD, 1998a.

71

most Member States the bulk of the burden has its origin in non-wage labour costs. On average more than two-thirds of total direct taxes on labour in the EU are accounted for by non-wage labour costs, compared with less than half in the US. Apart from Denmark, where SSC are rather marginal, the most outstanding exceptions are Ireland and the UK, with relatively low NWLC. In France, the Netherlands, Portugal and Austria about four-fifths of total direct taxes on labour correspond to NWLC, with the proportion being close to 100 per cent in Greece. Generally speaking, the statutory burden is borne almost equally between employers and employees. However, in Finland, Italy, Spain and Sweden the employers share the bulk of contributions, while in Germany, the Netherlands and Denmark much of the burden is paid by the employees.

Figures in Table 3.8 should not be compared with those corresponding to Tables 3.4, 3.5 or A3.1, since the rates have been calculated on the basis of totally different methodologies. Basically, effective rates are the ratio of average tax revenues collected per worker to the average gross wage, while Table 3.8 reports on those taxes that a worker earning a given gross wage (67 per cent of the wage received by the average production worker – APW) and with a given marital status (single no children) should pay. Moreover, the average gross wage and the wage of the APW are not necessarily the same. The relevant comparison references are also provided by the OECD (1998a), namely direct taxes on a single person with no children earning the APW. The second column of each panel of Table 3.8 expresses taxes paid by workers earning 67 per cent of the wage of the APW as a percentage of taxes paid by the APW. This suggests that the progressivity of the tax systems is relatively low. In many countries the difference in the tax burden at the lower end and at the middle of the wage scale is lower than 10 percentage points. Such lack of progressivity finds its origins in the rates of SSC paid by the employers, owing to the existence of lump-sums independent of wages, whereas – except for Ireland – SSC paid by the employees are rather proportional and the personal income tax is progressive.

More information about progressivity of tax systems is also given by the marginal tax rates and the marginal increase in net incomes as calculated by the OECD (1998a). Unskilled workers could face rather high marginal tax rates in a number of countries such as in Austria, Belgium, Denmark, Finland, Germany, France and the Netherlands (Table 3.9). In Belgium and Germany these marginal rates (on wage earnings) are close to that of the APW whereas, in Austria and France, OECD estimates point to a regressive tax system at the low end of the wage scale. The same is true for Spain and Sweden, although their marginal tax rates for low-skilled workers are considerably lower. In Denmark, the UK, Greece, Portugal and the US both average production and low-skilled workers face equal marginal tax rates on wage earnings, while the rest of the Member States display more progressive tax systems.

Table 3.9 Marginal tax rates, 1997

	On gross wage earnings[1] 1997–96		On gross labour costs[2]				Increase in net income on wage earnings[3] 1997–96		1997–96	
	67%	67% pps	100%	67%	100%	67%	67% pps	100%	100% pps	
B	54.8	0.0	55.9	66.5	67.3	0.68	0.00	0.75	0.00	
DK	52.1	0.4	52.1	52.2	52.2	0.82	0.00	0.87	0.00	
D	51.9	3.1	55.2	60.2	63.0	0.76	–0.04	0.78	–0.04	
EL	20.1	0.0	20.1	37.6	37.6	0.96	0.00	0.97	0.00	
E	31.2	0.9	26.8	47.4	44.0	0.81	0.00	0.92	0.08	
F	49.4	15.5	35.4	74.0	53.9	0.67	–0.19	0.90	0.01	
IRL	30.5	–2.0	54.7	35.9	59.6	0.85	0.00	0.61	–0.01	
I	34.4	0.2	40.7	55.2	59.5	0.88	0.01	0.83	0.00	
L	34.1	0.1	43.1	41.9	49.8	0.83	0.01	0.77	–0.02	
NL	46.8	–0.2	55.1	51.8	57.4	0.81	–0.01	0.74	0.00	
A	51.5	4.0	42.5	63.2	56.4	0.62	–0.05	0.80	–0.03	
P	26.0	0.0	26.0	40.2	40.2	0.86	0.00	0.90	0.00	
FIN	45.0	–2.5	50.7	56.2	60.7	0.78	0.02	0.77	0.00	
S	38.9	0.9	35.7	54.0	51.6	0.90	–0.01	0.98	0.36	
UK	33.0	–1.0	33.0	39.1	39.1	0.85	0.01	0.90	0.01	
US	**29.9**	**0.0**	**29.9**	**34.9**	**34.9**	**0.92**	**0.00**	**0.95**	**0.01**	
JP	16.5	1.5	21.6	22.0	26.8	0.97	0.00	0.92	–0.01	
EUR-11	45.5	4.6	44.9	60.5	57.9	0.76	–0.06	0.82	–0.01	
EU-15	**43.4**	**3.6**	**42.8**	**56.9**	**54.8**	**0.78**	**–0.05**	**0.84**	**0.01**	

Notes:
(1) Marginal tax rate covering employees' social security contributions and personal income tax, with respect to a change of gross wage earnings.
(2) Marginal tax rate covering employees' and employers' social security contributions and personal income tax, with respect to a change of gross labour costs.
(3) Increase in net income after a one per cent increase in gross wage earnings (elasticity of income after tax). Net income is calculated as gross earnings minus employees' social security contributions and personal income tax. In a proportional tax system the elasticity would equal 1. The more progressive the system, the lower the elasticity.

Source: *The Tax Benefit Position of Employees*, OECD, 1998a.

High marginal rates reduce net income at the margin by almost 20 per cent in many Member States. In Belgium and France unskilled workers receive less than 70 per cent of the last monetary unit earned, once direct taxes on labour have been deducted. In Austria net income at the margin goes down by 40 per cent for unskilled labour. Net income increases are the highest in Japan (97 per cent), the US (92 per cent), Greece (96 per cent) and Sweden (90 per cent). In

Ireland, going from the low end to the middle of the wage scale may imply a significant reduction in marginal earnings. On the contrary, in France and Austria, and, to a lesser degree, in Spain, Sweden, Belgium, Denmark and the UK, climbing the wage scale results in higher marginal earnings.

According to OECD data, France curbed NWLC for low-skilled workers by almost five percentage points between 1996 and 1997. Conversely, Austria and the UK exhibited rises of about four and two percentage points respectively. In addition, the relative position of low-skilled with respect to average workers was improved significantly (the gap narrowed) in France and Belgium but worsened (the gap widened) sharply in the UK. As a result of these measures, unskilled workers in France faced marginal tax rates on gross wage earnings 16 percentage points higher in 1997 than in 1996, whereas in the UK these were trimmed down marginally. Very significantly, Austria increased NWLC for unskilled labour and still arrived at marginal rates in 1997 above those recorded in 1996. As a consequence of higher marginal tax rates, French unskilled workers saw their net income at the margin being reduced strikingly by about 20 percentage points with respect to the previous year. Austria followed suit the trend (down by 5 percentage points), with unskilled workers receiving just about 60 per cent of their last monetary unit earned. Finally, climbing the wage scale in Spain resulted in significantly higher net income earnings at the end of 1997 compared with 1996. The case of Sweden is nevertheless the most startling. In only one year it moved from being the country where going from the bottom to the top of the wage scale implied the highest reduction in marginal earnings to be the one where average production workers displayed the highest gains in net income.

4 TAXATION, SPENDING, EMPLOYMENT AND UNEMPLOYMENT

We have argued in section 2 that there is a link between expenditures and taxes. Some other similar links have also been suggested between welfare spending and social security contributions or, equivalently, labour taxes. Furthermore, in section 3 we have seen that the effective taxation on labour has followed almost the same path as the tax ratios. Therefore, there is a case for asking why effective taxation changes. The main task at hand is to reveal something about the capacity of public authorities to change tax rates on labour in a discretionary way without creating budgetary imbalances. If total taxes and effective tax rates on labour follow expenditures, any exogenous change on tax codes affecting labour income might leave effective taxation on labour unaffected, unless other adjustments are made on the spending side.

On the other hand, a number of recent empirical works (*viz*. Daveri and Tabellini, 1997; Elmeskov *et al.*, 1999, and Blanchard and Wolfers, 1999), by using different specifications and panel data techniques, have found fairly robust relationships between indicators of effective taxation on labour, on the one hand, and employment and/or unemployment, on the other. In general, high effective taxes on labour seem to be correlated with low employment and/or high unemployment, implying that a reduction of the labour tax wedge may reduce unemployment and/or increase employment. The economic channels seem to involve labour market institutions, social protection and the effects of taxes on labour supply. Overall, it is expected that taxes are wage-pressure factors, thereby reducing the demand for labour. Moreover, the lowering of taxes on labour may result in a reduction of replacement rates, which would increase the incentives to take up jobs, thus making work pay and reducing the risk of unemployment traps. Finally, lower taxes on labour could have a positive impact on the supply of labour at the margin, which would increase the incentives to participate in the labour market and/or to supply more hours of work, especially for workers at the top end of the wage scale, as well as for other population groups, such as married women. Such institutional factors, which temporally evolve in a discontinuous way, are difficult to include in time-series models, while they can be more accurately represented in panel data models. However, in this kind of model it is difficult to disentangle the effects of taxes from the effects of shocks, which simultaneously affect taxes and employment performance. More specifically, panel data relationships are of a contemporaneous nature and, although the corresponding econometric models may pass endogeneity tests or use instrumental variable techniques, in our view, the question of whether effective taxes cause labour market outcomes, or the other way round, remains unresolved. The relevance of this question for economic policy seems to be evident.

Within this framework, this section presents empirical evidence of the causal relationships between three groups of variables. First, we analyse the link between expenditures and tax revenues. Second, we present empirical evidence on the causal link between spending and effective taxation on labour. Finally, we analyse causal relationships between effective tax rates on labour and labour market outcomes, namely unemployment and employment.

There seems to be quite strong evidence that the fiscal indicators considered here, namely, the ratio of total expenditures to GDP (SPENDING), the ratio of transfers to households to GDP (TRANSFERS), the ratio of total taxes (BURDEN), and the two most representative effective tax rates on labour analysed in section 3 (NWLC and LETR), behave as stochastic processes integrated of order 1, so that their first differences are stationary. Since the evidence of the existence of deterministic trends, with or without structural breaks, is somewhat more ambiguous, robustness analyses were carried out by adding such trends in the relevant models.[8]

Causality analyses have been carried out by testing block exogeneity in bivariate VARs. Block-exogeneity tests are actually Granger-causality F-tests (Judge *et al.*, 1988). This allows us to test whether lagged values of a given variable are significant when explaining the present value of another variable. Given the short time span of the series,[9] we have only considered VAR models with 1 and 2 lags, including and excluding deterministic linear trends, with and without structural breaks. Overall, such deterministic trends and structural breaks appeared to be unnecessary in obtaining well-specified models. Although we do not change the names of the series, the following refers to the first differences of their logarithmic transformations. In so doing we recognize that, where the links between spending and effective taxation on labour and the links between effective taxation on labour and employment performance are concerned, not only has the change in the series an impact on the results but its effect also depends on the initial level of the variable.

4.1 Causal Relationships between Expenditures and Tax Receipts

The first column of Table 3.10 presents summary statistics of the reduced form for the tax burden corresponding to the bivariate VAR with SPENDING. Apart from the Breusch–Godfrey LM-tests of orders 1 and 2,[10] the table also gives the VAR-based Granger-causality/block-exogeneity F-test for the equation displayed in the table (SPENDING causes BURDEN, in this case) and for the other equation in the bivariate VAR (BURDEN causes SPENDING). It is worth noting that VARs including 2 lags, as well as the ones including deterministic trends, were not superior to the model in the table on the basis of the Schwartz-Bayes Information Criterion (SBIC), while, in some cases, specification tests suggested the presence of misspecification errors.

There is evidence of a causal relationship going from the spending ratio to the tax burden in the EU. Moreover, no reverse causality is detected, while the explicative power of the model is relatively high given its parsimony and the fact that the series are in first differences. Shocks to the spending ratio are translated to the tax burden one year later, while the reverse is not true. Furthermore, if in the same regression the contemporaneous change in the spending ratio is introduced, the corresponding estimate is not significant. Analogously, the introduction of the current change in the tax burden in the regression for spending induces clear misspecification errors on the basis of the Breusch–Godfrey and ARCH criteria. This may suggest that shocks on spending are not immediately translated into the tax burden, but only with a one-year lag, implying that shocks to spending in the EU would come first and subsequently taxes would adjust. Therefore, there seems to be some empirical evidence that across-the-board tax cuts may be unsuccessful unless spending trends are reversed. Tax cuts could simply lead to an increase of public deficits, which, given the constraints imposed by the Stability and Growth Pact, would bring higher taxes in the future. This has obvious implications for the long-run sustainability of the tax systems in the EU and their effects on employment performance.

Table 3.10 Relationships between SPENDING and taxes

	BURDEN	NWLC	LETR
Intercept	0.004	0.003	0.004
	(1.88)**	(0.96)	(1.19)
$Y(-1)^{(1)}$	0.28	0.33	0.53
	(1.49)	(2.05)*	(2.55)*
SPENDING(−1)	0.16	0.50	0.24
	(2.06)*	(5.20)*	(2.19)*
R^2	0.32	0.68	0.53
$LM1^{(2)}$	0.21	0.13	0.39
	[0.65]	[0.72]	[0.53]
$LM2^{(3)}$	0.99	0.99	0.00
	[0.61]	[0.61]	[0.99]
$GC^{(4)}$	4.26	29.14	4.69
	[0.05]	[0.00]	[0.04]
$R\text{-}GC^{(5)}$	0.22	0.51	2.85
	[0.64]	[0.48]	[0.10]
$USGC^{(6)}$	5.00	0.59	1.95
	[0.03]	[0.45]	[0.17]
$USR\text{-}GC^{(7)}$	1.47	6.36	7.49
	[0.24]	[0.02]	[0.01]

Notes: *significant at 5%, **significant at 10%. P-values between square brackets
(1)   Lagged dependent variable (BURDEN/NWLC/LETR).
(2) and (3) Breusch–Godfrey LM test for autocorrelation of orders 1 and 2, respectively.
(4)   Block-exogeneity/Granger-causality test (SPENDING causes BURDEN/NWLC/LETR).
(5)   Block-exogeneity/Granger-causality test (BURDEN/NWLC/LETR causes SPENDING).
(6)   Same as (4) for the US.
(7)   Same as (5) for the US.

Although the same causal relationship is apparent in the US, there are no more valid analogies between this country and the EU. While in the latter the correlation between changes in spending and changes in taxes is positive, in the US it is surprisingly negative, suggesting that higher spending one year would correspond to lower taxes the year after. The explanation for such an illogical relationship seems to be that the consideration of contemporaneous relationships between changes in the spending ratio and changes in the tax burden together with their first lags improves the model. The explicative power of the model which includes the current change in SPENDING is twice that including only the lagged changes. Furthermore, the coefficient of SPENDING(−1) becomes non-significant at 5 per cent. In other words, it seems that in this country the government changes expenditures and taxes simultaneously and that there is no clear way to identify the origin of fiscal shocks,

Table 3.11   Relationships between TRANSFERS and taxes

	BURDEN	NWLC	LETR
Intercept	0.004	0.003	0.003
	(1.56)	(0.72)	(0.84)
$Y(-1)^{(1)}$	0.28	0.26	0.53
	(1.49)	(1.33)	(2.74)*
TRANSFERS(−1)	0.13	0.39	0.15
	(2.08)*	(3.97)*	(1.64)
R^2	0.32	0.58	0.49
$LM1^{(2)}$	0.01	0.16	1.19
	[0.94]	[0.69]	[0.28]
$LM2^{(3)}$	0.58	0.27	0.90
	[0.75]	[0.88]	[0.64]
$GC^{(4)}$	4.32	16.3	2.85
	[0.04]	[0.00]	[0.10]
$R\text{-}GC^{(5)}$	1.13	0.58	7.03
	[0.30]	[0.45]	[0.01]
$USGC^{(6)}$	0.74	0.68	0.09
	[0.40]	[0.42]	[0.77]
$USR\text{-}GC^{(7)}$	5.62	1.39	11.9
	[0.03]	[0.05]	[0.00]

Notes: *significant at 5%, **significant at 10%. P-values between square brackets.
(1)   Lagged dependent variable (BURDEN/NWLC/LETR).
(2) and (3) Breusch–Godfrey LM test for autocorrelation of orders 1 and 2, respectively.
(4)   Block-exogeneity/Granger-causality test (TRANSFERS causes
             BURDEN/NWLC/LETR).
(5)   Block-exogeneity/Granger-causality test (BURDEN/NWLC/LETR causes
             TRANSFERS).
(6)   Same as (4) for the US.
(7)   Same as (5) for the US.

whether from the spending side or from the tax side. This seems to be in agreement with recent findings by Blanchard and Perotti (1999). By using a totally different data set in the framework of a structural VAR which includes quarterly data on spending, taxes and growth for the US, Blanchard and Perotti conclude that the ordering of the shocks to the two first variables makes little difference to the impulse response of output.

It could also be argued that a rise in welfare spending corresponds directly to a rise in taxation. The direct link between welfare spending and taxes is difficult to test on the basis of National Accounts data, in which transfers to households is the only indicator of social protection explicitly displayed, while being only a fraction of total welfare spending. Furthermore, databases on social spending available in EUROSTAT and in the OECD are unfortunately too short, only covering the period 1980 to 1995/6. As shown in the first column of Table 3.11, the same econometric analyses applied to the relationships between transfers to households and the tax burden reveal the same kind of causal relationship running from the former to the latter. This should not be surprising since transfers to households have followed the same path as expenditures. As a matter of fact, their share in total government spending increased by more than six percentage points between 1970 and 1998.

4.2 Effective Taxation and Spending

The fact that effective tax indicators, as shown by MRT (1994), are consistent with the representative agent behaviour begs the question as to what extent such tax wedges can be changed in the long run without requiring additional adjustments in the public budget. Section 3 showed that effective tax rates on labour have been following quite similar paths as some tax ratios, in particular the total tax burden, while we have seen that in the EU the tax burden seems to follow the spending and transfers ratios. There is therefore good reason to ask whether the causal relationships detected between expenditures and tax revenues also link expenditures and effective tax rates on labour. One could argue that since effective taxation on labour seems to be following the tax burden and since this ratio follows spending, it is not necessary to pursue this analysis further. However, causality analyses between labour effective tax rates and the tax burden suggest that, leaving apart possible contemporaneous relationships, no dynamic relationships exist between them. However, in Europe there is quite strong evidence of feedback between the total tax wedge and BURDEN. This should not be surprising since, as shown in sections 2 and 3, the bulk of taxes in the EU are collected from labour, including personal income taxes on labour income, and consumption, while in the US capital taxes are relatively high and indirect taxes relatively low. Therefore, unless a radical change in the tax structure takes place, any increase in the total tax burden is translated into a higher total tax wedge for labour. Given such a close link between the tax burden and the tax wedge, we will exclude the latter series in the subsequent analyses.

The last two columns in Table 3.10 show relevant statistics for the equations of the two main effective labour tax rates, namely NWLC and LETR, in their respective bivariate VAR models including the ratio of total expenditures to GDP. The corresponding reduced forms seem to be well specified and their explicative power rather high, especially for NWLC and LETR. Furthermore, the causal relationship running from spending to the effective tax rates is strong, while no reversal causality is detected. It is worth noting that the opposite result is found in the US, where, as a general rule, changes in expenditures are not related to changes in effective taxation the subsequent year.

Turning to the EU, the relationship between government spending and non-wage labour costs and, to a lesser extent, the effective tax rate on labour is particularly strong. Almost 70 per cent of the variance of this series is explained by changes in expenditures (more than 50 per cent for LETR). Therefore, it seems that the conjecture about an insurance principle linking social spending and social security contributions (NWLC) is very much supported by the data. Accordingly, quite similar results hold for the relationship between this latter series and the ratio of transfers to GDP. Although the explicative power is lower, almost 60 per cent of the variance of the changes in NWLC is explained by the past change in TRANSFERS. Interestingly, the coefficient of the lagged change in NWLC is non-significant. This suggests that, for reductions in social security contributions to result in a significant fall in effective non-wage labour costs, a reversal of the past trend in transfers to households seems to be needed. All in all, Tables 3.10 and 3.11 suggest the existence of a strong insurance principle between social security contributions and welfare spending in the EU, which is not found in US data.

4.3   Labour Market Outcomes and Effective Taxes

It has been argued that taxes and, particularly, taxes on labour may hamper job creation and have perverse effects on unemployment. We want to understand to what extent such perverse effects can be described by using effective tax indicators and how they compare with the effects of spending.

We start with the relationship between the employment rate (EMPR) and fiscal policy, as represented by the tax burden, the effective taxation on labour (NWLC and LETR), the spending ratio and the transfers ratio. All in all, the relationships between the employment rate and fiscal indicators are less clear-cut than the relationships between taxes and spending analysed above. In no country did causal relationships exist between NWLC and EMPR in either direction. Moreover, while the bivariate VARs in the previous sub-section were well specified by introducing just one lag, the relationships between the employment rate and taxes needed two lags in order to avoid misspecification errors.

Table 3.12 presents summary statistics for reduced forms corresponding to the employment rate in the bivariate VARs with the five fiscal indicators mentioned above. Leaving aside the series on NWLC, which does not cause the employment rate and has no impact on it, it seems that the explicative power

Table 3.12   Relationships between the employment rate and fiscal indicators

	Burden	NWLC	LETR	Spending	Transfers
Intercept	−0.00	−0.009	−0.00	0.001	0.00
	(−0.14)	(−0.37)	(−0.30)	(0.40)	(0.05)
EMPR(−1)	0.69	0.60	0.73	0.34	0.64
	(3.31)*	(2.89)*	(4.18)*	(1.71)**	(2.04)*
X(−1)[1]	−0.23	0.03	−0.40	−0.15	−0.03
	(−1.85)**	(0.26)	(−3.50)*	(2.05)*	(−0.31)
EMPR(−2)	−0.29		−0.27		−0.38
	(−1.44)		(−1.64)		(−1.26)
X(−2)[1]	0.24		0.35		−0.05
	(1.35)		(2.84)*		(−0.59)
R^2	0.49	0.31	0.63	0.41	0.41
LM1[2]	0.55	3.09	1.20	0.00	0.80
	[0.46]	[0.08]	[0.27]	[0.98]	[0.37]
LM2[3]	5.02	3.78	2.75	5.34	2.27
	[0.08]	[0.15]	[0.25]	[0.07]	[0.32]
GC[4]	2.04	0.07	6.81	4.21	0.34
	[0.16]	[0.80]	[0.01]	[0.05]	[0.72]
R–GC[5]	0.33	2.50	0.24	3.59	1.40
	[0.72]	[0.13]	[0.79]	[0.07]	[0.27]
USGC[6]	1.04	1.49	3.62	4.02	5.16
	[0.37]	[0.23]	[0.04]	[0.06]	[0.02]
USR–GC[7]	1.07	1.37	2.10	5.63	9.09
	[0.36]	[0.25]	[0.15]	[0.03]	[0.00]

Notes: *significant at 5%, **significant at 10%. P-values between square brackets.
(1)   Lagged independent variable (BURDEN/NWLC/LETR/SPENDING/TRANSFERS).
(2) and (3) Breusch–Godfrey LM test for autocorrelation of orders 1 and 2, respectively.
(4)   Block-exogeneity/Granger-causality test
           (BURDEN/NWLC/LETR/SPENDING/TRANSFERS causes EMPR).
(5)   Block-exogeneity/Granger-causality test (EMPR causes
           BURDEN/NWLC/LETR/SPENDING/TRANSFERS).
(6)   Same as (4) for the US.
(7)   Same as (5) for the US.

of taxes is higher than expenditures when comparing the regressions including BURDEN and LETR with those including SPENDING and TRANSFERS. Overall, increases in total taxes, labour taxes and spending lagged one year have a negative impact on the employment rate, and it seems that it is higher for taxes than for spending, while the coefficient of TRANSFERS is non-significant. However, when looking at the total impact, it is worth noting that changes in effective taxation on labour lagged two years are positively correlated with changes in the employment rate, so that the positive effects of lowering taxes on employment would tend to be offset in the longer term. Although the coefficient is statistically non-significant, the same applies to total tax revenues.

It is worth pointing out that the same regressions including the contemporaneous change in the fiscal indicators (BURDEN, NWLC, LETR), although they did not exhibit any misspecification errors, were not superior to the corresponding reduced form shown in Table 3.13. While this new variable worsened or did not improve the SBIC and the adjusted R^2, its coefficient was not significant at 10 per cent. Consequently, we could claim that changes in taxation and changes in employment do not take place simultaneously. It therefore seems that, if governments are able to cut taxes, especially the total tax burden and the labour effective tax rate, they could induce positive short-run effects on employment. However, such short-term effects on the change of the employment rate would disappear in time. Indeed, given the relationship between taxes and spending, such an ability seems to depend on the government's capacity to cut total spending, which, as suggested by Table 3.12, could also induce positive dynamics on employment.

The assessment of the relationships between the unemployment rate (UNEMP) and fiscal policy leads to more ambiguous results. There is evidence of causal relationships running from total taxes and the effective tax rate on labour to unemployment. Across-the-board tax cuts, as well as the reduction of the tax burden on labour, would reduce unemployment in the short run. Analogously, there seems to be a positive correlation between effective non-wage labour costs and the unemployment rate, but causality runs in the opposite direction. It seems that higher unemployment increases the effective share of social security contribution in the gross wage.

The last two columns in Table 3.13 indicate that cutting total and welfare spending could also have positive effects on unemployment. However, Granger-causality tests indicate that changes in the unemployment rate also induce changes in the spending rate. In fact, the model of the corresponding reduced form plus the contemporaneous change in government expenditures suggests that there exists a significant, well-specified and positive contemporaneous correlation between the change in the unemployment rate and the change in the spending rate. It would therefore be possible to infer that, in the EU, higher unemployment increases total spending through unemployment and other benefit (*viz.* disability, early retirement) systems, but this is something that cannot be *estrictu sensu* worked out on the basis of Table 3.13.

Table 3.13 Relationships between the unemployment rate and fiscal indicators

	Burden	NWLC	LETR	Spending	Transfers
Intercept	0.02	−0.004	−0.01	0.03	0.02
	(0.73)	(−0.12)	(0.40)	(1.87)**	(1.02)
UNEM(−1)	0.29	0.59	0.31	−0.43	−0.21
	(1.38)	(2.65)*	(1.63)	(−1.84)**	(−0.58)
X(−1)[(1)]	5.73	0.13	5.18	4.26	2.41
	(2.70)*	(0.07)	(3.73)*	(4.52)*	(1.92)**
UNEM(−2)	−0.45	−0.56	−0.41		
	(−2.13)*	(2.04)*	(−2.30)*		
X(−2)[(1)]	−0.52	2.97	−1.59		
	(−0.24)	(1.86)**	(−1.02)		
R^2	0.43	0.34	0.54	0.55	0.27
LM1[(2)]	0.78	1.70	0.65	0.57	0.14
	[0.38]	[0.19]	[0.42]	[0.45]	[0.71]
LM2[(3)]	1.12	3.35	5.11	5.52	2.71
	[0.57]	[0.19]	[0.08]	[0.06]	[0.26]
GC[(4)]	3.64	1.83	7.04	20.4	3.70
	[0.04]	[0.19]	[0.00]	[0.00]	[0.06]
R-GC[(5)]	1.57	4.53	0.63	8.73	3.08
	[0.23]	[0.02]	[0.54]	[0.01]	[0.09]
USGC[(6)]	1.73	2.96	5.19	1.21	4.27
	[0.20]	[0.07]	[0.01]	[0.28]	[0.05]
USR–GC[(7)]	1.88	1.61	1.73	1.68	8.55
	[0.18]	[0.22]	[0.20]	[0.21]	[0.00]

Notes: *significant at 5%, **significant at 10%. P-values between square brackets.
(1)   Lagged independent variable (BURDEN/NWLC/LETR/SPENDING/TRANSFERS).
(2) and (3) Breusch–Godfrey LM test for autocorrelation of orders 1 and 2, respectively.
(4)   Block-exogeneity/Granger-causality test
            (BURDEN/NWLC/LETR/SPENDING/TRANSFERS causes UNEM).
(5)   Block-exogeneity/Granger-causality test (UNEM causes
            BURDEN/NWLC/LETR/SPENDING/TRANSFERS).
(6)   Same as (4) for the US.
(7)   Same as (5) for the US.

Interestingly, on the other side of the Atlantic, the causal relationship between the effective tax rate on labour and labour market performance, as measured by the employment and the unemployment rates, is similar to that observed in the EU. In both countries the causal relationship running from LETR to labour market outcomes is significant and the corresponding models indicate a negative correlation between changes in taxes on labour and changes in the employment rate, and a positive correlation between changes in taxes on labour and changes

in the unemployment rate. This seems to challenge some panel data specifications, such as those by Daveri and Tabellini (1997), where the relationship
between taxes on labour and employment performance depends on the labour
market institutions, indicating that taxation of labour has no effect on labour
market performance in countries with fully decentralized labour markets. The
empirical evidence in Tables 3.12 and 3.13 rather seems to support the
Blanchard and Wolfers (1999) approach, where the marginal effect of taxation
does not depend on other market institutions, but interacts with them and with
adverse shocks to explain labour market performance.

5   CONCLUSIONS

This chapter has analysed the evolution of the tax wedge across EU Member
States, the US and Japan over the period 1970–98. Effective tax rates are
calculated on the basis of AMECO (National Accounts) data by using a variant
of the MRT method. Effective tax indicators allow for calculations of the
average effective tax wedges driven by taxes on production factors and the tax
wedge driven by indirect taxes between the consumer aggregate price index
and the producer aggregate price index. The tax wedge – the difference between
the gross wage deflated by the producer's price and the wage net of taxes
deflated by the consumer's price – has been decomposed here into total non-
wage labour costs (NWLC), a part of which are social security contributions
paid by the employers (SSCER), personal income taxes (PIETR) and consumption taxes (CETR). NWLC and personal income taxes on labour income
make up the labour effective tax (LETR).

Although the long-run trend of NWLC has been unambiguously positive
since the early 1970s, it seems to be reversing after the early 1990s crisis. This
fall could be related to recent efforts to reduce taxation on labour through cuts
in SSC. The long-run evolution of the LETR is also clearly positive but, as with
NWLC, the direct tax burden on labour has been decreasing slightly in the EU
during the 1990s.

Of the EU Member States which reduced NWLC rates between 1994 and
1998, only the Netherlands, Finland, Ireland and, to a lesser extent, Denmark
show a fall in the total tax wedge. That is, in Italy, Spain and France the fall in
NWLC has been compensated by rises in consumption taxes and, additionally
in the case of France, by a very strong upsurge in personal taxes. While the
main components of the reduction in Finland were both NWLC and personal
income taxes, in the Netherlands, Ireland and Denmark the bulk of the fall in
the tax wedge is due to a sharp reduction of personal taxes. In the four countries
NWLC fell, although not as much as they did in Finland. In addition, in all four
of them consumption taxes (CETR) increased, but without offsetting the
reductions achieved in NWLC and in personal income taxes.

We have explored empirical relationships linking a number of indicators, including taxes, expenditures and labour market outcomes. The evidence of a causal relationship going from the spending ratio to the tax burden is rather strong in the EU. There is no evidence of a causal relationship in the opposite direction, while no contemporaneous relationships seem to exist between both variables. Therefore, there seems to be some empirical evidence that across-the-board tax cuts may be unsuccessful unless spending trends are reversed. Interestingly, in the US, the government seems to be able to change expenditures and taxes simultaneously while there is no clear way to identify the origin of fiscal shocks, whether they come from the spending or the tax side. The causal relationships running from total and welfare spending to effective taxation are strong, especially for non-wage labour costs. Therefore, it seems that the insurance principle linking social spending and social security contributions (NWLC) is very much supported by the data. In other words, European governments have little room for manoeuvre to reduce NWLC and LETR in the longer term without cutting spending, which seems to follow long-run paths independent of tax revenues.

Overall, increases in total taxes, labour taxes and spending have a negative impact on the employment rate and a positive effect on the unemployment rate. It therefore seems that if governments are able to cut taxes, especially the total tax burden and the labour effective tax rate, they could enhance employment performance in the short run. Indeed, given the relationship between taxes and spending, the effects of a tax cut should be greater the larger the reduction in expenditures. Where unemployment performance is concerned, our empirical results suggest that reductions of the effective tax burden on labour might have significant impacts on unemployment. In addition, there is evidence of feedback between expenditures and unemployment. According to this, higher unemployment would increase total spending through unemployment and other (*viz.* disability, early retirement) benefits. Overall, the effects of taxation on employment performance in the US are similar to those in the EU. It therefore seems that, in line with Blanchard and Wolfers (1999), such effects do not depend on other market institutions, as proposed by Daveri and Tabellini (1997), but interact with them and with adverse shocks to explain labour market performance.

Indeed, although illustrative, these are just partial relationships, which might not hold true if a more complete analysis is carried out. Future research on the impacts of taxation on employment performance should progress in this direction by, for instance, considering a structural VAR approach allowing for the interplay between employment performance (*viz.* unemployment), fiscal policy variables (total spending, the tax burden, effective tax rates), as well as monetary policy shocks (inflation) and output. Recent work by Blanchard and Perotti (1999) combined with models for unemployment, as in for instance

Dolado and Jimeno (1997), could lead to structural VARs to analyse the response of unemployment to shocks in taxes on labour and their interaction with shocks in expenditures, inflation, output and other structural factors determining the NAIRU.

NOTES

1. Comments made by M. Buti, M. McCarthy, F. Orlandi, J.H. Schmidt and H. Wijkander, are gratefully appreciated. The views expressed are those of the authors and do not commit the European Commission or its services.
2. Indeed, we are consciously excluding here lump sum taxes. For the purposes of this chapter we implicitly refer to proportional as well as to progressive and regressive tax systems, which are the typical characteristics of most taxes on labour income.
3. The consumption tax rate is calculated here as the difference between the consumer price and the producer price expressed in terms of the former.
4. Thus including SSC.
5. Of course, the total operating surplus of the economy should then be adjusted by an amount equal to the average gross wage times the number of self-employed.
6. See sub-section on the tax burden on low-skilled labour below.
7. Only in Denmark (12%) and Austria (15%) was the share of taxes on payroll and workforce to total social security contributions greater than 10% in 1996.
8. The results are available upon request.
9. Furthermore, no quarterly series are available on effective taxation.
10. Tests for heteroskedasticity, Ljung-Box tests for autocorrelation of orders 1 and 2, ARCH for auto-regressive conditional heteroskedasticity of order 1, and Jarque-Bera and Shapiro-Wilk for normality were also calculated. Since none of these alternative tests led to different results, they are not included in the tables to lighten the presentation.
11. The labour share is calculated as the ratio of total gross labour costs to GDP (the labour share of employees) multiplied by the ratio of total employment to employees. In this way, we assume that the opportunity cost of the self-employed equals the average gross wage of the employees.
12. Latest available year in OECD (1998b).
13. This hypothesis holds as a general rule, since the composition of TSSC records very marginal changes from one year to another. Indeed, if drastic reforms of SCCER or SCCEMP took place in the last year the estimates of NWLCEL will not be able to reflect them.
14. We assume that the value of the depreciation is not distributed and, thus, does not enter the personal income.
15. Some relatively minor differences can arise between data in Table A3.3 and those calculated by EUROSTAT since, although the definition is the same, data sources are different.

REFERENCES

Blanchard, O. and J. Wolfers (1999), *The Role of Shocks and Institutions in the Rise of European Unemployment: The Aggregate Evidence*, mimeo.

Blanchard, O. and R. Perotti (1999), *An Empirical Characterization of the Dynamic Effects of Changes in Government Spending and Taxes on Output*, mimeo.

Daveri, F. and G. Tabellini (1997), *Unemployment, Growth and Taxation in Industrial Countries*, mimeo.

Dolado, J.J. and Jimeno, J.F. (1997), 'The causes of Spanish unemployment: a structural VAR approach', *European Economic Review*, **41**: 1281–1307.

Dreze, J. and H. Sneessens (1996), 'Technological development, competition from low-wage countries and low-skilled unemployment', in D.J. Snower and G. de la Dehesa (eds), *Unemployment Policy: Government Options for the Labour Market*, Cambridge, UK: Cambridge University Press.

Elmeskov, J., J.P. Martin and S. Scarpetta (1999),' Key lessons for labour market reforms: evidence from OECD countries' experience', *Swedish Economic Policy Review*.

European Commission (1997), *Effective Taxation and Tax Convergence in the EU and the OECD*, note to the EPC II/603/97-EN/Rev.2.

European Commission (1998), *Structures of the Taxation Systems in the European Union, 1970–1996*, Luxembourg: OOPEC.

European Commission (1999), *Commission's Recommendation for the Broad Guidelines of the Economic Policies of the Member States and the Community*, COM(1999) 143 final.

Gordon, K., and H. Tchilinguirian (1998), *Effective Average Tax Rates on Capital, Labour and Consumption Goods: Cross Country Estimates*, DAFFE/CFA/WP2/RD(98)14, Paris: OECD.

Hamermesh, D.S. (1993), *Labour Demand*, Princeton: Princeton University Press.

Judge, G.G., R.C. Hill, W.E. Griffiths, H. Lutkepohl and T. Lee (1988), *Introduction to the Theory and Practice of Econometrics*, New York: Wiley.

Liebfritz, W., J. Thornton and A. Bibbee (1997), *Taxation and Economic Performance*, OECD Economics Department Working Paper, 176, Paris: OECD.

Lucas Jr., R. E. (1990), 'Supply-side economics: an analytical review', *Oxford Economic Papers*, **42**: 293–316.

Martínez-Mongay, C. (1998), *On effective taxation*, DAFFE/CFA/WP2/RD(98)17, Paris: OECD.

Martínez-Mongay, C. (1999), *Effective Tax Rates Based on AMECO Data. Updating of December 1999*, mimeo, European Commission, DG ECFIN/508/99.

Martínez-Mongay, C. and R. Fernández-Bayón (1999), *Effective Taxation in the EU. Effective Tax Rates Based on AMECO Data*, ECFIN/508/99-EN, Brussels: European Commission, DG ECFIN.

Mendoza, E.G., A. Razin and L. Tesar (1994), 'Effective tax rates in macroeconomics. Cross-country estimates of tax rates on factor incomes and consumption', *Journal of Monetary Economics*, **34**: 297–33.

OECD, (1997), National Accounts: Detailed Tables, Paris: OECD.

OECD, (1998a), *The Tax/Benefit Position of Employees*, Paris: OECD.

OECD, (1998b), Revenue Statistics, Paris: OECD.

OECD, (1998c), National Accounts, Part 1: OECD.

Volkerink, B. and J. de Haan (1999), *Tax Ratios: A Critical Survey*, DAFFE/CFA/WP2(99)4/REVI, Paris: OECD.

APPENDIX   EFFECTIVE TAXATION INDICATORS

The most operational solution to the problem of analysing the sources of the changes in tax revenue structures is to construct synthetic indicators of broad, aggregate tax bases and tax rates. Mendoza, Razin and Tesar (1994), based on a seminal work by Lucas (1990), have produced effective average tax rates for broad tax groups, which generate the majority of the government's tax revenue, based on data on actual tax payments and national accounts. Although less rigorous in the treatment of the economic effects of changes in tax laws than marginal tax rates, such effective rates are consistent with the representative agent assumption and, by looking at the aggregate data, they also take account of the effective, overall tax burden resulting from each of the major tax categories. In addition, the method is easier to implement in multi-country research projects because it exploits the international consistency of available data sources on national accounts and revenue statistics.

By using a comparable methodology, the Commission (see European Commission, 1998) publishes regularly the so-called implicit tax rates for employed labour, other production factors and consumption. The latest update of this publication covers the period 1970–97 for most Member States. In a note to the Economic Policy Committee (see European Commission, 1997), DG ECFIN services applied the Mendoza-Razin-Tesar (MRT) method to obtain effective taxation indicators for personal income, labour, capital, corporate income and consumption for the period 1965–95. Within quite a similar methodological framework, the OECD is also developing a data bank on effective taxation (see Gordon and Tchilinguirian, 1998, and Martínez-Mongay, 1998). The issue of effective taxation has also been discussed by Volkerink and de Haan (1999).

In European Commission (1997) effective tax rates and tax bases are obtained by finding for each tax category the corresponding total tax revenue in the OECD data bank 'Revenue Statistics for OECD Member Countries' (see OECD, 1998b), and the corresponding tax base in the OECD data bank 'National Accounts' (see OECD, 1997 and 1998c). The ratio between both (tax revenues and the corresponding tax base) is the effective (average) tax rate. In Martínez-Mongay and Fernández-Bayón (1999), we have followed the same methodology by using as much as possible AMECO data, which allows us to calculate effective tax indicators coherent with official macroeconomic data used by the Commission in its Autumn and Spring forecasts and in the multilateral surveillance process.

This Appendix uses the latest update available of the databank (see Martínez-Mongay, 1999). It is based on raw data from the version of AMECO corresponding to the *Commission Forecast of Autumn 1999*, as well as on the latest available version of the OECD databank on tax revenues (OECD, 1998b), which includes data until 1997. For a deeper understanding of the methodology used in this paper, one should refer to Martínez-Mongay and Fernández-Bayón (1999) or Martínez-Mongay (1999). The following summarizes the formula and definitions used in these papers.

Effective Non-Wage Labour Costs

The effective rate of non-wage labour costs (NWLC) is the ratio of total social security contributions (TSSC) to total labour costs. The rate includes the imputed wage of the self-employed, as well as the social security contributions paid by this category of labour. If TSSC is the ratio of social security contributions to GDP, and LSH is the labour share, which includes gross wages imputed to the self-employed,[11] the effective average non-wage labour costs for total employment can be obtained as:

$$NWLC = (TSSC/LSH)$$

See Table 3.4 of the main text.

Since the OECD Revenue Statistics decomposes total social security contributions (SSC) into SSC paid by the employers (*SSCER*), SCC paid by the employees (*SSCEMP*), SSC paid by the self-employed (*SSCSELF*), taxes on payroll and workforce (*TPRWF*) and others (*SSCOTH*), it is possible to obtain the part of TSSC published in AMECO attributable to employed labour

$$(SSCER + SSCEMP + TPRWF = SSCEL)$$

Then, the effective non-wage labour cost rate on employed labour is:

$$NWLCEL = (SSCEL/SHEL)$$

This rate can be calculated until 1997,[12] and extrapolated to 1998 by assuming that the shares of SSCER, TPRWF and SSCEMP to TSSC in 1997 hold in 1998.[13]

On the other hand, the effective rate of social security contributions paid by the employers (non-wage labour costs paid by the employers – *NWLCER*) can be calculated as

$$NWLCER = (SSCER/SHEL)$$

Again the series can be currently calculated until 1997 and was extrapolated to 1998 by assuming that the share of SSCER to TSSC in 1997 holds in 1998. The summary table for this indicator is shown in Table A3.1:

Effective Tax Rate on Personal Income and Labour Effective Tax Rates

Once non-wage labour costs have been deducted from gross wages, workers pay personal taxes on their remaining labour income. Thus, the effective

Table A3.1 NWLC paid by the employers

	1998–70	1998–94	1995	1996	1997	1998*
B	4.7	0.0	19.9	20.0	20.2	20.1
DK	−0.1	0.0	0.9	0.9	0.9	0.9
D	5.8	1.0	17.3	17.7	18.3	18.2
EL	6.8	−1.2	18.3	18.9	17.5	17.4
E	6.3	−0.2	18.0	18.5	18.6	18.5
F	1.2	−2.2	22.9	22.8	22.9	20.8
IRL	4.5	−0.2	8.5	7.9	8.1	8.1
I	2.8	0.1	22.7	24.4	25.1	22.2
L	N/A	N/A	N/A	9.6	9.3	N/A
NL	−5.7	0.1	5.4	5.4	5.0	4.9
A	5.2	0.5	13.4	13.7	13.8	13.6
P	9.9	2.4	14.3	14.6	15.7	16.3
FIN	14.2	−4.1	23.9	22.5	21.8	21.3
S	8.5	−1.9	20.7	20.8	19.4	19.2
UK	3.6	−0.1	7.7	7.7	7.5	7.6
US	**2.7**	**−0.3**	**8.2**	**8.2**	**8.0**	**7.9**
JP	4.7	1.1	9.3	9.3	9.5	9.8
EUR-11	3.3	−0.2	18.7	19.3	19.6	18.6
EU-15	**3.5**	**−0.5**	**16.9**	**17.4**	**17.3**	**16.4**

Note: *Estimation based on the assumption that the share of SSC paid by the employers to total SSC has remained unchanged since 1997.

Source: OECD (1998b) AMECO, DG ECFIN, European Commission.

taxation on labour should include non-wage labour costs and personal income taxes paid by labour income. AMECO only provides the aggregate series on direct taxes on income and wealth (DITW), which actually include four categories of taxes: taxes on personal income from labour, taxes on personal income from capital, taxes on corporate income and taxes on property and wealth. On the other hand, the OECD Revenue Statistics (RS hereafter) provide a more detailed breakdown of taxes on income and wealth: taxes on income, profits and capital gains of individuals (PITRA), corporate taxes on income, profits and capital gains (CITRA) and revenues from any kind of property taxes (PWTRA). The last two are exclusively capital taxes, while PITRA includes direct taxes on both labour and capital. Therefore, on the basis of such breakdown, it is possible to decompose DTIW from AMECO into the same three categories of direct taxes found in RS, by calculating the shares of the three components of direct taxes from the RS and then by applying those ratios to AMECO's DITW.

Again, since the series in RS only provide coverage up to 1997, the values of the series on PITRA, CITRA and PWTRA for 1998 have been obtained by assuming that the values of TRIIR, TRCIR and PROPR observed in 1997 hold in 1998. Once this has been done, we decompose PITRA into the personal income tax attributable to labour income and the personal income tax attributable to capital income. We follow here a slightly modified version of the approach proposed by MRT (1994) who consider that the effective tax rate on personal income is the same regardless of the income source, be it either labour or capital. We define personal labour income as gross wages less non-wage labour costs. In short, we assume that only the net wage (take-home pay) is subject to the personal income tax. To estimate the personal income from capital we deduct from the total net operating surplus of the economy (NOS),[14] which is available from AMECO, the imputed labour income of the self-employed and other direct taxes on capital, namely the corporate income tax and taxes on property and wealth. Therefore the personal income tax base is calculated as:

$$PITB = LSH - TSSC + NOS - (LSH\text{-}SHEL) - CITRA - PWTRA$$

or, equivalently,

$$PITB = SHEL + NOS - TSSC - CITRA - PWTRA$$

Then, the effective tax rate on personal income is:

$$PIETR = PITRA/PITB$$

The summary table for this indicator is shown in Table A3.2.

Thus, the total personal income effective tax rate is calculated as the ratio of tax revenues from income taxes paid by individuals to the total income received by them, a part of which is revenues from capital. Such personal income is the sum of total labour costs, including the imputed wages of the self-employed and net of social security contributions, and the net operating surplus of the economy, adjusted for the imputed wages of the self-employed and net of taxes on corporate income and on property and wealth.

On the other hand, the effective tax rate on labour income is the ratio of the sum of non-wage labour costs *plus* the personal income tax revenues attributable to labour income to the pre-tax labour income. The latter is, obviously, total gross wages, including gross wages imputed to the self-employed, while the second component of the tax revenues can be estimated by multiplying

Table A3.2   Personal income effective tax rates

	1998–70	1998–94	1995	1996	1997	1998*
B	11.2	0.9	22.4	22.3	22.6	23.3
DK	12.2	−1.5	41.1	41.6	41.1	40.0
D	4.5	0.3	17.1	16.9	16.5	16.8
EL	5.9	2.2	6.4	6.3	7.2	7.9
E	8.3	−0.8	10.8	10.8	10.4	10.2
F	7.1	3.2	9.6	10.4	10.9	13.0
IRL	8.4	−2.6	14.1	14.2	14.2	13.7
I	13.5	− 0.3	17.3	17.7	19.2	17.2
L	N/A	N/A	N/A	11.9	10.1	N/A
NL	−2.3	−4.2	14.6	13.8	12.1	11.9
A	8.1	3.5	17.5	18.7	19.8	20.2
P	4.3	0.4	8.9	9.4	9.2	9.3
FIN	10.6	−3.8	27.5	28.8	26.2	26.4
S	7.8	5.9	29.7	30.7	31.2	34.0
UK	−2.1	0.7	13.9	13.2	12.8	14.2
US	**3.5**	**2.5**	**12.0**	**12.8**	**13.5**	**13.9**
JP	2.3	−1.2	7.3	6.9	7.3	6.7
EUR-11	7.1	0.5	15.0	15.2	15.3	15.5
EU-15	**5.4**	**0.6**	**15.7**	**15.8**	**15.8**	**16.2**

Note: *the share of tax revenue from income taxes paid by individuals to total direct taxes remained constant to the 1997 level.

Source: OECD, (1998b), AMECO, DG ECFIN, European Commission.

PIETR by the net wages, once non-wage labour costs have been discounted. Then the effective tax rate on labour income is

$$LETR = (TSSC + PIETR*(LSH - TSSC))/LSH$$

See Table 3.5 of the main text.

If one is more concerned about the effective tax rate on the income of employed labour, a slight modification gives:

$$LETREL = (SSCEL + PIETR*(SHEL - SSCEL))/SHEL$$

Effective Tax Rate on Consumption and the Tax Wedge

Following the general concept of effective taxation, the effective tax rate on consumption should be the ratio of tax revenues from consumption taxes to the pre-tax value of consumption (MRT, 1994). However, if the goal is to calculate the total tax wedge, a more useful indicator of the effective taxation on consumption (CETR) can be obtained on the basis of the after-tax value of consumption. The effective tax rate on consumption can then be calculated as the ratio of indirect taxes to the value of final (private and public) consumption, including indirect taxes. Such an indicator coincides with the so-called implicit tax rate on consumption calculated by EUROSTAT (see European Commission, 1997). Such a rate is the difference between the consumer price (a post-tax price) and the producer price (a pre-tax price) expressed as a percentage of the former

$$CETR = (P_c - P_p)/P_c$$

Table A3.3 presents summary statistics for this indicator.[15]

Table A3.3   Consumption effective tax rates

	1998–70	1998–94	1995	1996	1997	1998
B	−1.3	0.6	16.2	16.8	17.2	17.2
DK	−0.4	1.4	22.1	22.8	23.1	23.5
D	−3.6	−0.3	14.9	14.7	14.8	15.2
EL	− 0.1	1.3	15.3	15.9	16.3	17.0
E	4.0	1.3	13.1	13.1	13.7	14.5
F	0.3	1.3	19.4	20.1	20.4	20.4
IRL	2.5	2.0	19.0	19.6	20.1	20.7
I	5.6	4.5	15.7	15.5	16.0	19.9
L	N/A	N/A	24.4	24.4	24.4	N/A
NL	2.9	1.3	14.7	15.3	15.8	16.0
A	−1.0	0.9	18.6	18.7	19.5	19.8
P	3.9	0.7	18.1	18.1	18.3	18.3
FIN	0.3	0.7	17.5	18.2	19.0	19.6
S	3.5	2.2	17.9	18.5	19.1	20.3
UK	−0.4	0.9	15.8	15.9	16.4	16.4
US	**−2.2**	**−0.6**	**8.5**	**8.3**	**8.2**	**8.1**
JP	−0.3	0.2	11.6	11.8	11.6	11.6
EUR-11	0.3	1.3	16.2	16.3	16.7	17.6
EU-15	**0.2**	**1.2**	**16.3**	**16.5**	**16.8**	**17.6**

Source: AMECO, DG ECFIN, European Commission.

The tax wedge on labour is the difference between the producer's wage and the consumer's wage expressed as a percentage of the producer's wage. It arises because labour income is first taxed through social security contributions; then, workers have to pay income taxes on the remaining income, which in turn, once direct taxes have been deducted, will be subject to indirect taxes when the income is consumed. In other terms, the tax wedge on labour is the difference between the gross wage deflated by the producer's price (real producer wage $-w_p$) and the gross wage net of social security contributions and personal income taxes on labour income deflated by the consumer's price (the real consumer wage $-w_c$). As explained in section 3, the tax wedge can be calculated as:

$$WEDGE = 1 - (1 - NWLC)(1 - PIETR)(1 - CETR)$$

See Table 3.6 of the main text.

The effective tax wedge on employed labour is thus:

$$WEDGEEL = 1 - (1 - NWLCEL)(1 - PIETR)(1 - CETR)$$

4. Net replacement rates of the unemployed: comparisons of various approaches[1]

Aino Salomäki[*]

INTRODUCTION

Unemployment and Welfare: the Framework for Analysing Work Incentives of Benefit Systems

Large-scale unemployment has become the prime social, economic and political issue in Europe. It is a waste of human potential and national product, it increases inequality and poverty and it creates social and political tensions. Economists, social scientists, government advisers and policy-makers have been asked to analyse the problem and the causes of unemployment, and to derive policy responses, in order to reduce unemployment and increase employment opportunities.

Different countries have dealt with the problem in different ways. Some have concentrated on demand-side policies in order to create more demand for products and services necessary for the creation of new jobs. Others have relied on supply-side policies, aiming to improve the productivity of the work-force and to change institutional settings with a view to relaxing labour market regulation so as to reduce unemployment. The choice of the mix of policy responses in different countries has been affected by the diversity of economic institutions and policy goals as well as by the balance achieved between efficient policy measures and political concerns.

It is reasonable to expect that unemployment arises from several different causes operating simultaneously. It would then be unreasonable to expect any single theory to explain exhaustively the causes of unemployment; neither is there a single right policy to respond to the problems. Notwithstanding this, economic theories can provide a variety of useful insights about where

[*] The views expressed in this chapter are those of the author and do not commit the European Commission or its services.

promising policy approaches are to be found. Moreover, a reasoned analysis of the underlying problem is needed for policy advice.

This chapter is devoted to the analysis of one part of the unemployment problem, namely, the relationship between unemployment and benefit systems. The economic thinking on this relationship rests on institutional theories depicting unemployment as a result of market failures. These theories attempt to explain how the functioning of the labour market is affected by labour market regulation including such features as union power, wage bargaining, labour market rigidities caused by employment protection legislation and the incentive effects of tax and benefit systems. The associated policies are related to the changes in underlying labour market institutions such as bargaining, employment and unemployment protection systems (Snower 1997).

The unemployment benefit system is a cause of concern because the gains from provision of unemployment insurance are accompanied by efficiency losses at the same time. The main deficiency of unemployment benefit systems is that while they provide income security during unemployment, they make the underlying problem worse. The reasons are that unemployment benefits i) discourage job search because, if an unemployed person finds a job, the benefit is withdrawn; and ii) put upward pressure on wages, thereby improving incumbent workers' negotiating position. Together, these effects entail inherently inefficient and inequitable elements in the unemployment benefit system.

Regarding unemployment benefit systems, equity and efficiency objectives are the major concerns. The equity goal is to redistribute income while the efficiency goal is to respond to market failures in the provision of unemployment insurance. With regard to equity, it is worth discussing whether unemployment benefit targets the poor and is the best way to redistribute income. For an unemployed person, employment is often the best way to overcome poverty. Thus it is particularly unfortunate that unemployment benefit discourages employment and makes employment opportunities more unequal.

With regard to efficiency, the advantages of income security must be set against the efficiency losses that arise from the discouragement of employment. An unemployment insurance system to correct the failures in the labour market is far from optimal: the design of such systems, with floors, ceilings and dependence on past earnings, matches better with redistributive objectives than with the aim of reducing unemployment. Moreover, labour market theories based on wage bargaining, the role of labour unions and insider–outsider effects identify market failures that prevent a good balance between employment and wages from being reached. The unemployment benefit system is found to exacerbate these failures by driving wages up further, and by yielding an excessively low rate of employment. The consequent imbalances in wages and employment can be further worsened by the dynamic effects of prolonged unemployment, such as loss of skills and discouragement from job search and hence increasing reluctance on the part of potential recruiters, to take up the long-term unemployed.

For all these reasons, unemployment benefit reforms have become a topic of growing policy concern. The need for reform is clear but the critical question is how to provide a safety net for the unemployed without unduly reducing people's incentives to fend for themselves. A general principle for unemployment benefit reforms is to set an objective to overcome the disincentive effects for work and the deficiencies in targeting the poor.

In order to be able to provide guidance for reforms of the unemployment benefit system, some evidence of disincentives is required. Even though the conclusions regarding the existence of disincentives from observed data are subject to judgements of analysts and sensitive to different interpretations, the basic facts can be derived by economic analyses. The measurement of the income level when out of work in comparison with the level of income achieved at work is the first task in the process. The relationship between out-of-work and in-work incomes is known as *net replacement rate*, the basic concept of this study.

The problem which arises from high replacement rates is known as the unemployment trap. This is a situation where benefits paid to the unemployed and their families are high relative to earnings, and, more precisely, when disposable income gained from benefits is high relative to that gained from work so that working 'does not pay'. A high benefit level reduces the economic incentive to move from unemployment to paid employment or can push individuals, especially those at a lower wage level, to turn to social benefits or to withdraw entirely from the labour market.

Purpose of the Analysis

Several methodologies have been and can be applied in order to assess the living standard during unemployment compared with that in employment. One approach is to calculate so-called net replacement rates. This means that the wage will be replaced by an unemployment benefit to which the given wage entitles. In addition, the reaction of tax and other benefit schemes, notably means-tested ones, will be taken into account. Assuming an 'in-work' situation as a starting point, this analysis allows *ex ante* replacement rates to be computed. Calculations for stylized households assuming a given set of wage levels and family types can illustrate the shape and structure of replacement rates over an income range for various family types.

Another approach to comparing the living standard of unemployed and employed persons or families is possible on the basis of household surveys, as they provide information on the disposable income of various types of families. This approach offers an opportunity to show what income levels people in different labour market states actually receive. It relies on the assumption that the population of the unemployed with given qualifications represents adequately the population of the employed with the same qualifications in the sense that the average out-of-work income of the unemployed is equal to the income that the employed people would receive on average if they became unemployed, or *vice versa*. The ratio of disposable income of unemployed households to that of employed households can be interpreted as the statistical equivalent of net replacement rates, even though it compares different households in different situations and not the same households in different labour market situations.[2]

These two methodologies described above try to capture the same issue, namely, to compare the living standard of unemployed individuals in comparison with those in work. Yet, the approaches have major differences:

1. the first uses hypothetical households as source data; the second uses statistical data;
2. the first calculates the net income from given wage levels according to the rules which apply in the benefit and tax legislation; the second relies on actual observations of wages, taxes and benefits;
3. the first compares a person in two different labour market situations; the second, when cross-sectional data is used, compares two different populations in different labour market situations.

The methodologies emphasize different aspects. The first emphasizes the mechanisms included in the tax and benefit rules but the representativeness of the results in the population is limited to the selection of stylized families. The second relies on the fact that the multiplicity of family and labour market situations as well as the diversity in benefit take-up are captured.

This study will analyse the living standard of the unemployed in comparison with those in work having in mind two policy questions:

1. whether unemployment benefit systems discourage employment;
2. whether unemployment benefits target the poor.

The study focuses mainly on problems in measuring the net replacement rates. Various approaches to compute net replacement rates are discussed, as well as their comparability and reasons for possible differences in results. Furthermore, the study aims to find empirical evidence as to whether the unemployment benefits target the poor.

Section 1 of this study compares earlier studies of net replacement rates for stylized households. The approach of stylized calculations on hypothetical data describes the structures and levels of tax and benefit schemes. In order to make these descriptions internationally comparable, a number of studies have adopted a so-called 'Average Production Worker' (APW) wage level as the benchmark. The approaches and results of three different studies are compared, namely those of the Seven Countries Group, the Central Planning Bureau of the Netherlands and the OECD.

Section 2 discusses studies on observed data. The European Community Household Panel survey offers a new framework for international comparisons. The Commission services have used the first wave of this data in two different studies in order to verify the net replacement rates obtained from stylized calculations. The results of these studies are compared here. Moreover, the receipt of unemployment benefits is analysed with a view to gaining insights into the take-up and targeting of benefits.

1   STUDIES BASED ON HYPOTHETICAL DATA

1.1   OECD, Seven Countries Group and Central Planning Bureau: Net Replacement Rates for Stylized Household Types

There is a large interest in gaining greater insight into the question of whether benefit and tax systems offer an adequate safety net in case of unemployment and whether they involve disincentives for work. While the figures of one country are sensitive to different interpretations of 'high' and 'low', international comparisons provide an opportunity to assess the results on the basis of the position relative to other countries. Given the lack of suitable statistical data and the complexity of and differences in tax and benefit systems, there has been a need to develop other methodologies which take account of comparability across countries and of the interaction of tax-benefit systems in a detailed and country-specific manner.

A few studies have tried to accomplish comparisons of unemployment benefit replacement rates among different countries. First, comparative studies have been carried out by a group of national experts (Seven Countries Study) and the Central Planning Bureau in the Netherlands (CPB). Subsequently, the OECD has started to regularly calculate net replacement rates for stylized households covering a larger set of countries. In all these studies the structure of benefit and tax systems and the outcome of their interaction is analysed under the legislation at a given date and assuming that the benefit and tax rules are applied as they stand in the legislation.

The common feature of the studies presented below is that all calculations have been carried out with an *ex ante* approach: stylized family types entitled to protection of the welfare systems in a reference year have been defined, and the potential replacement income has been calculated in a standardized way, in both gross and net terms, thus taking into account income taxation. In other words, the basic assumption in these calculations is that a person works at a certain wage level and, in the second phase, the person becomes unemployed and begins to receive the unemployment benefit to which he/she is entitled. Family benefits, housing allowances and other means-tested benefits are taken into account as they are determined on the basis of gross income (wage or unemployment benefit) in each case.

Net replacement rates are defined in all the studies considered as the ratio of disposable income when unemployed to the disposable income when in work (out-of-work income to in-work income). They have been calculated for a number of typical cases, choosing as a benchmark for comparisons the OECD's 'average production worker' (APW), and calculating the replacement rates for a selection of family types based on an income range below and above the APW.[3] The replacement rates then measure the percentage of previous earnings that each of these family types will receive in case of unemployment.

As to the choice of income concept and levels for comparison, all the studies refer to the choice made in 'The tax/benefit position of production workers' (OECD 1995). The average wage of a production worker in each country is chosen as the benchmark of income level and the income range investigated is related to the average wage level. To describe the economic position of an unemployed person in comparison with an employed one, disposable income is then calculated in a standardized way across countries: average wages or gross unemployment benefits, standard deductions and allowances in the taxation system as well as inherent means-tested benefits are involved. However, there are differences in details on how exactly and upon which assumptions the disposable income has been calculated, for example, concerning housing costs and benefits and payments for day care for children. The OECD and CPB studies strictly follow the usual definition of disposable income, that is, housing benefits are included as means-tested benefits but no deductions are made on the basis of necessary consumption such as moderate housing costs or childcare payments. Instead, the Seven Countries Study applies a 'Family purse' concept of the disposable income. It differs from the usual disposable income as it deducts moderate housing costs and measures the disposable income which can be regarded as available for free-choice consumption. Additionally, for some countries, 'Family purse' income has been calculated after childcare payments (net of subsidies).

1.1.1   OECD

The OECD studies are of particular interest since they present the most established practice and have the largest coverage (OECD 1998a, 1997a and 1997b, Martin 1996). The 1995 study presents the replacement rates for 18 OECD countries, including 14 EU countries (see Table 4.1). All replacement rate calculations are based on the level of previous earnings defined with reference to the APW. The calculations are made for the most common family types. Different calculations have been made for the first month of unemployment and for the sixtieth month of unemployment. Where in the case of the sixtieth month of unemployment the level of social assistance is higher than that of unemployment benefit, and where the unemployed family would be entitled to have it, social assistance is assumed to be paid on top of the primary benefit.

The main conclusions can be summarized as follows:

- Net replacement rates at average wage level are above 80 per cent in Luxembourg (for all family types), the Netherlands (for all families) and in Finland, Sweden and Germany (for families with children). They are above 70 per cent also in France, Portugal and Spain. The lowest rates are found in Ireland and Italy.
- Net replacement rates at low wage level are above 80 per cent in Denmark, Finland, France, Luxembourg, the Netherlands and Portugal (for all family types), and additionally, in Sweden and the United Kingdom (for families). Net replacement rates for low-income families (single persons and couples without children) are below 70 per cent only in Austria, Ireland and Italy, and for families with children only in Italy.
- In all countries, except Belgium and Portugal, net replacement rates are higher for families with children than for those without children, often due to higher or additional benefits paid to families with children. Similarly, earners with a dependent spouse tend to have higher net replacement rates than single persons.
- Net replacement rates for low-income families (at two-thirds APW earnings level) are significantly higher in some countries (Belgium, Denmark, Finland, Ireland, Portugal, UK) and at about the same level in some other countries (Austria, Germany, Italy, Luxembourg, Spain, Sweden) than for those at average earnings level.
- After 60 months, unemployment benefits are lower than in the first month of unemployment in some countries (France, Spain) or not paid at all to families without children (Italy, Portugal). In the majority of EU countries (10 out of 15), the net replacement rate for a single person at average wage level is lower in the sixtieth than the first month of employment, but less so for low-wage earners and families with children.
- In many countries social assistance eligibility results in higher net replacement rates than unemployment benefits alone, especially for families with children. In Belgium, Finland, Germany, Netherlands, Sweden and the UK, net replacement rates including social assistance in the sixtieth month of employment are higher for low-paid families with children than in the first month of unemployment (social assistance not included).

Table 4.1   OECD, 1995: net replacement rates for single-earner households

| EU countries | APW level of earnings | | | | | |
| | First month of unemployment | | | 60th month of unemployment | | |
	Single	Couple, no children	Couple, 2 children	Single	Couple, no children	Couple, 2 children
Austria	57	60	71	54	60	69
Belgium	65	57	60	46	66	63
Denmark	65	68	77	49	77	97
Finland	68	71	87	62	82	100
France	76	74	79	43	43	51
Germany	70	66	80	62	63	73
Ireland	33	49	64	33	49	64
Italy	36	42	47	0	4	11
Luxembourg	86	86	90	54	66	77
Netherlands	75	81	82	60	76	78
Portugal	79	78	77	0	0	6
Spain	73	74	76	27	33	46
Sweden	75	75	85	62	83	100
UK	52	63	67	52	63	76

| EU countries | Low level of earnings (two-thirds of APW) | | | | | |
| | First month of unemployment | | | 60th month of unemployment | | |
	Single	Couple, no children	Couple, 2 children	Single	Couple, no children	Couple, 2 children
Austria	57	62	77	54	59	74
Belgium	84	76	76	78	90	91
Denmark	90	94	95	68	98	80
Finland	83	86	92	84	100	100
France	85	85	87	57	56	58
Germany	73	74	76	76	87	92
Ireland	45	64	72	45	64	72
Italy	35	42	46	0	6	14
Luxembourg	85	85	91	75	89	89
Netherlands	86	90	86	85	95	96
Portugal	89	88	87	0	0	8
Spain	71	71	73	37	47	63
Sweden	78	78	85	89	116	122
UK	75	88	80	75	88	91

1.1.2   Seven Countries Group

The Danish and Dutch authorities co-ordinated a comparative study on unemployment benefits and social assistance in seven European countries (Denmark, Finland, France, Germany, the Netherlands, Sweden and the UK), (Seven Countries Group 1996). The study presents a standardized description of tax and benefits rules, as well as standardized calculations of net replacement rates in stylized cases of various family types and income levels (see Table 4.2). The national experts from each participating country combined their efforts in order to agree upon a common methodology and to carry out the necessary calculations by themselves in each country. This was considered to ensure good international comparability and high quality of data, together with in-depth understanding of national circumstances.

More specifically, the countries involved calculated the actual gross and net income support which unemployment would provide in the contingency that one member of the household becomes unemployed. In some countries the social assistance establishes a norm of the social minimum income, and thus, gives a subjective right to that level of income maintenance, irrespective of the labour market situation. In the case where it provides a higher level of assistance than the unemployment benefit, it is included as means-tested benefit in the calculation of net replacement rate of unemployment benefit. Complementary housing benefits less housing costs and children allowances are taken into account when and where applicable. The disposable income is defined as 'Family purse' income indicating that necessary housing costs are deducted. These net replacement rates show the economic living standard after the housing costs when unemployed relative to that when working. The calculations of benefits and disposable income are based on information on unemployment, other benefit and tax schemes in 1994.

The main conclusions of these calculations are:

- Replacement rates for unemployed vary considerably between countries, family types and income levels, for example, for a single person at average wage level from 21 per cent in the UK to 71 per cent in Sweden.
- In all countries, replacement rates in many cases are above 80 per cent or even reaching 100 per cent at the lower end of the income scale, which might influence work incentives.
- In most countries, having a dependent spouse does not change substantially the net replacement rates, the only exceptions being Finland and the UK where the differences reach more than ten percentage points, and in Germany for low-income households where the difference reaches almost 30 percentage points.

The facts

- In all countries, benefits for the unemployed favour families with children, thus giving them higher replacement rates. The most striking differences are seen in Germany, Finland and the UK; couples with children have even higher replacement rates than single parents except in Denmark and Sweden.
- Families that are exempted from day care costs when unemployed may even be better off receiving benefits than working, which indicates severe distortion of work incentives.

Table 4.2 Seven Countries Group, 1994: net replacement rates for one-earner households

| | APW level of earnings | | | | |
| | Single | | | One-earner couple | |
	No children	2 children	2 children, incl. child care costs[1]	No children	2 children
Denmark	58	79	88	61	65
Finland	53	86	90	75	96
France	64	68	–	65	79
Germany	44	64	–	46	71
Netherlands	65	67	70	66	69
Sweden	71	87	93	68	83
UK	21	44	–	34	58

| | Low level of earnings (67.5% of APW) | | | | |
| | Single | | | One-earner couple | |
	No children	2 children	2 children, incl. child care costs[1]	No children	2 children
Denmark	85	95	97	88	89
Finland	64	89	89	100	100
France	80	82	-	78	89
Germany	45	89	-	73	95
Netherlands	60	78	84	86	88
Sweden	70	86	91	64	80
UK	34	65	–	54	

Notes: (1) The children are assumed to be 3 and 8 years old, full day care is provided for the youngest child.

1.1.3 Central Planning Bureau

The Central Planning Bureau of The Hague, developed for the Commission, services a tax-benefit model enabling the estimation of, on one hand, the social contributions and taxes payable by individuals at different levels of gross earnings, and on the other hand, the unemployment benefit or social assistance receivable by the same individual in case of unemployment. Through the calculation of replacement rates, the study allows an overview to be obtained of the income position of unemployed workers for the EU Member States and three states of the US with a reference date of 1 July 1993 (Central Planning Bureau, 1995). (See Table 4.3.)

Replacement rates have been calculated for three kinds of households: single persons, married couples without children and married couples with children; in the case of married couples, it is assumed that only one spouse is in employment. As in the OECD study, the person is assumed to be 40 years old, but with only ten years of work experience (as against 22 in OECD). Different replacement rates are also calculated according to the duration of unemployment (at various stages of unemployment, from the initial situation to that which occurred after 60 months of unemployment).

The main conclusions of these calculations are:

- Generally, at the minimum wage level, income loss was minimal in the case of becoming unemployed, because of the minimum assistance levels set. In two countries (Portugal and Spain) there was no income loss for any family type, nor was there in many other countries (Germany, Ireland, Luxembourg, Netherlands) for families with children in the first month of unemployment. In the majority (7 out of 12) of the European countries examined, the average income loss was less than 10 per cent, and over 20 per cent only for single person households in some countries.
- After five years of unemployment, in over half the countries considered, the net income dropped markedly for single persons but only in Greece, Portugal and Spain for families with children. The remaining countries preserved about the same income level.
- In general, having a dependent spouse does not change the amount of gross wage or unemployment benefit; however, often special tax advantages, higher housing benefits and means-tested assistance are available for sole earners.
- For couples with children, replacement rates are even higher; tax advantages, child benefits, additional assistance, etc. lead to higher disposable incomes, especially among low-income households.

Table 4.3 Central Planning Bureau, 1993: net replacement rates for single-earner households

	AWP earnings level					
	First month of unemployment			60th month of unemployment		
	Single	Couple, no children	Couple, 2 children	Single	Couple, no children	Couple, 2 children
Belgium	67	59	63	47	59	66
Denmark	80	88	87	80	82	87
France	80	78	80	47	56	65
Germany	61	63	74	55	59	69
Greece	48	50	55	7	8	10
Ireland	44	59	74	44	59	74
Italy	56	62	66	28	44	63
Luxembourg	85	84	89	45	62	77
Netherlands	74	79	82	57	73	77
Portugal	79	77	76	0	0	5
Spain	84	79	77	23	29	41
UK	41	54	70	41	52	70

	Minimum wage level					
	First month of unemployment			60th month of unemployment		
	Single	Couple, no children	Couple, 2 children	Single	Couple, no children	Couple, 2 children
Belgium	77	81	81	65	81	85
Denmark	95	96	97	95	96	97
France	89	89	90	63	78	88
Germany	79	97	112	79	97	112
Greece	79	79	89	12	12	16
Ireland	73	93	115	73	93	115
Italy	79	83	87	43	63	87
Luxembourg	89	103	102	79	90	92
Netherlands	85	100	100	85	100	100
Portugal	112	112	111	0	0	10
Spain	107	107	106	47	61	81
UK	80	89	86	79	86	86

1.2 Comparison Between Net Replacement Rates for Stylized Households

The net replacement calculations for stylized households use similar approaches and are methodologically comparable. However, there are differences in detailed assumptions and the years considered are not exactly the same. Both of these factors are likely to induce slightly different results, but one can assume that the overall picture should be similar. The most essential differences between these calculations concern the treatment of housing costs and benefits, the possible topping-up of social assistance, and the selection of the low-wage level. (See Table 4.4.)

The OECD and CPB studies apply the general disposable income concept, that is, including housing benefits but without deducting housing costs, whereas the Seven Countries Group applies a wider disposable income definition, that is, so-called 'family purse' income which is measured including housing benefits and deducting moderate housing costs. Here, the assumption of 'moderate' housing costs, which were slightly different between countries, additionally affects the final outcome.[4] The OECD and CPB studies assume that social assistance is not granted during the first month of unemployment and the possible topping-up of social assistance is included only in the calculations of the net replacement rates for the sixtieth month of unemployment, whereas the Seven Countries Group also includes social assistance in the net replacement rate for the first month's unemployment. The low-wage level is interpreted as two-thirds of the average wage level in the OECD and Seven Countries Group studies, but the minimum wage in the CPB study.

There are significant variations in the replacement rates of different family types in all countries, implying that one could weight them differently to compute an alternative summary measure. For instance, instead of taking a simple average of all the replacement rates, an alternative approach would be to weight them in line with the actual demographic, family and duration composition of unemployment in each country. In addition to the fact the population weights are not easily available, using them also implies problems, namely, that the population sizes respond to incentives in benefit systems and thus potentially give rise to bias in the summary measure. Here, for comparison of different stylized calculations, a simple average of the first month's replacement rates for three different family types (single person, couple without children, couple with two children) is presented.[5]

The replacement rates calculated by the Seven Countries Group were, in general, clearly lower than those in the OECD calculations, mainly due to the fact that moderate housing costs were deducted from the disposable income of households. For families with children, especially in Finland, Germany and the UK, the rates were, however, higher, due to the topping-up of social assistance having been taken into account. In general, the ranking order of countries according to replacement rates was largely the same in these two studies.

Table 4.4   *Summary measure of net replacement rates in the first month of unemployment*

EU countries	APW wage level			Low wage level		
	OECD 1995	CPB 1993	Seven Countries 1994	OECD 1995	CPB 1993	Seven Countries 1994
Austria	63	–	–	65	–	–
Belgium	61	63	–	79	80	–
Denmark	70	85	61	93	96	87
Finland	75	–	75	87	–	88
France	76	79	69	86	89	82
Germany	72	66	54	74	96	71
Greece	–	51	–	–	82	–
Ireland	49	59	–	60	94	–
Italy	42	61	–	41	83	–
Luxembourg	87	86	–	87	98	–
Netherlands	79	78	67	87	95	78
Portugal	78	77	–	88	112	–
Spain	74	80	–	72.	107	–
Sweden	78	–	74	80	–	71
UK	61	55	38	81	85	58

Note: The summary measure of net replacement rates has been calculated as a simple average of the net replacement rates for three family types (single earner, couple without children and couple with two children). Low wage level is the minimum wage in CPB study and in others two-thirds of APW wage level.

The calculation of net replacement rates at minimum wage level (CPB) provides additional information, because it is a stricter condition than a low wage level in the OECD calculation. In many countries, the net replacement rates at minimum wage level, especially for families, exceeded the income from the minimum wage; in Portugal and Spain, also, a single person was better off on benefits than on minimum wage. The results concerning net replacement rates at the minimum wage level should be interpreted with regard to the minimum wage level relative to average wage level, which differs markedly between countries.[6] Notably in Portugal, Spain, Ireland and Italy, the net replacement rates were far above those for two thirds of APW wage level calculated by the OECD.

In summary, the different calculations of net replacement rates of unemployment benefits lead to broadly similar conclusions. While there are differences between the levels of various calculations, the country rankings are strongly correlated. All studies show the same patterns of net replacement variation, namely, higher rates for low-income households and higher rates for families with children. The comparison of summary figures allows the distinction to be made between groups of countries with – arbitrarily defined – high, intermediate and low replacement rates. The high replacement rates are found in Luxembourg, Netherlands, Denmark, Finland, Sweden, France and Portugal. Intermediate replacement rates are found in Austria, Belgium, Germany, Spain and the UK and the low replacement rates in Greece, Ireland and Italy.

2 STUDIES BASED ON OBSERVED DATA

2.1 A Study Based on the European Community Household Panel (ECHP)

2.1.1 The methodology
Data   The basis of this analysis is the rich micro-data collected in the European Community Household Panel (ECHP), designed by EUROSTAT in close consultation with Member States.[7] The first wave (1993) of the panel survey provides information on the social dimension of 12 member countries in the European Union, covering income, demographic and labour force characteristics, health, education, housing, migration and other topics. The following tables and analysis are based on the sample with a size of 61 106 households (with around 127 000 individuals over 15 years of age) for the 12 EU Member States.

Target populations   The analysis will focus on the active population, that is, employed and unemployed people in households of working age. This means that households whose largest source of income is any kind of pension (old-age, survivor or invalidity) or income from investment, savings or property are excluded. First, a population of individuals belonging to households whose head is of active age (below 65 years) and whose members are available for labour market is defined. Second, a sub-group of low-income households is derived including those active households whose disposable income is less than two-thirds of the average household disposable income.

Observation units   The key observation unit in this analysis will be the individual, whether employed or unemployed. However, in order to simplify the analysis and to compare the regular income in and out of work, only dependent workers are taken into account. The self-employed and unpaid workers in family enterprises are not taken into consideration, because their income includes irregularities and elements other than compensation of work. Also apprentices and trainees are excluded because their labour market status is not yet established.

The analysis is made by comparing the two groups of individuals, namely, employed individuals in active households, that is, people over 15 years who received an income from paid work, and unemployed individuals in active households, that is, people over 15 years who were unemployed at the time of the interview according to the declaration of the interviewed person.

In- and out-of-work income   The comparison is made between employed and unemployed individuals with the same observable characteristics, assuming that the income that an individual who loses his/her job would receive is the same as that received by an unemployed person with the same characteristics (level of household income, sex, age, education, sector of last occupation, and so on).

For the purpose of this analysis the concept of individual net income is defined. It takes into consideration regular income from employment (when it is the case) plus all typical benefits that the individual receives. Irregular income from employment, income from self-employment, pensions (old-age/retirement, survivors' and invalidity), income from investment, savings or property, or any kind of gift, are not taken into account when calculating the individual income. Family allowances and housing allowances, which in the questionnaire were attributed to the household, were redistributed in each household among all active (i.e., employed or unemployed) individuals. All earnings and benefit amounts are indicated net of possible tax and other deductions already in the questionnaire. This means that if there have been yearly adjustments in taxation at the end of the year, these changes have not been taken into account.

2.1.2   Main results of the analysis

Incidence of unemployment   Table 4.5 and 4.6   In the ECHP data the incidence of the unemployment is defined as a percentage of the unemployed of the sum of the unemployed and the employed in dependent work. The incidence of unemployment, was 15 per cent on average in 12 Member States whereas the unemployment rate according to the LFS was 10.7 per cent.

According to the ECHP Survey, there were 18.7 million unemployed people in 12 Member States in 1993. This figure is 15 per cent higher than the unemployment figure in LFS (16.2 million). In some countries, the differences are moderate and may reflect differences similar to those found between the national

Table 4.5   *Numbers of the unemployed and the unemployment rates according to ECHP and Labour Force Surveys in 1993*

| | **All households** | | | |
| | ECHP Survey | | Labour Force Survey (LFS) | |
	Number of the unemployed in 1000	Incidence of unemployment, % of the labour force[1]	Number of the unemployed in 1000	Unemployment rate, % of the labour force
Belgium	540	14	329	8.1
Denmark	343	13	305	10.9
France	3113	15	2788	11.4
Germany	3081	9	2975	7.7
Greece	617	23	347	8.8
Ireland	248	22	208	15.9
Italy	3874	21	2300	10.4
Luxembourg	7	5	4	2.3
Netherlands	916	16	386	6.3
Portugal	438	12	240	5.5
Spain	3006	25	3388	22.4
UK	2481	11	2919	10.4
EU 12	18 663	15	16 188	10.7

Note: (1) The labour force is here defined as sum of the unemployed and the employed, excluding self-employed.

administrative sources and the LFS. But, notably in Greece, Italy, the Netherlands and Portugal, the differences were unexpectedly large: the ECHP showed approximately double the unemployment figures.

The differences are due to different surveys which have different sample bias and somewhat different definitions, for example, of the concept of unemployed. In the ECHP survey the unemployed is defined at the time of interview according to the declarations of the persons interviewed, whereas the LFS defines unemployment on the basis of job search and labour market availability. Hence, one can assume that declaring oneself as unemployed in an interview like ECHP does not follow such strict rules, for instance, concerning the availability of labour markets, as the LFS.

Low-income households were defined as households having less than two-thirds of the average household income. Denmark and Germany had the smallest shares of individuals in low-income households, 22 and 24 per cent respectively, and the UK and Portugal the largest shares, 38 and 40 per cent, respectively. The rest of the countries had a relatively similar figure of around 30 per cent of all individuals. The small share of individuals in low-income households reflects a compressed income distribution. The general picture of the shares of the individuals in low-income households largely follows the general perception on overall income differences across countries. Countries with the most equal income distribution had the lowest shares of individuals in low-income households, and vice versa.

Table 4.6   Share of individuals, number and share of the unemployed and the incidence of unemployment in 1993

| | **Low-income households** | | | |
	Share of individuals in low-income households	Number of the unemployed in 1000	Share of all unemployed	Incidence of unemployment, % of the labour force
Belgium	28	273	51	39
Denmark	22	128	37	52
France	33	1704	55	34
Germany	24	1803	59	30
Greece	33	300	49	53
Ireland	33	151	61	57
Italy	34	2342	60	43
Luxembourg	28	4	61	12
Netherlands	30	436	48	36
Portugal	40	247	56	23
Spain	34	1753	58	52
UK	38	1873	76	33
EU 12	32	11 014	59	37

Note: (1) The labour force is here defined as sum of the unemployed and the employed (excluding self-employed) in the sub-population of low-income households.

The share of unemployed people in low-income households was 59 per cent on average, almost double the share of all individuals. In most countries the shares of the unemployed were between 50–60 (exactly 48–61) per cent. Only Denmark with the lowest (37 per cent) and the UK with the highest figure (76 per cent) clearly differed from the other countries studied. The greatest concentration of unemployment in low-income households, measured by the difference (38 percentage points) between shares of the unemployed and all individuals, was found in the UK, followed by Germany and Luxembourg. The smallest concentrations of unemployment in low-income households were found in Denmark, Greece and Portugal.

Take-up rates   Table 4.7   In order to analyse incentive impacts of the benefit system, it is important to know the take-up rates of benefits, that is, how many persons who fulfil the benefit eligibility criteria actually take up the benefit. One is interested to know whether the receipt of benefits can be taken for granted or whether only some of those fulfilling the primary eligibility condition in fact receive the benefits as well as whether there are large differences across countries.

According to the household panel survey, the average take-up rate of unemployment benefits was 33 per cent amongst all unemployed and at about the same level amongst the unemployed in low-income households. Three countries had high take-up rates of unemployment benefits, namely Belgium (83 per cent for both all and low-income unemployed), Denmark (80 per cent for all and 85 per cent for low-income unemployed), and Ireland (76 and 80 per cent). After these countries, only in Germany did a relatively large number of unemployed receive unemployment benefits (60 per cent). In the rest of the countries the take-up rate did not exceed 40 per cent.

It is evident that the take-up rates are below 100 per cent because people do not qualify for benefits immediately. The reasons for this may be that i) an insurance scheme requires contributions and some time of work history before becoming entitled to benefit, ii) the benefit periods are limited, iii) entitlement of the second bread-winner or other family members than the principal bread-winner may be restricted or means-tested, and iv) provision of substituting schemes such as social assistance and schemes for laid-off people may play a different role from country to country (Martin 1996).

Still, it is worth examining more carefully the statistical information concerning the take-up rates of benefits. The absolute numbers of unemployment benefit recipients are broadly similar to those reported in the LFS. The ECHP reports somewhat higher figures for Belgium, Ireland and the Netherlands, and lower figures for Germany and France. The figures for the UK in 1993 are missing from the LFS but later figures from 1994 onwards suggest that either the ECHP figures are far too low or the LFS includes in unemployment benefits also social assistance or other similar benefits. Despite this overall consistency between absolute figures in the ECHP and LFS, one has to keep in mind that the unemployment was over-reported in the ECHP, notably in Greece, Italy, Luxembourg and the Netherlands. Hence, the take-up rates become undervalued merely for this reason.

There is evidence that the LFS also under-reports receipt of benefits. Studies show that for some countries the LFS reports a coverage of benefit recipients only half, or even less, what the national administrative sources report as ben-

Table 4.7   Numbers and take-up rates of all benefits and unemployment benefits

	A. All households			
	Recipients of all benefits		Unemployment benefits	
	Number in 1000	Take-up rate, % of all unemployed	Number in 1000	Take-up rate, % of all unemployed
Belgium	498	92	446	83
Denmark	337	98	273	80
France	2707	87	1218	39
Germany	2974	97	1846	60
Greece	267	43	70	11
Ireland	227	92	189	76
Italy	830	21	148	4
Luxembourg	5	78	1	8
The Netherlands	445	49	264	29
Portugal	300	69	110	25
Spain	1874	62	1028	34
UK	2183	88	502	20
EU 12	12 647	68	6095	33

	B. Low-income households			
	Recipients of all benefits		Unemployment benefits	
	Number in 1000	Take-up rate, % of all unemployed	Number in 1000	Take-up rate, % of all unemployed
Belgium	257	94	228	83
Denmark	125	98	109	85
France	1466	86	637	37
Germany	1735	96	1084	60
Greece	133	44	25	8
Ireland	138	91	120	80
Italy	437	19	80	3
Luxembourg	3	81	1	13
The Netherlands	212	49	128	29
Portugal	165	67	53	22
Spain	1093	62	596	34
UK	1691	90	379	20
EU	7454	68	3439	31

eficiary totals (OECD 1998b). It is likely that in countries with developed administrative register system and register-based statistics, there are fewer differences in reporting the receipt of benefits.

In summary, caution is needed in interpreting benefit coverage rates because they seem to be under-reported in interview surveys in general. Moreover, the over-reporting of unemployment worsens the problem. Notwithstanding these reservations, some conclusions can be drawn regarding the patterns of benefit receipt. First, the receipt of unemployment benefits in case of unemployment cannot be taken for granted in all countries. Second, there seem to be strikingly large differences in the take-up rates of unemployment benefits across countries. Third, there do not seem to be major differences in the take-up rates between the low-income and all unemployed within any country.

Net replacement rates   Net replacement rates are analysed in Table 4.8 according to educational level.[8] Preferably, the skill level would be used as the most appropriate criterion to distinguish people by their probable wage level. In the absence of this information, the educational level is used as a proxy.

The average net replacement rate (weighted by the number of unemployed receiving benefits) was 52 per cent in the EU countries. In six countries the rates were somewhat below 50 per cent (44 to 49 per cent in Spain, Italy, Greece, Belgium, France and the Netherlands), in four other countries somewhat above 50 per cent (51 in Ireland, 54 in Portugal, 55 in Germany and 56 per cent in the UK). Luxembourg had the lowest rate (38 per cent) and Denmark was far above the other countries (74 per cent).

The net replacement rate for the subset of unemployed belonging to low-income households was 64 per cent on average, 12 percentage points higher than that for all unemployed. High rates were found in Denmark (87 per cent), Ireland (76 per cent), Germany (72 per cent) and United Kingdom (70 per cent). The highest increases for low-income unemployed in comparison with the rate for all unemployed were noted in Ireland (by 25 percentage points), and in Germany and Spain (by 17 percentage points). Only in France and Italy were the net replacement rates at about the same level as those for all unemployed and Italy was the only country where the rate was clearly low (42 per cent).

In fact, in most European countries, the average out-of-work income for the unemployed in low-income households was, in absolute terms, almost the same as that on average for all unemployed. The unemployed in low-income households received only 10 per cent less than all unemployed, whereas the employed in low-income households received on average 25 per cent less than all employed.

In all countries (except the Netherlands) unemployment is concentrated amongst people with a low education level. On average, 71 per cent of the unemployed had a low education level, 19 per cent a medium and 9 per cent a

Table 4.8   Net replacement rates according to level of education

	All households						
	All	*Educational level*					
	Average	Share of the unemployed[1]			Net replacement rates[2]		
	net repl. rate	Low	Medium	High	Low	Medium	High
Belgium	47	59	24	11	49	49	51
Denmark	74	68	16	15	79	75	63
France	49	70	14	12	57	43	36
Germany	55	86	7	6	60	60	45
Greece	46	45	40	15	54	44	40
Ireland	51	76	18	5	58	51	31
Italy	45	62	29	5	47	39	52
Luxembourg	38	87	3	11	41	N/A	66
Netherlands	49	34	54	12	50	54	54
Portugal	54	91	7	1	65	41	33
Spain	44	78	11	12	50	45	33
UK	56	77	16	7	61	58	49
EU 12[3]	52	71	19	9	57	50	42

	Low-income households						
	All	*Educational level*					
	Average	Share of the unemployed[1]			Net replacement rates[2]		
	net repl. rate	Low	Medium	High	Low	Medium	High
Belgium	59	63	22	8	60	60	63
Denmark	87	71	13	16	89	85	75
France	53	76	14	7	58	41	27
Germany	72	89	6	4	74	58	66
Greece	56	56	34	10	64	38	49
Ireland	76	79	17	3	76	75	32
Italy	42	65	27	3	44	39	19
Luxembourg	49	95	N/A	5	50	N/A	N/A
Netherlands	53	41	51	7	56	54	51
Portugal	68	94	6	N/A	70	78	N/A
Spain	61	83	8	9	61	69	55
UK	70	81	14	4	76	50	73
EU 12[3]	64	76	17	6	67	51	53

Notes:
(1) The shares may not always add up to 100 because of missing information on education level.
(2) The net replacement rates have been calculated for the unemployed with benefits. The average out-of-work income of each group has been calculated separately and compared with the average in-work income of the respective group of employed.
(3) Weighted by the number of unemployed receiving benefits.

high education. The share of low-educated unemployed was over 80 per cent in Germany, Luxembourg and Portugal and additionally amongst low-income households also in Spain and the UK. The Netherlands was a clear outlier; over 50 per cent of the unemployed had a medium education level and 40 per cent had the lowest education level. The reason behind this may be in the high share of female unemployment (two-thirds); this, however, is likely to include a large number of inactive people as the number of the unemployed is over-reported.[9] The pattern of unemployment according to education level was very similar in the sub-population of low-income households, being only a little more concentrated at low education levels.

2.1.3 Summary of the results
The main conclusions of the analysis above are the following:

- According to the ECHP, the number of unemployed was considerably higher than according to Labour Force Surveys: on average by 15 per cent in 12 Member States, but almost double in Greece, Italy, the Netherlands and Portugal.
- Receipt of benefits was probably under-reported in the ECHP survey as seems to be the case with interview surveys in general.
- Despite the above general reservation, the following patterns of benefit receipt hold: i) there are large differences across countries in benefit take-up rates, ii) there are no notable differences in benefit take-up rates between the unemployed in low-income and the unemployed in all households within any country. Unemployment benefits are not especially targeted towards the poor.
- The take-up rate of benefits of all sorts (unemployment, housing, family allowances, social assistance etc.) amongst the unemployed was 68 per cent on average, twice as high as that of unemployment benefits alone, 33 per cent. The take-up rate of all benefits was over 90 per cent in Belgium, Denmark, Germany and Ireland. The lowest rates were found in Italy (21 per cent), Greece (43 per cent) and the Netherlands (49 per cent).
- A third (32 per cent) of individuals belonged to low-income households, that is, those where the disposable income was less than two-thirds of the average disposable income, ranging from 22 per cent in Denmark to 40 per cent in Portugal. The proportion of the unemployed living in low-income households was 59 per cent, almost twice the share of all individuals, ranging from 37 per cent in Denmark to 76 per cent in the UK. This finding can be interpreted to support the perception of coincidence of unemployment and low-income.

- Unemployment was concentrated amongst the low-educated, and thereby also among the low-skilled: about three out of four unemployed people had a low education level. Almost half of the unemployed were young, under 30 years old.
- The net replacement rate was on average 52 per cent and among low-income households 64 per cent. The highest average net replacement rate for all unemployed was found in Denmark (74 per cent), whereas it was around 50 per cent in most countries.
- The highest average net replacement rates for the unemployed in low-income households were found in Denmark (87 per cent), Ireland (76 per cent), Germany (72 per cent) and the UK (70 per cent). The highest increases in replacement rates for low-income households in comparison with those for all households were found in Ireland (25 percentage points), and in Germany and Spain (17 percentage points).
- In the majority of countries net replacement rates were higher for low-educated people than for those with medium or high level education. The results support the pattern of higher net replacement rates for those with a lower wage and a lower education level.

2.2   Another Approach to ECHP Data

A study assigned by the Directorate-General for Employment, Industrial Relations and Social Affairs (later referred to as DG V study), also based on the ECHP data from 1993, compares the net income of the same persons who experienced both an unemployment spell and an employment period during the same observation year.[10] The income data relate to the average monthly net earnings from employment and the average monthly net income when drawing benefits during unemployment. As regards the benefits, those related to unemployment, whether as insurance-based benefits or as assistance, were covered. However, the family-related benefits including housing benefits were excluded. The population of this study was confined to those who had experienced at least a three months' unemployment spell and at least one month's full-time employment. The data did not allow the separation of those who had the unemployment period after employment from those who were unemployed before employment; both groups are included. For the latter group, the replacement rate is calculated from the accepted post-unemployment wage level.

This DG V study relates to individuals, as the study reported in Chapter 2.1 (later referred to as DG II study), but in contrast with the DG II study, compares the monthly income of the same individuals in different labour market situations, whereas the DG II study compares the yearly income of different persons in different labour market situations. The second major difference is that the DG V study excludes family-related benefits and can be interpreted to compare net unemployment benefit with net earnings. Both of these approaches primarily attempt to measure individual net income, whereas the model calculations attempt to capture the impact of unemployment on family income.

Table 4.9   *Net replacement rates and take-up rates of unemployment benefits in DG V and DG II studies*

| | Net replacement rate | | Take-up rate of unemployment benefits | | Take-up rate of all benefits |
	DG V	DG II, all households	DG V	DG II	DG II
Belgium	48	47	91	83	92
Denmark	70	74	98	80	98
France	66	49	67	39	87
Germany	55	55	89	60	97
Greece	26	46	28	11	43
Ireland	55	51	84	76	92
Italy	49	45	26	4	21
Luxembourg	–	38	–	8	78
Netherlands	–	49	–	29	49
Portugal	75	54	28	25	69
Spain	55	44	53	34	62
UK	20	56	89	20	88
EU 12	49	52	67	33	68

The number of unemployed people in 10 EU countries (Luxembourg and the Netherlands as well as the new Member States Austria, Finland and Sweden excluded) examined in the DG V study was 4.1 million of which 2.8 million received unemployment benefits. These unemployed represented 22 per cent of those examined in the DG II study.

The figures in Table 4.9, compared with the figures of the DG II study, show remarkable differences in results. The take-up rates of unemployment benefits were much higher (67 per cent) in the DG V study than in the DG II study (33 per cent) in all countries. Yet, the average take-up rate remained relatively low. This was affected by very low take-up rates, less than one-third, in Greece, Italy and Portugal, whereas they were over 80 per cent in five countries (Belgium, Denmark, Germany, Ireland and UK). The most striking difference between the two studies was apparent in the UK where the DG V study showed the take-up rate of 89 per cent whilst the DG II study showed 20 per cent. Italy, Greece and Portugal showed the lowest take-up rates in both analyses.

Average net replacement rates according to the DG V study are a little lower than according to the DG II study. This is unexpected because the DG II study covers all unemployed, whereas the DG V study covers only those who were both unemployed and employed during the reference year, and thus the majority of these unemployed are likely to have benefits which were not yet phased out owing to a lengthy unemployment spell. The result can be explained by a narrower disposable income concept, which in the DG V study included only net unemployment benefits and excluded family-related benefits. The expectation of higher replacement rates holds only in three countries, namely, France, Portugal and Spain. In these countries the inclusion of all unemployed (in the DG II study) may lead to a marked decrease of net replacement rates, because in these countries the benefit level is gradually phased out over the unemployment spell. For about half the countries, the net replacement rates were at about the same level as net replacement rates for all unemployed in the DG II study.

Moreover, the net replacement rates in Greece and the United Kingdom were far below those of the DG II study. The mismatch in results is most prominent in the UK where, according to the DG V results, the take-up rate was very high but the net replacement rate very low, whereas the DG II study showed rather the opposite results. It is likely that the exclusion of family-related benefits contributes much to a low net replacement rate in the DG V study. According to an OECD study (OECD 1997a), for instance, in a British family of a one-earner couple with two children, the income during unemployment consists of unemployment benefits only for one half and of housing and family allowances for the other half.

2.3 Comparison between Observed and Stylized Net Replacement Rates

When comparing observed and stylized net replacement rates, two completely different methodologies are applied and compared. Therefore, it is not easy to find proper summary measures for comparison purposes. In particular, the large variations in family and duration compositions of unemployment, which is captured in summary indicators derived from observed data, is difficult to capture with stylized measures, which, by definition, try to simplify complex situations. Additionally, stylized calculations based on hypothetical data were made at household level whereas the studies based on the observed data of the ECHP data focused primarily on individuals. Hence, the stylized calculations drew more attention to the economic impact at the household level and its consequences for work incentives of an individual.

A great number of variables affecting the comparison could not be controlled for in the above studies based on ECHP data. The strength of observed data in capturing the variation of family and unemployment situations is also a limitation in comparison with stylized calculations. There are notable difficulties in correctly defining the groups of households which can properly be compared with each other on the basis of observed data.

In the following, a tentative comparison between the approaches of DG II and DG V is made with the OECD calculations (Table 4.10). In the OECD calculations, there are two benchmarks: the net replacement rate of the first month of unemployment and that of the sixtieth month. While the DG II approach covers all unemployed, neither the first month's nor the sixtieth month's rate perfectly correspond to the 'average' duration of unemployment in real data. The approach of DG V is closer to the first month of unemployment, because the study was confined to those having been both unemployed and employed during the reference year.

Table 4.10   Comparison of observed and stylized net replacement rates

EU countries	Studies on hypothetical data OECD 1995 APW wage level		Studies on observed data ECHP data 1993	
	1st month of unemployment	60th month of unemployment	DG II study	DG V study
Austria	63	61	–	–
Belgium	61	58	47	48
Denmark	70	74	74	70
Finland	75	81	–	–
France	76	46	49	66
Germany	72	66	55	55
Greece	–	–	46	26
Ireland	49	49	51	55
Italy	42	5	45	49
Luxembourg	87	66	38	–
Netherlands	79	71	49	–
Portugal	78	2	54	75
Spain	74	35	44	55
Sweden	78	82	–	–
UK	61	64	56	20

The above tentative comparison allows one to make the following conclusions:

- There is a fair match between the observed and stylized net replacement rates in half the countries. The results regarding Denmark and Ireland are identical and there is a good match in Italy as well. In a number of countries, namely, France, Portugal and Spain, the results from observed data can be interpreted as being consistent with calculations based on hypothetical data in that they reflect the phasing-out of the benefit level over the unemployment spell: the net replacement rates from the observed data are lower than those based on hypothetical data for the first month's replacement but higher than for the sixtieth month's replacement. However, in the other half of the countries, the net replacement rates from observed data are significantly lower than those from hypothetical data. In particular, the results for the Netherlands and Luxembourg are inconsistent: the ECHP survey shows very low replacement rates, whereas the stylized calculations show high ones. Also in Belgium, Germany and the UK the results from observed data show somewhat lower replacement rates.

• The average net replacement rates based on observed data across countries tend to concentrate around the rate of 50 per cent (44–56 per cent), with the exceptions of Luxembourg (38 per cent) and Denmark (74 per cent). Instead, the stylized net replacement rates are spread over a wider range of 61–87 per cent in the first month of unemployment and over the range of 46–82 per cent in the sixtieth month (some exceptional values excluded).

3   CONCLUSIONS

A first comparison of net replacement rates based on observed data with those on hypothetical data does not give an unambiguous answer. There is a fairly good match between the overall results in half the countries, but in the other half the replacements rates on observed data were lower than those on hypothetical data. There were clear inconsistencies in more detailed results but one has to bear in mind several reservations regarding the different approaches. None of the approaches can be rejected on the basis of these results.

The different net replacement rates based on different types of data suggest different uses for the results. The net replacement rates on hypothetical data emphasize the mechanisms, interactions and outcomes of the tax-benefit systems. Instead, the rates on observed data are better able to cope with the diversity of family and labour market situations and to answer questions such as how many people there are in a given situation. For comparison purposes across countries, the stylized method on hypothetical data has the advantage of taking proper account of the complexities of tax-benefit systems in a comparable and identified manner. In order to compare the generosity of benefit systems between countries, it provides an appropriate method, given that the selection of stylized family types is justified. The studies of the OECD, the Seven

Countries Group and the Central Planning Bureau have contributed to finding a more established basis for calculations and created a framework for cross-country comparisons.

Studies based on observed data can shed more light on the question of the receipt of benefits, which in fact cannot be answered on the basis of hypothetical data. The results suggest that the take-up rates of unemployment benefits are notably low in many countries and that there are marked differences between countries. At the same time, however, the take-up rates of benefits of all sorts are considerably higher. There are reasons to believe that the actual take-up rates are not as low as the results suggest. It seems evident that the ECHP over-reports unemployment, which is clearly seen in a comparison with the figures of the LFS. It is also very likely that both the ECHP and the LFS under-report the receipt of benefits; comparisons between the LFS and national administrative sources have found evidence of this.

With regard to labour market policy matters, there are two important findings in this study. First, both methods applied in the cited studies prove that the net replacement rates for low-paid workers are higher than in general. Hence, low-paid people are most discouraged from taking up a job and, consequently, most likely to be found in an unemployment trap. On the basis of stylized calculations, a conclusion regarding high net replacement rates for some family types, in particular, families with children, can be drawn. Second, the statistics show that there is no difference in the incidence of unemployment benefits between the poor and in general. Thus, the unemployment benefit systems do not target specifically the equity objective. Instead, all countries provide a wide range of other schemes, which, in addition to redistribution and complementary goals, can also substitute for unemployment benefits.

In order to tackle better the comparison problems encountered in this study, there is ample room for further work, starting from unnecessary inconsistencies in concepts and definitions, paying more attention to the scope of the analysis and substituting benefit schemes for the unemployed, taking better control of individual and household characteristics affecting the composition of the groups to be compared, making better use of improving provision of longitudinal statistical data and, finally, developing more sophisticated methods.

International comparisons of the incidence and distribution of high net replacement rates have suffered from the lack of appropriate data. The ECHP improves the situation because, in future, it will allow the same individuals to be followed over time and thus will provide information on the transitions in and out of employment as well as on the income received in different situations. One may assume as well that the quality of data improves when it becomes more established.

Some countries have already applied simulation techniques together with observed data. Such models enable account to be taken of all interactions of taxes and benefit systems in a equally detailed manner as in stylized calcula-tions and, in addition to this, enable experiments to be conducted by changing the labour market status of actual persons. Thus, for each individual and household in the sample, the impact on net income can be simulated when a transition from employment into unemployment or vice versa is assumed. When the model is based on micro-data, it results, in this example, in new informa-tion on the actual level and distribution of net replacement rates for actual unemployed people. In order to increase the power of these models, behav-ioural responses to policy changes need to be known and incorporated. This would allow more to be said about the actual influence of benefits on labour market transitions.

NOTES

1. This article is based on work carried out by the author and Teresa Munzi who worked in the European Commission in 1995–7. The complete work of the same title has been published in the series of *Economic Papers of the European Commission*, 133, February 1999.
2. Sometimes this actual ratio is referred to as the *ex post* replacement ratio. However, in literature the *ex post* replacement rate is used to mean the ratio between benefit income during unem-ployment and the post-unemployment wage income. Therefore, we prefer to use the concepts of stylized and observed replacement rates in order to describe differences in approaches.
3. All studies to be compared include calculations over a wide income range, Here, however, for comparison purposes only the APW and two-thirds of the APW wage levels have been chosen.
4. See Eight Countries Group (1998), 'Note on methodology: The Importance of Housing Cost Assumption' in the report 'Income Benefits for Early Exit from the Labour Market in eight European Countries', *European Economy, Reports and Studies* No. 3, 1998, European Commission.
5. There are significant differences in the weights of different household types across countries, thus implying also differences in family patterns. For instance, the share of single person households varied between 20–50 per cent, couples without children between 20–30, and couples with children between 20–50 per cent in European countries (OECD 1997b).
6. According to an OECD Study, the minimum wages relative to the full-time mean earnings in 1997 ranged from about 30 per cent (in Spain) to 55 per cent (in France) in a group of EU countries. See 'Making the Most of the Minimum: Statutory Minimum Wages, Employment and Poverty', in OECD Employment Outlook, 1998.
7. See ECHP documentation, e.g. European Commission (1996a and b).
8. More detailed analyses by other characteristics of the unemployed and by the distribution of net replacement rates are available in the complete paper by Salomäki and Munzi, 1999.
9. See Salomäki and Munzi (1999), pp. 41–2.
10. European Commission (1998).

REFERENCES

Central Planning Bureau (1995), 'Replacement Rates – A Transatlantic View', CPB Working Paper, 80, September.

Eight Countries Group (1998), 'Income Benefits for Early Exit from the Labour Market in Eight European Countries', *European Economy, Reports and Studies* 3, 1998, European Commission, Brussels.

European Commission (1996a), 'The European Community Household Panel (ECHP): Survey Methodology and Implementation, Volume 1', EUROSTAT, Luxembourg.

European Commission (1996b), 'ECHP Wave 1 Documentation', Doc. Pan 15.2.1996, EUROSTAT, Luxembourg.

European Commission (1998), 'Social Protection in Europe 1997', Brussels.

Martin, J.P. (1996), 'Measures of Replacement Rates for the Purpose of International Comparisons: A Note', *OECD Economic Studies*, 26, January: 99–114.

OECD (1995), 'The Tax/Benefit Position of Production Workers, 1995 Edition', Paris: OECD.

OECD (1997a), 'The OECD Jobs Strategy: Making Work Pay. A Thematic Review of Taxes, Benefits, Employment and Unemployment', Paris: OECD.

OECD (1997b), 'Benefits and Incentives in OECD Countries, 1995', Working Party on Social Policy, Paris: OECD.

OECD (1998a), 'Benefit Systems and Work Incentives', Paris: OECD.

OECD (1998b), 'The Public Employment Service in Greece, Ireland and Portugal', OECD 1998.

Salomäki, A. and T. Munzi (1999), 'Net Replacement Rates of the Unemployed. Comparison of Various Approaches', *Economic Papers* 133, European Commission, Brussels.

Seven Countries Group (1996), 'Unemployment Benefits and Social Assistance in Seven European Countries', *Werkdocumenten* 10, Ministerie van Sociale Zaken en Werkgelegenheld, The Netherlands.

Snower, D.J. (1997), 'Evaluating Unemployment Policies: What Do the Underlying Theories Tell Us?', in D.J. Snower and G. de la Dehesa (eds), *Unemployment Policy. Government Options for the Labour Market*, Cambridge University Press.

5. The retreat of the welfare system: myths and reality – a broad comparison of trends in social protection expenditure across EU countries

Paolo Sestito and Michele Ca'Zorzi[1]

1 INTRODUCTION

The build-up of the welfare system has lasted several decades and has been characterized, in general, by what may be described as 'incremental' steps. According to a widespread view, this process has come to a halt during the last decade and is due, at least, to three broad forces:[2]

- short-run budgetary strains, particularly relevant because of the discipline imposed by the Maastricht Treaty and because of the increased speed of capital movements;
- long-run budgetary concerns linked to current demographic trends[3] and to what may be referred to as the 'maturity' of the system;[4]
- fears that the disappointing employment performance of many EU countries may be, at least partly, due to the excessive generosity of their welfare systems or to the consequent excessive fiscal burden.[5]

To evaluate whether a welfare system retreat is the appropriate response to these concerns, one should balance the relevance of these concerns with the goals traditionally attached to the welfare system. Extensive social insurance, even when it causes a higher natural rate of unemployment, may still be more desirable than an alternative configuration with lower unemployment but widespread income insecurity among the workforce.[6] Moreover, any discussion on a given welfare programme should not confine itself to establishing its overall 'optimal size'. To reduce adverse incentives, it is even more important to consider how each programme functions in detail (also taking account of the interactions with the other programmes).

The more limited aim of this study is to test the presence of a welfare retreat, not by examining the effectiveness of single welfare reforms, but by putting forward a systematic assessment of recent changes in broad expenditure patterns. The analysis will then resort to a simple regression framework, so as to net out the fluctuations in expenditure from the effects of employment fluctuations.

Our analysis distinguishes among eight broad categories of expenditure as defined by the methodology used by EUROSTAT which is known as ESSPROS. This methodology offers, consistently across the 15 EU Member States, a breakdown of gross expenditure flows[7] into the eight following categories: unemployment, invalidity, social exclusion (which includes several mixed items), family, housing, sickness, old-age and survivors (and other dependants). A joint analysis of these expenditure flows allows one to take account of the possible substitution effects between different expenditure categories. This point is also most relevant when comparing different countries given that different schemes and institutions may come to play functionally similar roles.[8]

While leaving to EUROSTAT (1996) a more detailed description of the data at our disposal,[9] it is important here to begin by referring to the general philosophy underlying the ESSPROS methodology. First, the data covered by ESSPROS are gross of taxes. They measure the gross amount of resources transiting through a non-market channel (the social protection system).[10] Second, the social protection schemes covered, while not necessarily 'public', exclude insurance policies which are not compulsory such as private life insurance schemes.[11]

Each of the eight categories of expenditure corresponds to a different social protection objective. According to this methodology, in classifying each individual expenditure flow under one of the above headings, what matters most is the single most relevant social goal pursued. As an example, all income support expenditures in favour of old people[12] should be classified in the old-age category, even when they formally derive from an invalidity scheme. Similarly, ESSPROS rules indicate that all expenditures financing early retirements with a basic economic motivation should be included as part of the unemployment (and not the old age) category. The unemployment category should also include those supplementary allowances related to the housing and family needs of the unemployment benefits claimants. On the other hand, housing and family related expenditures which are available to everyone, including employed people, should be included in the family and housing categories, respectively. Finally, as far as the distinction between invalidity and sickness is concerned, the dividing line should be, in principle, between, on the one hand, expenditures supporting the income of disabled people and, on the other, expenditures more closely targeting health needs.

Throughout this chapter the eight different categories of expenditures are ranked according to their presumed relationship with unemployment. In this respect, the first category is clearly unemployment, followed by the categories of invalidity and social exclusion, as they represent a supplementary source of income for individuals whose earning ability is very low. More debatable is whether any similar role is played by the family and housing categories, as they should not include those expenditure flows explicitly targeted to support the non-employed. Given the difficulties of properly implementing the ESSPROS methodology, these two expenditure categories are nevertheless likely to act as indirect forms of income support in favour of the non-employed of working age. The remaining three categories of expenditure should be less connected to the support of the non-employed of working age.[13]

Some limitations of our approach have to be signalled as expenditure trends alone do not provide a full characterization of welfare reforms in terms of the quality of the services provided and possible disincentives to work effects. Further, our analytical framework is relatively simple, since it does not separate supply and demand factors in the evolution of expenditure as we only consider the aggregate expenditure for each category, in the absence of separate information on per capita expenditure and the number of beneficiaries.[14] Finally, the period covered here (ending in 1996 for most countries and only 1995 in the others), may be too short for detecting major effects of the most recent reforms. For this reason, we carefully examine the presence of a break in our estimates at the end of the sample period and we complement the statistical analysis of this study with some qualitative assessment of welfare reform already presented by other researchers.

The chapter is organized as follows. Section 2 offers a broad descriptive characterization of current social protection expenditure patterns across EU countries by examining the size and internal breakdown of expenditure. Even if limited to the expenditure side, several national features emerge. As for the expenditure's evolution over time, in section 3 we document the piecemeal nature of social welfare reforms and the broad expenditure trends in the last two decades. The evolution of expenditures is further analysed in section 4 through a simple econometric analysis which accounts for cyclical effects.

2   A BROAD SUMMARY OF EXPENDITURE FLOWS

This section summarizes the recent situation of social protection expenditures across EU countries.[15] A broad analysis of expenditure flows in the 1993–6 sample period is in Table 5.1, which presents gross expenditure flows as a percentage of GDP for the aforementioned eight categories for each of the 15 EU countries. We have focused on expenditure data expressed as a percentage of GDP in order to facilitate the comparison between countries (and over time,

Table 5.1 Social protection expenditure flows (average percentage of GDP across the 1993–6 period)

Country	Unemployment	Invalidity	Social exclusion	Family	Housing	Sickness	Old-age	Survivors	Total
				Expenditure category					
Belgium[1]	3.93	1.80	0.70	2.31	–	7.07	8.60	3.03	**27.43**
Denmark[1]	5.30	3.42	1.37	4.05	0.82	6.02	12.60	0.02	**33.25**
Germany	2.77	1.96	0.61	2.33	0.18	8.62	11.28	0.59	**28.34**
Greece[1]	0.96	1.67	0.15	1.33	0.41	5.24	8.29	1.57	**19.63**
Spain	3.55	1.68	0.11	0.40	0.10	6.42	8.70	0.95	**21.91**
France	2.51	1.70	0.47	2.61	0.90	8.44	10.59	1.91	**29.13**
Ireland	3.27	0.87	0.36	2.26	0.60	6.62	3.98	1.16	**19.13**
Italy	0.53	1.75	0.01	0.87	0.00	5.36	12.88	2.72	**24.11**
Luxembourg[1]	0.71	3.15	0.34	3.12	0.04	5.96	7.35	3.53	**24.20**
Netherlands	3.03	4.74	0.73	1.46	0.33	8.85	9.83	1.66	**30.64**
Portugal[1]	0.99	2.47	0.08	1.07	0.00	6.23	6.28	1.34	**18.47**
United Kingdom[1]	1.76	3.13	0.26	2.41	1.86	6.92	9.21	1.45	**27.00**
Austria	1.60	2.15	0.36	3.27	0.09	7.27	10.75	3.04	**28.52**
Finland	4.92	4.87	0.70	4.22	0.44	6.97	9.44	1.28	**32.85**
Sweden	4.03	4.18	1.15	4.12	1.21	7.91	12.62	0.87	**36.08**
European Union[2]	2.38	2.29	0.43	2.10	0.58	7.41	10.65	1.53	**27.35**

Notes:
(1) 1993–5 period.
(2) Weighted average using as weights GDP (in 1990 ECUs) during the 1993–6 period.

129

as will be seen in subsequent paragraphs). The choice of a multi-year average aims at minimizing cyclical factors.

Not surprisingly, the well known[16] distinction between Nordic (and NL) and Mediterranean (and IR) countries in terms of total expenditure holds. PO and SW stand at the two opposite extremes, with total expenditure equal respectively to 18.5 and 36.1 per cent of GDP. Below the 20 per cent threshold we also find IR and GR. Immediately above are ES (21.9 per cent) and, but at a greater distance, IT and L (both about 24 per cent). SF, DK and NL are above the 30 per cent level. The remaining countries are character-ized by total expenditure in the 27–2 per cent range, quite close to the EU average of 27.4 per cent.

Cross-country differences in total social protection expenditure are mainly explained by the discrepancies existing for the first five categories, namely unemployment, invalidity, social exclusion, family and housing. The smallest degree of variation across countries emerges for the sickness category. For the two remaining categories (old-age and survivors), cross-country ranking turns out to be rather different from the one described for the total. In the case of old-age expenditure, which is the largest category of expenditure overall, IT overtakes SW as the biggest spender. Among the big spenders for this category, we also find DK, FR, DE and OS. Overall, the presence in the first five categories of some countries which are consistently low (as for instance IT) or high spenders (the Nordic countries) brings about a positive cross-country cor-relation in the amount of these five categories of expenditure. However, the relatively high expenditure for unemployment in countries such as BE, ES and IR is compensated by low values of expenditure in the other four categories. The opposite emerges for countries like UK and PO, where expenditure appears to be relatively high for invalidity and (in the case of UK) housing, being relatively low for unemployment.

To some extent the cross-country differences discussed here may be related to the differences in the GDP level itself. In Figure 5.1 we therefore look at the scatter plot of the bivariate relationship between total expenditure as percentage of GDP and the GDP level (in Purchasing Power Parities), and also report the fitting line obtained by considering the 14 major countries (excluding Luxembourg which appears as a clear outlier). As expected, the outcome is that of a positive correlation.[17] As such this broadly shows that several social protection expenditures can be described as 'luxuries'. However, the correla-tion is not sufficiently strong to safely infer a general theory on the relationship between social protection expenditure and GDP. The result obtained is partic-ularly sensitive to the position of a few individual countries. For instance, if L is included, there would be a much weaker correlation with GDP. From a more general perspective, these positive correlations tend to depend, to a great extent, on the well-known discrepancy between the welfare policy of Nordic and Mediterranean countries rather than anything else. Even taking at face value the expenditure–GDP correlation, it turns out that most of the already depicted features of national welfare systems may not be simply attributed to the GDP level of each country. For instance, the characterization of Nordic countries as 'big spenders' is not simply a question of their higher GDP level (on the other hand, the low expenditure level for ES and PO may be somehow related to their low GDP level, while a country which appears to be a small spender when its GDP level is taken into account is IT).

How do these results fit with the welfare systems classifications developed by the economic and sociological literature? While these classifications differ among each other,[18] most of them are based on a few basic characteristics:

1. Whether welfare systems are based on 'citizenship' or 'professional status'. In the first case, as opposed to the second, the right to claim benefits tends to be universal and benefits are less related to contributions and earnings.
2. The extent of income redistribution. In welfare systems based on 'citizenship', resources come from the general fiscal system and there tends to be greater income redistribution among individuals. This is not to say that

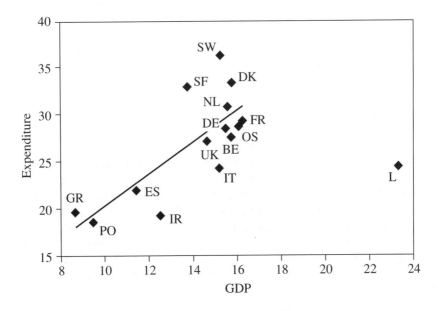

Figure 5.1   Total expenditure as percentage of GDP against GDP per capita in PPP

systems based on 'professional status' cannot be characterized by a high amount of redistribution.

3. The pervasiveness of welfare systems, that is, the degree of participation of the active population to welfare systems. This criterion contrasts those welfare systems where a great part of the population pays contributions and receives benefits to those where essentially only the very poor receive some, usually means tested, public assistance.

4. Finally, the organizational structure of welfare systems, in terms of reliance on public and private structures.

On the basis of these criteria, it has become common practice to classify welfare systems into three broad models, plus a fourth model that is less clearly identified: a) the Anglo-Saxon 'residual welfare' model, characterized by small public assistance schemes for the very poor, b) the continental European 'occupational' or 'Bismarckian' welfare model, characterized by larger schemes based on occupational categories and with limited redistribution of income, c) the Nordic 'universal' ('social-democratic' or 'Beveridgeian') welfare model, characterized by larger universal schemes and an important redistributory role, d) a less clearly identified (and less developed) Mediterranean model, smaller in size, and generally organized along occupational schemes, but also implicitly relying on the role of family as a complementary institution.

Overall, the evidence so far exposed fits rather well into this categorization. Its 'added value' is in the presence of several nuances when it comes to individual countries and individual benefit categories, as it is often the case that a benefit category substitutes for another one.

3   THE DYNAMICS OF EXPENDITURE FLOWS[19]

A preliminary overview of the reforms undertaken by EU countries during the 1980s and 1990s is presented in Tables 5.2a and 5.2b, which are both based on evidence assembled by the De Benedetti Foundation.[20] The first table considers the number of legislative reforms in a broad array of welfare fields (excluding old-age); the second table considers more specifically the number of reforms in connection with old age pensions. Two periods, namely 1986–93 and 1993–7, are distinguished. The direction of the arrows, up or down, indicates respectively an upward or downward movement in generosity. For each period 'marginal' and 'radical' reforms are distinguished and we also computed a summary index, adding up marginal (with a weight of +/–1) and radical (with a weight of +/–3) interventions.

The general result that seems to emerge is that radical reforms have been very few compared with the number of marginal interventions. Moreover, inter-

Table 5.2a   Number of marginal and radical reforms in the EU in social welfare reforms, excluding old age, in the 1986–97 period

Country	Marginal reforms 1986–93	1993–7	Radical reforms 1986–93	1993–7	Index 1986–93	1993–7
Belgium	↗↘↘↘	↗↘↘			−2	−1
Denmark	↗↘			↗↘↘	0	−3
Germany	↗↗↗	↗↘↘↘↘			3	−3
Greece	↗	↗			1	1
Spain		↗↘↘	↘		−3	−1
France	↘	↘			−1	−1
Italy	↗↗↘	↗↗↗↘			1	2
Ireland	↗↗↘	↗↗↘↘↘			1	−1
Netherlands	↗↗↘	↗↘↘↘	↘		−2	−2
Portugal	↗↗	↗			2	1
United Kingdom	↘↘↘			↘	−3	−3
Austria	↗	↗↗↗↗ ↘↘↘↘			1	0
Finland		↗↘↘↘↘			0	−3
Sweden	↗↗	↗↗↘↘ ↘↘		↗↘	2	−2
European Union[2]	–	–	–	–	0.08	−1.84

Notes:
(1) The direction of the arrow indicates the direction in the generosity of welfare. The index provides a rough summary number by assigning +/–3 values to radical reforms and +/–1 to marginal reforms.
(2) Weighted average using as weights GDP (in 1990 ECUs) during the 1993–6 period.

Source: Fondazione De Benedetti.

ventions have often followed opposite directions, with arrows going both up and down in the same period for the same broad social protection category and country. While this 'mostly marginal' and 'not fully consistent directionality' pattern holds true for both social welfare categories and for both periods, in the case of welfare not related to old age there seems to be a net shift toward less generosity in the latest period. With respect to the old age category results are instead more differentiated across countries, with restrictions in some countries, such as Italy, contrasted by opposite interventions in some other EU countries.

Table 5.2b   *Number of marginal and radical reforms in the EU in the old age category in the 1986–97 period*[1]

Country	Marginal reforms 1986–93	Marginal reforms 1993–7	Radical reforms 1986–93	Radical reforms 1993–7	Index 1986–93	Index 1993–7
Belgium	↗↘	↗↘	↗		3	0
Denmark	↗↘				0	0
Germany		↗↗↘	↗↘		0	1
Greece		↗	↘↘		–6	1
Spain	↗	↗		↘	1	–2
France	↘	↗↗↗↗↘			–1	3
Italy	↘	↘↘	↘	↘	–4	–5
Netherlands	↘↘↘↘	↗↗↘	↗	↗	–1	4
Portugal	↗↗↗↗↗			↘	5	–3
United Kingdom	↗↘		↗	↗	3	3
Austria	↗	↗↗↘			1	1
Finland	↘	↗↘↘↘↘			–1	–3
Sweden	↗↘			↘↘	0	–6
European Union[2]	–	–	–	–	–0.29	0.19

Notes:
(1) The direction of the arrow indicates the direction in the generosity of welfare. The index provides a rough summary number by assigning +/–3 values to radical reforms and +/–1 to marginal reforms.
(2) Weighted average using as weights GDP (in 1990 ECUs) during the 1993–6 period.

Source: Fondazione De Benedetti.

Overall, the conclusion which may be drawn is that a piecemeal approach to reform has been widespread in Europe. This result can be easily understood when taking into account that welfare systems represent the *status quo*, as emphasized, among others, by Pierson (1996) and Saint-Paul (1995a and b). Great uncertainty, especially in large and complex welfare systems, about the aggregate benefits of reform and which social groups are adversely affected, make it difficult to establish a coalition supporting a complete overhaul of the system. From a normative point of view, a piecemeal approach is not in itself to be condemned, as the fine-tuning of welfare legislation may be necessary given the institutional complexity of all welfare systems.

Precisely because of this piecemeal nature of welfare reform, a direct look at the actual expenditure's evolution becomes necessary. A characterization of the trends in social protection expenditure is presented in Tables 5.3a and 5.3b, where the incidence for each expenditure category in the 1993–6 period, shown in section 2, is compared with previous average levels, attained respectively during the 1990–92 and the 1980–84 sample periods.

Table 5.3a   Dynamics of the social protection expenditure flows as percentage of GDP (change between the 1990–92 and the 1993–6 periods)

Country	Unemployment	Invalidity	Social exclusion	Family	Housing	Sickness	Old-age	Survivors	Total
				Expenditure category					
Belgium[1]	0.38	0.03	0.30	-0.04	N/A	0.06	0.87	0.21	**1.81**
Denmark	0.22	0.44	0.25	0.45	0.07	-0.03	1.37	0.00	**2.77**
Germany	0.31	0.33	0.12	0.15	0.00	0.30	0.54	0.03	**1.78**
Greece[1]	-0.18	-0.22	0.07	0.06	-0.07	-0.10	-0.04	-0.03	**-0.51**
Spain	0.16	0.09	0.05	0.05	0.00	0.29	0.86	0.03	**1.52**
France	0.17	0.10	0.11	0.15	0.13	0.48	0.83	0.09	**2.07**
Ireland	0.28	0.02	0.03	0.10	-0.03	0.13	-0.45	-0.10	**-0.02**
Italy	0.10	0.02	0.00	-0.15	0.00	-0.69	1.08	0.18	**0.54**
Luxembourg[1]	0.12	-0.04	0.00	0.60	-0.01	0.18	0.16	-0.12	**0.88**
Netherlands	0.42	-0.36	-0.13	-0.21	-0.02	-0.11	-0.14	-0.02	**-0.56**
Portugal[1]	0.53	0.17	0.02	0.05	0.00	1.44	1.09	0.21	**3.50**
United Kingdom[1]	0.10	0.78	0.06	0.26	0.45	0.51	0.47	0.16	**2.79**
Austria	0.32	0.31	0.02	0.48	-0.02	0.39	0.72	0.02	**2.24**
Finland	2.09	0.47	0.08	0.38	0.16	-0.59	0.98	0.10	**3.67**
European Union[2]	0.24	0.24	0.08	0.10	0.09	0.16	0.69	0.09	**1.69**

Notes:
(1) The latest period refers to 1993–5.
(2) Weighted average using as weights GDP (in 1990 ECUs) during the 1993–6 period. Sweden is excluded because data start with 1993.

135

Table 5.3b Dynamics of the social protection expenditure flows as percentage of GDP (change between the 1980–84 and the 1993–6 periods)

| Country | Unemployment | Invalidity | Expenditure category | | | | | | Total |
			Social exclusion	Family	Housing	Sickness	Old-age	Survivors	
Belgium[1]	-0.39	-0.48	0.35	-0.73	N/A	0.32	1.38	-0.33	**0.11**
Denmark	0.68	0.78	0.50	1.07	0.38	-0.98	2.19	-0.09	**4.53**
Germany	0.46	0.18	0.28	-0.27	0.02	0.10	-0.07	-0.25	**0.45**
Greece[1]	0.19	0.05	0.12	-1.17	-0.35	-0.72	1.82	0.12	**0.06**
Spain[2]	0.84	0.22	0.03	-0.45	0.09	1.20	1.82	0.09	**3.85**
France[3]	0.31	0.12	0.26	-0.33	0.32	0.79	1.91	-0.23	**3.14**
Ireland	0.55	0.14	0.06	0.14	-0.23	-1.98	-1.03	-0.32	**-2.67**
Italy	-0.12	0.24	-0.02	-0.59	0.00	0.15	3.45	0.71	**3.81**
Luxembourg[1]	-0.04	-1.04	0.02	0.57	0.02	-0.40	-0.65	-0.91	**-2.43**
Netherlands	-0.15	-0.58	-0.24	-1.06	-0.03	-0.14	2.00	0.17	**-0.01**
Portugal[1]	0.75	0.26	0.02	-0.02	0.00	2.30	2.44	0.41	**6.17**
United Kingdom[1]	-0.66	1.55	0.12	0.01	1.36	0.68	0.94	-0.68	**3.32**
Austria[4]	0.76	0.48	0.05	0.11	-0.08	0.19	1.30	-0.19	**2.61**
European Union[5]	0.15	0.35	0.15	-0.32	0.28	0.38	1.45	-0.09	**2.34**

Notes:
(1) The latest period refers to 1993–5.
(2) For housing the 1980s data refer to 1983 and 1984.
(3) For sickness the 1980s data refer to the 1981–4 period.
(4) For the 1980s the data refer to 1980 and 1985.
(5) Weighted average using as weights GDP (in 1990 ECUs) during the 1993–6 period. Sweden and Finland are excluded because there are no data for the 1980s.

Comparing 1993–6 with the 1990–92 period, only GR and NL appear to have significantly decreased total social protection expenditure in terms of GDP. In the case of IR, expenditure has been stabilized, while IT and L have both contained the rise of total expenditure below the one percentage point of GDP. All other countries have, however, experienced significant rises, the greatest being those registered by SF and PO (equal respectively to 3.7 and 3.5 percentage points). With the exception of a few countries, where the change in expenditure between 1990–92 and 1993–6 have represented an inversion from a previous rise (GR and NL) or a deceleration from a previously more buoyant rise (IT and, to a minor extent, ES), for all remaining countries the recent changes represent an acceleration with respect to the previous trend. Comparing the 1993–6 period to the first half of the 1980s (Table 5.3b), L, IR and (marginally) NL, are the only countries where there has been an overall decline in total expenditure as a percentage of GDP.

There is no doubt that cyclical factors may have played a role in such an evolution. It could be argued that averaging data over a three to five year time span might not be sufficient to eliminate this influence. While leaving to the next section a more analytical treatment of this issue, a first rough idea of the importance of cyclical factors may be obtained by looking at the individual expenditure categories. For instance, the rise in the expenditure on unemployment in the whole sample period, namely between 1980–84 and 1993–6, is generally explained by its rise in the most recent period (between 1990–92 and 1993–96), during which cyclical factors may have played some role. However, the rise in the unemployment category constitutes only a fraction of the total rise in expenditure. The biggest rise, when the latest period is considered and when comparing the 1993–6 period to the first half of the 1980s, takes place in the old-age category. A continuous rise is also evident for other categories, such as invalidity, social exclusion, housing and sickness.

Another relevant aspect is that restricting the attention to those categories of expenditures which most likely act as forms of income relief in favour of working-age individuals (the first three categories, plus family and housing), it appears that in some cases the changes are opposite to those taking place in the unemployment category.

Overall, it appears possible to conclude that the likely built-in business-cycle effect regarding the expenditure for unemployment does not appear to be the most important reason for the rise in the incidence of social protection expenditure during the latest period. On the other hand, insofar as business-cycle effects are important, it is likely that they are also present for those expenditure categories which may have acted as substitutes for the unemployment expenditure.

Finally we address the issue whether the evolution of expenditure may have also been influenced by its starting level. Indeed, if there is a long run equilibrium expenditure level, the evolution over a given period should be negatively related to the starting expenditure level. A sort of catching-up effect would be in action. We have therefore verified the relevance of such an effect by regressing the rise in the GDP incidence for each expenditure category on its initial average level in the 1980–84 period (Figure 5.2 illustrates this for the case of total expenditure). It turns out that while for total expenditure some evidence can be found of a negative relationship, mainly related to the large rises in some Mediterranean countries from very low levels, the individual analyses of the expenditure categories seem to deny any strong evidence of a catching-up effect at work (these results are not reported here for brevity). The weak evidence of a catching-up effect for some particular categories (i.e. invalidity, sickness and, to a minor extent, survivors) is, more than anything else, explained by the presence of a few countries who have reduced, but not fully eliminated, their extremely marked characterization as being high or low spenders in those specific categories.[21]

Our conclusion is that while some extreme spending patterns have been markedly reduced, each country still appears to have its own spending pattern (both in terms of overall level and of internal composition). In other words,

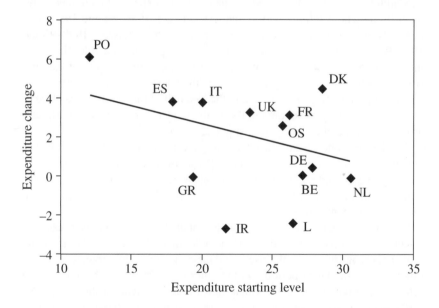

Figure 5.2   *Expenditure change between the 1980–84 and the 1993–6 sample periods against the 1980–84 expenditure level as percentage of GDP*

there has been no evolution over time towards a unique 'European' model with differences across countries explained simply by the stage of economic development in each country.[22] The absence of a unique equilibrium spending pattern suggests the need to analyse the evolution of each single country without superimposing too much initial structure to the data. This is what we will do in the following section.

4   A REGRESSION APPROACH FOR MEASURING TRENDS AND THE CYCLICAL BEHAVIOUR OF EXPENDITURE FLOWS[23]

The evidence presented in the previous section on the changes over time in the incidence of social protection expenditure is too rough a procedure for reaching the definite conclusion that a reduction of welfare expenditures in EU countries has not occurred. The average of multiple observations may not entirely remove the business-cycle effects. In addition, the relationship between the cycle and welfare expenditures is intrinsically interesting and worth examining. Therefore, in order to identify more accurately both long-run trends and business-cycle effects this section resorts to a regression technique.

For each category of expenditure and country, we have separately regressed expenditure, as a percentage of GDP, on a measure of employment performance and a linear trend. Employment performance was measured by the ratio of employment to working age population.[24] Its role is to capture both the general effects of the cycle and the extent to which a given category of expenditure reacts to an increased demand for income support arising from an employment shortfall. In view of the limited data availability – we have annual observations over the 1980–96 sample period – we avoid attempting to consider these two effects separately.

Most of our discussion has been based on the presumption that the causal effect, from employment to expenditure, is negative as a fall in employment increases demand for social protection and hence actual expenditure. It is theoretically possible, however, that a fall in employment, by reducing available resources, could instead lead to a fall in social protection supply, as authorities may need to pursue a policy of expenditure restraint. Therefore, it is conceivable that the overall causal effect, from employment to expenditure, may turn out to be positive rather than negative. Moreover, even neglecting the possibility of a positive 'supply' effect, from employment to expenditure, the employment–expenditure relationship does not shed any light on the channel through which an increased 'demand' for social protection affects expenditure. This leaves open the question whether this is due to a rise in the number of benefits claimants, or whether the administration applies less stringent criteria in evaluating their claims or, as a final possibility, whether the government formally relaxes the eligibility criteria or increases benefits.

Besides including employment and trend in our regression, we have also considered additional effects for the family and the old-age categories, by including among the right-hand side variables, respectively, the number of children and the number of aged people relative to the working-age population. In both cases these variables are natural 'activation variables', that is, variables capturing the demand for social protection not directly related to business-cycle or to employment performance. For the remaining cases we have not found any activation variable worth employing. When a long-run relationship exists between expenditure and the level of economic development, as measured by GDP, this will be caught by the trend. Given the descriptive nature of our exercise, and the weak evidence of a long-run GDP-expenditure relationship, we have preferred avoiding any attempt to impose such a parameterization on the data.

For each regression we have conducted a dynamic specification search, attempting to capture the presence of possible lags for both expenditure and employment variables. Our aim has been to single out the short and long-run effect of an employment change. Limited data availability prevents implementing a thorough preliminary analysis of the time series at our disposal. As we had a maximum of 17 observations, any attempt to establish the order of integration of the series would not have led to very conclusive results. Therefore, the procedure we followed is to be considered as an approximation to a proper dynamic analysis.

In assessing the results one has to be aware also of an underlying identification problem. While social protection expenditure is likely to respond to employment performance, employment itself may react to the degree of generosity and the institutional design of social protection. For instance, expenditure for unemployment and employment performance may be negatively correlated for two very different reasons: because aggregate demand shocks increase the number of benefits claimants, because a very generous unemployment compensation system leads to a lower 'equilibrium' employment level.[25] Technically, we have the standard problem of simultaneity-bias resulting from the presence of shocks affecting both employment and expenditure at the same time.

However, the practical relevance of this problem should not be overplayed. It is likely that a given institutional change leading to a more generous benefits system, while having some immediate effect on expenditure, will affect employment only with longer lags.[26] Provided the residuals of the estimated equations are white noises, the empirical relevance of the simultaneity bias is hence reduced. Under these circumstances simple OLS estimates would fully reflect the causal link from employment performance to expenditure. As a matter of fact, we have also experimented with instrumental variable estimators, in particular for the case of the unemployment expenditure category where the existence of a causal link, going from the benefit system to the performance of employment, has stronger theoretical grounds. The instruments we have considered are an adjusted world trade variable (capturing the shocks to aggregate demand and employment unrelated to the national benefits system)[27] and the change in the population of working age (capturing the demographic shocks that, at least in the short run, may have a negative impact on the employment to working age population ratio). As expected, the results of instrumental variable estimation are not very precise because the estimates are characterized by a very limited number of degrees of freedom. Nevertheless, they are generally supportive of OLS estimates, signalling the presence of a very limited amount of bias.[28] Thus, for reasons of brevity, these results are not reported here.

Generally, the OLS estimates are quite satisfactory. The selected models not only make good sense but show moreover some interesting regularities. Even if very basic, the estimated models explain the data sufficiently well, and the standard diagnostic tests are for the most part acceptable. However, the limited number of degrees of freedom has drastically reduced the precision of these estimates, leading us, as a general rule, to retain in the final specification all regressors whose statistical significance is above a 25 per cent threshold. As already mentioned, we paid particular attention to avoid serial correlation in the residuals. While, in general, the dynamic specification selected is meaningful, in a few isolated instances the economic interpretation could be described as puzzling.[29]

Let us focus on a few relevant features of the 95 equations estimated.[30] In Tables 5.4 and 5.5 we investigate the presence of, respectively, a long-run trend and of structural breaks in the expenditure pattern during the last three years of the sample period (i.e. in the 1993–6 period). In Table 5.6 we concentrate on the short and long-run effect of employment on expenditure. Given the specification adopted here, the tables have a straightforward economic interpretation, the effects there reported being expressed as (multiples of) percentage points of GDP.[31] Table 5.4, as those that will follow on later, may be read either by country (rows) or by expenditure category (columns). With the first method the broad result is that for only two countries (NL and L) negative trends are definitely dominant, once cyclical effects, as measured by the employment rate, are accounted for. In the Dutch case negative trends are particularly sizeable for those expenditure categories (invalidity and sickness) where NL was an outlier at the beginning of the period (and partly remains so today). A majority of negative signs is also present for IR while a broadly balanced result characterizes BE, DE (where for most cases there is no significant trend at all) and

Table 5.4 Trends in the expenditure flows (controlling for employment) (estimation period 1980–96)

Country[1]	Unemployment	Invalidity	Expenditure category						
			Social exclusion	Family	Housing	Sickness	Old-age	Survivors
Belgium	–	–2.4^a	3.4^a	–6.3^a	N/A	4.3^a	7.1^b	–1.1^c
Denmark	–	6.3^a	4.1^a	7.7^a	3.0^c	–8.4^a	21.2^b	–0.7^a
Germany	–	–13.2^a +1.2t^a	2.0^a	2.1^b	–	–	–2.2^a	–2.0^b
Greece	–	–10.9^a	0.9^a	21.5^b	–	–4.5^a	–	–3.6^b
Spain	7.8^a	1.8^a	0.3^a	3.8^a	64.1^a –138.0e^a	13.2^a	–	0.8^a
France	–	0.7^b	3.0^b	–	2.0^a	11.7^c	16.6^a	–
Ireland	–	0.8^a	0.7^a	–	–	–	–9.3^a	–2.0^a
Italy	–	–	–0.3^a	–4.5^a	–	10.8^a	26.9^a	5.6^a
Luxembourg	5.9^a	–6.5^a	0.3^a	–7.3^a	–	–10.4^a	–20.4^a	–5.1^a
Netherlands	–	–11.8^a	–3.6^a	–7.7^a	0.8^a	–25.9^a	–	–1.8^c
Portugal	8.5^b	2.0^a	0.5^a	2.5^c	2.1^a –3.2e^a	18.2^c	–	3.8^a
United Kingdom	–2.4^a	18.5^a	1.1^a	–	12.6^a	9.7^a	–	–

Notes:
(1) Besides a linear trend (t) the selected model for the expenditure flow (in % of GDP) may include several lags of the dependent variable (x) and of the employment to 15–65 years population ratio (e); an activation variable has also been considered for the old-age and the family expenditure flows (respectively the ratio to the 15–65 years population of the over 65 years people and of the under 6 years children). The actual estimation period may be shorter than the 1980–96 period (1980–95 for BE, GR, L, PO and UK).

The table reports the coefficient (multiplied by 100) of a linear trend; where the model is specified in terms of changes in x, it reports the drift term (which may be itself a function of a linear trend or employment). The term in brackets reports the level of statistical significance; where no effect has been reported it is because its statistical significance is worse than the 25% level and it has been removed.
a: < 5% statistical significance; b: 5–10% statistical significance; c: 10–25% statistical significance.

Table 5.5 *Presence of structural breaks in the last three years of the sample period (estimation period 1980–96)*

Country[1]	Unemployment	Invalidity	Expenditure category					
			Social exclusion	Family	Housing	Sickness	Old-age	Survivors
Belgium	12.4[d]	4.3	14.5[b]	7.5[d]	N/A	25.4[d]	39.4[a]	25.1[a]
Denmark	−62.0[a]	26.6[a]	13.2[b]	17.2[d]	−3.5[a]	39.3[c]	120.2[a]	3.4[c]
Germany	−16.8[c]	−0.9	2.5[d]	4.4	−0.3	64.3[a]	−21.7[c]	9.4[a]
Greece	−5.5	19.7[c]	4.9[a]	−43.4[c]	−15.1	−11.4[d]	−2.5	12.9[d]
Spain	−54.7[a]	−2.5[c]	4.0[c]	−4.8	−0.4	−6.4	−11.0[c]	1.6[d]
France	1.3	3.5[d]	−0.9	0.1	2.1	−33.7[a]	8.1	2.8[d]
Ireland	3.3	1.2	2.1[c]	12.1[b]	4.6[d]	−3.5	−11.7[c]	0.0
Italy	−4.7[a]	−4.9[d]	0.3	5.1	−0.2[d]	−28.5[c]	3.7	−9.6[c]
Luxembourg	9.0[b]	7.2	−1.1	34.7[a]	−0.5[c]	7.1	−7.9	0.0
Netherlands	32.9[c]	−18.7[b]	−0.0	0.1	−3.2[c]	−56.0[a]	−33.4[b]	−7.2[c]
Portugal	35.8[a]	11.8[c]	−0.8	1.5	−0.0	98.6[c]	38.8[b]	0.8
United Kingdom	6.5	11.9[d]	0.7	1.9	−3.4	20.4[c]	24.2	6.4[d]

Notes:
(1) Besides a linear trend (t) the selected model for the expenditure flow (in % of GDP) may include several lags of the dependent variable (x) and of the employment to 15–65 years population ratio (e); an activation variable has also been considered for the old-age and the family expenditure flows (respectively the ratio to the 15–65 years population of the over 65 years people and the under 6 years children). The actual estimation period may be shorter than the 1980–96 period (1980–95 for BE, GR, L, PO and UK).

For each country it has been reported the coefficient (multiplied by 100) of a dummy variable equal to one in the 1994–6 period (1993–5 for BE, GR, L, PO and UK) inserted in the selected model. The term in brackets reports the level of statistical significance; where none has been reported it is because the statistical significance is worse than 50%.

a < 5% statistical significance; b 5–10% statistical significance; c 10–25% statistical significance; d 25–50% statistical significance.

143

GR. Pluses and minuses alternate with each other, but with a majority of pluses, for DK, IT and UK. Finally, ES and PO show positive trends, of considerable size and for almost all the different expenditure categories, while FR shows positive trends but for only a few categories.

Reading the table by expenditure categories is even more interesting. Starting with unemployment, once employment fluctuations are accounted for, UK is the only country with a negative trend in expenditure. Even in this single case, the negative trend appears to be of a modest entity. Moreover the positive and larger trend for some other expenditure categories among the first five, namely invalidity and social exclusion, signals the possibility that a substitution effect is at work. In the majority of cases, expenditure for unemployment shows no significant trend. For PO and ES it has been rising over time, which may be due partly to the later development in these countries of a proper unemployment compensation scheme. A rising trend also characterizes the unemployment expenditure trend for L.

For invalidity, there is again a majority of positive trends, particularly sizeable in DK and even more in the UK. A negative trend appears for the Benelux countries and, particularly strongly, as already discussed, in the Dutch case. For social exclusion, all countries but NL have increased their expenditure. The most sizeable rises were attained by BE, DK and FR. A less clear-cut picture emerges for the family category. NL, L, BE and IT have reduced their expenditure in this field; conversely GR, ES, PO, DE and DK have increased theirs. When present a positive sign applies generally to the housing category (particularly sizeable for UK) but in most of the cases no trend appears to be present.

Attempting a global reading of the first five expenditure categories, which are those most likely to be acting as income support for jobless people, one cannot avoid noticing that there are only four countries that have really managed to decrease their expenditure: IT, BE, L, and NL and only the latter in a very noticeable manner. A moderate rise has characterized instead DE, FR and IR while the largest rises have been reached by DK, GR, ES, PO and, notwithstanding the reduction in the unemployment category, UK.

The last three years of the sample, moreover, do not seem to suggest that this broad picture changed significantly in the mid 1990s. As shown in Table 5.5, for these first five categories significant structural breaks are very few and contrary to the hypothesis of a welfare retreat, there is no evidence that negative signs prevail. Only in a few instances, notably in the case of ES, the sign of a structural break appears to offset the long-run trend identified over the whole 1980–96 period, meaning that, on the basis of this evidence, expenditure on that particular category has fallen after a sustained period of expansion. Table 5.5 offers evidence of a predominance of reductions, besides ES, only in IT.[32] On the other hand, positive signs typically emerge for BE, L and PO. Less clear cut, even if the signs tend to remain overall positive, is the pattern that emerges for IR and UK. A mixed balance emerges instead for DK, DE, GR, FR and NL.

This broad picture does not change significantly when we examine trends in the remaining three categories of expenditure. Starting with the sickness category, Table 5.4 suggests that in six countries out of 12, namely BE, ES, FR, IT, PO and UK, there is a positive trend of expenditure on sickness. Table 5.5, however, qualifies this result by warning us that FR and IT might have experienced some cutbacks in the most recent period. A negative trend emerges for DK, GR, L and NL, while IR and DE have no trend at all. For the old-age category, IT is the country with the most buoyant rise in expenditure, followed by DK and FR. The trend is also positive for BE. A negative trend appears for DE (but it is quite small), IR and L. On the contrary, the survivors category is generally characterized by a negative trend, the exceptions being ES, PO and IT, with a positive trend (but again for IT there is some cutback in the latest period), and UK and FR, with no trend at all.

Also for these three remaining categories, structural breaks are few. For instance, in the case of sickness, this seems to have happened for FR and IT, which have recently managed to reduce expenditure after a sustained positive trend. The opposite has, however, happened to DE, which has experienced a large and significant rise at the end of the period examined here. For the old-age and survivors categories, there appear to be a few cases of an upsurge in expenditure (for BE, DK and PO) and only very few cases of a reduction in expenditure (NL is the most relevant one).

Overall, results in Tables 5.4 and 5.5 seem to contradict the widespread notion of a retreat of social protection expenditure. Neither the trends over the whole 1980–96 period, nor the evidence concerning possible breaks in the most recent years, suggest any systematic evidence of a reduction in expenditure as a percentage of GDP. At a more detailed level, it appears that those expenditure flows, which act as income support in case of joblessness, have tended to increase (above the level directly caused by the rise of joblessness itself), even if some exceptions emerge (among which the Dutch case is the most important).

As already stated, this analysis is not meant to provide any normative judgement about the appropriateness of such an evolution. There is no simple numerical benchmark for the 'appropriate' level of expenditure for the several categories. Neither are we able, on the basis of such results, to evaluate whether a given scheme, for instance, the expenditure in the old-age category, has to be considered financially and economically viable in the future. What the evidence here presented simply suggests is that, whatever the changes introduced in the welfare system rules have been, they have not yet led to a generalized reduction, nor a stabilization, of gross expenditure flows.

These findings are not always consistent with the qualitative evidence on welfare reforms described in the previous section. While the absence of a

Table 5.6 *Employment effects on the expenditure flows (estimation period 1980–96)*

Country[1]	Unemployment	Invalidity	Social exclusion	Family	Housing	Sickness	Old-age	Survivors
				Expenditure category				
Belgium	-38.2^a	-14.9^a	-12.7^a	–	N/A	-18.7^b	-43.8^a	-23.2^a
		-11.0^a			N/A	7.4^b	-23.9^b	-4.4^b
Denmark	-24.1^a	-4.8^a	-4.4^a	-6.0^a	-0.8^a	-15.4^a	-8.4^c	-1.4^a
		-4.4^a	-3.3^a					-0.8^a
Germany	-17.2^a	-3.8^a	-1.2^b	–	-1.6^a	–	-16.7^a	-1.3^c
	-17.2^a	-3.8^a					-19.9^a	-2.4^c
Greece	-9.6^a	–	–	–	–	11.6^c	–	-5.1^c
	-9.6^a					11.6^c		
Spain	-18.2^a	-2.4^a	-1.0^b	-2.5^b	-1.9^a	25.9^a	-15.0^a	-1.3^a
		-1.0^a		-1.1^c			-11.7^a	
France	-12.3^a	-4.9^a	–	3.5^b	-5.2^a	7.5^b	-24.4^a	-8.6^a
		-1.6^b		21.8^b	-3.1^a	46.1^b		
Ireland	-5.6^c	-1.6^a	-1.3^a	–	-4.6^a	-13.5^c	–	-6.6^a
Italy	–	–	-0.3^c	–	–	13.5^b	-29.7^a	-6.0^a
						34.3^a		
Luxembourg	-12.3^a	-21.2^a	–	3.4^b	–	-17.5^a	-22.5^a	-37.2^a
	-5.4^a			3.4^b		9.1^a	18.7^a	
Netherlands	-10.5^a	–	-1.0^c	-4.0^a	–	7.7	–	–
	-6.0^b	6.5^b			-1.0^a	24.1^a		3.6^a

146

Portugal	-2.5^c	–	-0.4^a	–	–	–	-7.1^a	–
	–	–	–	–	–	–	-12.1^a	–
United Kingdom	-26.9^a	-6.9^a	-1.2^a	-4.5^a	-9.9^a	-5.7^a	–	-5.0^a
	-12.4^a	–	-0.8^a	–	-11.4^a	–	-8.0^c	–

Notes:

(1) Besides a linear trend (t) the selected model for the expenditure flow (in % of GDP) may include several lags of the dependent variable (x) and of the employment to 15–65 years population ratio (e); an activation variable has also been considered for the old-age and the family expenditure flows (respectively the ratio to the 15–65 years population of the over 65 years people and the under 6 years children). The actual estimation period may be shorter than the 1980–96 period (1980–95 for BE, GR, L, PO and UK).

For each country the first row reports the short run impact of a change in the employment to 15–65 years population ratio. The second row reports the long-run effect. Where only a short-run effect is present, the reported short-run effect may be actually lagged and not contemporaneous. Where the equation is specified in terms of changes in x, the long-run effect is not computable. The term in brackets reports the level of statistical significance; where no effect has been reported it is because its statistical significance is worse than the 25% level and it has been removed.

a: < 5% statistical significance; b: 5–10% statistical significance; c: 10–25% statistical significance.

147

sizeable expenditure retreat resembles closely the story discussed there, certain more detailed results do not seem to correspond perfectly to what we have seen in that section. In particular, the recent generalized shift towards less generosity – which characterizes the broad category of the non-age related benefits defined in Table 5.2a – is not matched by the evidence in Table 5.5 on expenditure flows. As for the old-age category, the collocation of individual countries in Table 5.2b is not always the same as that in Table 5.5.

Some of these discrepancies may be explained by a lack of full comparability. Some of them depend, however, on more fundamental issues. A first plausible explanation for these differences may be that welfare reforms, important as they may have been in other respects, have generally been marginal and hence probably not very effective in reducing expenditure. A second explanation may be that these reforms need time to produce sizeable effects on expenditure flows, especially in the case of the old-age expenditure.

Shifting our attention to the estimated impact of employment on expenditure, we find other results of interest emerge. As in previous cases, Table 5.6 can be read by both country and expenditure categories. With the former method one may capture the peculiarity of each national welfare system, while with the second, one may identify the expenditure categories that are more reactive to the employment cycle. As expected, expenditure for unemployment turns out to be the one most reactive to employment performance. IT is the only country where such expenditure does not negatively respond to employment (but rather appears to follow an autoregressive process probably linked to the tendency to rollover the eligibility to the benefits for those few workers who have the right to obtain them). Besides, it is generally true that the short-run reaction is stronger than that of the long run. Indeed, in several cases (BE, DK, ES, FR, IR and PO) the expenditure seems to react only to the change in employment rather than to the employment rate. Thus, in these countries expenditure strongly reacts to employment at the very beginning of the process, progressively reverting to its pre-shock level.

A similar negative pattern of reaction to employment emerges also for the invalidity category, with the exception of GR, IT and PO, where there is no reaction at all, and NL, for which the reaction was surprisingly positive (i.e. a rise in employment performance seems to have a positive effect on this category of expenditure).[33] In comparison with the unemployment category, the reaction is generally less marked when present and there is a smaller difference between short and long-run effects. This different pattern is consistent with the tendency for people who have exhausted their right to unemployment benefits to start claiming these other (generally less generous) benefits.

The pattern of reaction to employment for the social exclusion and the housing categories is similar to the one shown for invalidity, even if for both categories the very small level of expenditure makes it difficult to identify with any accuracy an economic relationship. For the family category, there are about the same number of cases with positive and negative reactions to employment. This may possibly be due to the fact that demand for more social protection, arising from a negative employment performance, may be compensated by supply-side factors leading to more restrictive policies. Less straightforward is also the interpretation of the estimates concerning the remaining three expenditure categories. For sickness, it is more frequent to have a positive long-run relationship between expenditure and employment. The reaction of expenditure to employment in the case of old-age and survivors is generally negative.

In short, the broad picture emerging is that the reaction of social welfare expenditure is, in several instances, not channelled through the standard schemes formally designed for such purposes (i.e. the unemployment expenditure category). It seems as if the unemployment category is the first to react to employment fluctuations but, in the long run, other categories react in a similar manner.

Finally, cross-country comparisons are of equal interest. There appears to be a broad resemblance between the results that we present here and the standard classifications of welfare systems, with a clear distinction between Nordic and Anglo-Saxon systems on the one hand, both characterized by high expenditure sensitivity to employment, and Mediterranean systems on the other. Actually the most extreme case is represented by IT, where the categories of expenditure, which in theory should be most sensitive, appear not to be related at all with the employment rate (while some sensitivity to employment is present for the old-age category possibly because of early retirements). Generally speaking, continental Bismarckian systems are placed in a mid-way position. The resemblance to the traditional classification is, however, not perfect as the countries where the expenditure reaction to employment is very strong are DK, UK but also BE.

FINAL REMARKS AND POLICY IMPLICATIONS

The results presented in this chapter would appear to contradict the widespread notion of a general retreat of social protection expenditure. After taking account of the possible impact of employment fluctuations on expenditure, no conclusive evidence of a reduction in social protection expenditure as a percentage of GDP seems to emerge over the 1980–96 period, nor in the final years of that period. The analysis has shown that expenditure flows supporting the income of jobless people have tended, if anything, to increase above what one could have expected from the latest employment performance.

While there are of course exceptions to this general description – the most notable being the Dutch case with across the board reductions – in several other cases, the reductions in some components of expenditure have been more than compensated by rises elsewhere in the welfare system. For example, for the UK, which is the only country to have managed a significant reduction of expenditure in the unemployment category, we have found an opposite trend at work in some expenditure categories.

This lack of a significant expenditure retreat is broadly consistent with the qualitative discussion in section 3 on the marginal nature of welfare reform and its contradictory direction. However, while in section 3 a weak shift toward a reduced generosity seemed to emerge in the latest period, actual expenditure flows do not show any negative trend as yet. One explanation for this may be that implemented reforms have generally been marginal. A second possible explanation for this is that reforms require time to produce sizeable effects on expenditure flows, an argument which is particularly relevant to expenditure on the elderly.

Equally interesting are cross-country differences in the reaction of expenditure to the employment cycle. A number of regularities emerge when one considers those expenditure flows most related to the demand for social protection arising from joblessness. At one extreme we find countries such as IT, GR and PO, where the reaction appears to be rather weak, while at the other extreme we find countries like BE, DK and UK.[34] These differences provide complementary information to what already emerges from a simple comparison of expenditure levels and their internal breakdown. It is well known, for example, that the Italian system has a very pronounced old-age bias and that the resources aimed at unemployment are very limited.

Finally, our analysis suggests that the expenditure category formally aimed at unemployment is not the only one which reacts to employment. While it is the most responsive in the short run, there are also several other categories of expenditure which appear to react, like invalidity, social exclusion and housing. In some instances the reaction of these categories is even more persistent than that of the unemployment category which tends to return to its initial level as soon as benefits claimants lose their right to claim benefits.

NOTES

1. The opinions here expressed are exclusively personal and are not necessarily shared by the European Commission where this work was carried out during the traineeship of Michele Ca'Zorzi. While we are responsible for all remaining errors, we have benefited from valuable comments on a previous version of this article by Mads Kieler, Aino Salomäki, Hans Wijkander and Leslee Stratta. Giancarlo Amerini, Teresa Bento and Flavio Bianconi helped us understand ESSPROS figures and methodologies. Finally, Anthony Smith helped us update the data set.

2. For a survey of the relevant issues see Buti *et al.* (1997).
3. Both population ageing and changes in households' composition have an influence on expenditure trends.
4. The actual maturity of welfare systems depends on two different factors. In the first place, insofar as a reduced number of social and demographic groups enter the system, the short run net financial inflow related to the contributions to pension schemes falls. A second factor emphasized by Lindbeck (1995), is that individuals and households progressively learn to fully exploit the opportunities offered by each welfare system.
5. For recent surveys and discussions on these issues see Blanchard (1998), Buti *et al.* (1998) and Nickell (1997).
6. Among others, see Atkinson (1995) on this. A call for an adequate general equilibrium assessment is also made by Holmlund (1998).
7. The ESSPROSS methodology provides also a breakdown of receipts, but here we restrict our attention to expenditure flows.
8. Functional substitutability within the welfare system is discussed, among others, by Schmid (1995) and Buti *et al.* (1998). Blondal and Pearson (1995) compare unemployment and other non-employment benefits across OECD countries.
9. There have been different releases of ESSPROS data. The classification scheme used here is the most recent one, fully available from 1990 (1993 for Sweden) to 1996 (when preparing this chapter, the latest data for Belgium, Greece, Luxembourg, Portugal and the UK are available to 1995). A reconstruction of data for the 1980–89 sample period along the lines of the new classification scheme was provided by EUROSTAT for Belgium, Germany, France, Italy, Luxembourg and the Netherlands; whereas for Denmark, Greece, Spain, Portugal and the UK we estimated the dynamics for the 1980s decade on the basis of the old methodology data (which followed a different breakdown along 11 categories). There is no available information concerning the 1980s for Finland and Sweden. For Austria the earlier data are only single observations, 1980 and 1985.
10. Adema *et al.* (1996) and the OECD (1998) show that cross-country differences in the incidence of social protection expenditure shrink considerably when the expenditure is evaluated net of the taxes paid by social protection recipients on those gross expenditure flows. Moreover, the unnoticed role of taxes paid on social protection benefits may weaken the strength of many statements on taxes and unemployment as in most natural rate of unemployment models the impact of taxes depends, to a large extent, on the existence of a different tax treatment between earnings and benefits (see Pissarides, 1998 and Martin, 1995).
11. This may limit across-countries comparability, as there are countries where a given social protection goal is obtained through tax breaks and tax rebates (as such not recorded in the ESSPROS current methodology) while other countries pursue the same goal by paying social protection benefits (recorded by ESSPROS). Similarly, the exclusion of private insurance schemes ignores the fact that social and private insurance schemes may be substitutes and that the need to establish 'social' insurance schemes is stronger where there is not a well developed private market (see Adema and Einerhand, 1998).
12. Defined as those individuals whose age is above the standard retirement age as established by legislation at the national level rather than those above a specific age threshold.
13. Even for them there may be counter examples, as there may be health-related benefits inappropriately used to finance lay-offs, early retirement schemes that only nominally have a 'non-economic' motivation and retirements that take place at relatively young ages but formally not classified as early retirements.
14. Some information on the number of beneficiaries with specific reference to a few EU countries was presented in NEI (1998).
15. For brevity the 15 EU countries will be identified by the following labels in both the text and figures: BE (Belgium), DK (Denmark), DE (Germany), GR (Greece), ES (Spain), FR (France), IR (Ireland), IT (Italy), L (Luxembourg), NL (Netherlands), OS (Austria), PO (Portugal), SF (Finland), SW (Sweden) and UK (United Kingdom).
16. See for instance the 1998 edition of the Social Protection Report (CEE).

17. By repeating the same exercise for each single category of expenditure, it turns out that the correlation is stronger for some specific categories (in descending order, old-age, sickness, social exclusion and family).
18. See, among others, the classic work from Titmuss, 1974, the papers collected in Flora, 1986, Esping-Andersen, 1990, and Ferrera, 1996.
19. The evidence presented in this section excludes SW (for which there are data only between 1993–6). In some tables it also excludes SF (for which there are no data for the 1980s). For OS the 1980s data refer only to 1980 and 1984.
20. See the note entitled 'Riforme delle Politiche Sociali' which can be found to date in the website www.rdb.uni-bocconi.it/
21. For invalidity this is the case of NL. For sickness the outliers were GR and PO. For the survivors category, the most extreme outlier was L.
22. We also repeated the same exercise allowing for an evolution of the equilibrium level of expenditure to be linked to the change of GDP (in PPP) over the corresponding period. Again the results, not reported here for brevity, do not give much support to the hypothesis of a close connection between GDP and expenditure. In just one case (family) the change in expenditure appears to be positively related to the change in GDP (in the other cases the coefficients turn out to be generally not statistically significant and negative). Overall, catching-up terms in the estimated equations are only slightly statistically significant for the total of expenditure and for two out of eight individual categories (invalidity and sickness).
23. The evidence in this section is based on 12 countries (OS, SW and SF were not considered for lack of sufficiently long time series).
24. By measuring the labour market performance directly with the employment rate (instead of considering the unemployment rate) we take account of possible 'discouraged worker' effects.
25. A standard result of practically all natural rate models is that the more generous the unemployment benefits (in terms of their level *vis-à-vis* wages, their duration over the unemployment spell or the case of obtaining access to them), the higher the natural rate of unemployment. Empirically, the measures of generosity of unemployment benefits as constructed by the OECD have become a standard explanatory factor in understanding cross-country unemployment differentials. In principle, however, it is also possible to have positive employment and output consequences arising from a more generous benefits system (because of 'entitlement' effects on labour force participation and improved firm–worker matching).
26. For instance, Lemieux and MacLeod (1998) document the presence of a learning effect concerning the impact of changes in the generosity of the Canadian unemployment benefits scheme on the individual workers' employment probability.
27. The variable represents the evolution of aggregate demand in the relevant export market of a given country. It is the country specific export activation variable used in the QUEST-II model, whose details can be found in Roeger and In't Veld (1997).
28. Generally, the coefficients for the employment variable obtained in the IV estimates were, in absolute value, slightly larger than those obtained by OLS estimates.
29. In two cases the *change* in expenditure appears to be a function of the *level* of employment and in another case the expenditure *change* appears to follow a linear trend, always signalling the presence of a drift term in the expenditure process not constant over time. Generally speaking, however, the *level* of expenditure is a function of employment (its *level* and/or its *change*, so that the short and the long-run effects may be different) and in a few other cases the *change* of expenditure is a function of the *change* of employment.
30. There are 8 categories by 12 countries equations. However, housing is missing in the case of Belgium.
31. Details of the selected estimates, including the dynamic specification and the parameters of the activation variables, are available in a EC-DG2 document (doc. II/1717/98.En).
32. Where the reduction is also small because the starting level of the expenditure was extremely low, the expenditure being concentrated in the old age category.
33. One possible explanation for this could be that a rise in employment increases the availability of resources to be spent.

34. We suspect that a similar conclusion may be reached also in the case of SW and SF, for which the absence of long enough time-series data has, however, prevented us from being able to conduct the regression exercises reported in section 4.

REFERENCES

Adema W. and Einerhand M. (1998), *The Growing Role of Private Social Expenditure*, Labour Market and Social Policy Occasional Paper, 32, Paris: OECD.

Adema W., Einerhand M., Eklind B. and Pearson M. (1996), *Net Public Social Expenditure*, Labour Market and Social Policy Occasional Paper, 19, Paris: OECD.

Atkinson A.B. (1995), 'The Welfare State and Economic Performance', Discussion Papers, 99, Suntory-Toyota Centre for Economics and Related Discipline, London.

Blanchard O. (1998), 'Thinking About Unemployment', Paolo Baffi Lecture on Money and Finance, Rome, 16 October 1998.

Blondal S. and Pearson M. (1995), 'Unemployment and Other Non-Employment Benefits', *Oxford Review of Economic Policy*, 1: 136–69.

Buti M., Pench L. and Franco D. (eds) (1997), 'The Welfare State in Europe: Challenges and Reforms', European Economy, 4, European Commission.

Buti M., Pench L. and Sestito P. (1998), 'European Unemployment: Contending Theories and Institutional Complexities', European Investment Bank, Economic and Financial Reports, 1, 1998.

Esping-Andersen G. (1990), *The Three Worlds of Welfare Capitalism*, New York: Polity Press.

European Commission (1998), *Social Protection in Europe 1997*, Bruxelles, 1998.

EUROSTAT (1996), *ESSPROS Manual, 1996*, Luxembourg, 1996.

Ferrera M. (1996), 'A New Social Contract?: The Four Social Europes – Between Universalism and Selectivity', EUI Working Paper, 36/96.

Flora P., (ed.) (1986), *Growth To Limits. The European Welfare States Since World War II*, Berlin–New York: De Gruyter.

Holmlund B. (1998), 'Unemployment Insurance in Theory and Practice', *Scandinavian Journal of Economics*, 113–42.

Lemieux T. and MacLeod W.B. (1998), 'Supply Side Hysteresis: The Case of the Canadian Unemployment Insurance System', NBER Working Paper, 6732.

Lindbeck A. (1995), 'Welfare State Disincentives with Endogenous Habits and Norms', *Scandinavian Journal of Economics*, 1: 1–19.

Martin J.P. (1995), 'Measures of Replacement Rates for the Purpose of International Comparisons: A Note', *OECD Economic Studies*, 26: 99–115.

NEI (1998), 'Inactivity/Activity Ratios. A Descriptive Analysis for Six European Countries, the USA and Japan', Netherlands Economic Institute, Rotterdam, February 1998.

Nickell S. (1997), 'Unemployment and Labour Market Rigidities: Europe versus North America', *Journal of Economic Perspectives*, 3: 55–74.

OECD (1998), 'Net Social Expenditure Indicators', mimeo.

Pierson P. (1996), 'The New Politics of the Welfare State', *World Politics*, 143–79.

Pissarides C.A. (1998), 'The Impact of Employment Tax Cuts on Employment and Wages: The Role of Unemployment Benefits and Tax Structure', *European Economic Review*, 155–83.

Roeger W. and In'T Veld J. (1997), 'QUEST II: A Multi-Country Business Cycle and Growth Model', *Economic Papers*, 123, European Commission.

Saint-Paul G. (1995a), 'Reforming Europe's Labour Market: Political Issues', CEPR Discussion Paper, 1223.

Saint-Paul G. (1995b), 'Labour Market Institutions and the Cohesion of the Middle Class', CEPR Discussion Paper, 1298.

Schmid G. (1995), 'Institutional Incentives to Prevent Unemployment: Unemployment Insurance and Active Labour Market Policy in a Comparative Perspective', *Journal of Socio-Economics*, **1**: 51–103.

Titmuss R. (1974), *Social Policy*, London, Allen & Unwin.

PART III

Evaluation Methods

6. Evaluating the labour supply responses to 'in-work' benefit reforms for low income workers

Richard Blundell[*]

---

1 INTRODUCTION

The aim of this chapter is to consider the issues surrounding welfare reform for low skilled and low wage workers, in particular, the recent move towards the use of 'in-work' benefits. Such policies take welfare reform in a new direction emphasizing the dual objectives of getting low skill workers into work as well as the need to supplement their incomes. Their effectiveness in achieving these two goals is the focus of this chapter.

The problem with most traditional systems of low income support, designed to relieve poverty among particular target groups of families, is that as individuals in these families start to earn, the withdrawal of benefit income creates an implicit tax rate of close to 100 per cent. Effectively, there is a dollar for dollar loss on the welfare benefit as earnings rise. In addition, in-kind transfers like free medical services, free dental care, free medical prescriptions, and subsidized housing are often lost with a move into employment. Thus, although supporting low incomes, they reduce the economic incentives for workers in such families to seek work.

The chapter begins by describing the changing economic environment and demographic structure of such households that can be seen as the motivating force behind the policy move to 'in-work' benefits. Attention is focused on three specific reforms that together cover most of the aspects and issues surrounding 'in-work' benefits: the Earned Income Tax Credit (EITC) in the US; the Family Credit (FC) and Working Families Tax Credit (WFTC) in the UK; and the Self Sufficiency Programme (SSP) in Canada.

[*] This chapter draws heavily on joint work with Alan Duncan, Julian McCrae and Costas Meghir. It is part of the programme of research of the ESRC Centre for the Microeconomic Analysis of Fiscal Policy at IFS. The financial support of the ESRC is gratefully acknowledged. The usual disclaimer applies.

The EITC is the oldest of these programmes and was originally developed in the 1970s as a way of introducing a negative income tax for poor US families, which also involved a work test.[1] It provides a tax credit supplement to earnings which increases proportionally with earned income until a maximum credit or maximum income limit is reached. With the falling real wages of the low educated in the US over the 1980s, and the increasing level of welfare dependency among certain demographic groups, the EITC took on a new role in welfare policy as a mechanism for encouraging work by supplementing the working wage for low wage workers.

This dual motivation of providing an income supplement for low wage families together with an incentive to work also lay behind the introduction of FC in the UK in the 1980s and the evolution of FC into WFTC in the late 1990s. The SSP in Canada is purely an experimental policy reform which not only requires a work test but is also only eligible to long-term welfare recipients and is time limited. The experimental nature of the SSP makes it particularly useful in assessing the effectiveness of these reforms in inducing welfare recipients to move in to work.

As we will document in more detail below, the design and implementation of such 'in-work' benefits is not altogether straightforward. There are a number of important issues: the overall size of the credit, whether some minimum hours limit should be placed on eligibility, how rapidly to reduce the credit as earnings rise beyond the maximum limit and whether the amount of credit should be based on individual or family earnings. These issues are addressed in this chapter within the overall discussion of the workings of the EITC, WFTC and the SSP.

The nature of these three reforms also highlights the alternative methods economic researchers have developed to evaluate their effectiveness. In many ways the most convincing method of evaluation is a randomized experiment in which there is a control (or comparison) group which is a randomized subset of the eligible population. Such is the design of the SSP and the recent work of Card and Robins (1998) has used the experimental nature of this reform to show its effectiveness in inducing welfare recipients into work.

Of course, experiments have their own drawbacks. First, they are rare and typically expensive to implement. Secondly, they are not very amenable to extrapolation. That is they cannot easily be used in the *ex ante* analysis of policy reform proposals. Finally, they require the control group to be completely unaffected by the reform typically ruling out spillover and general equilibrium effects. None the less they have much to offer in enhancing our knowledge of the possible impact of such reform and I shall draw on them in the discussion below.

Another popular method of evaluation is the 'natural experiment' approach. This considers the reform itself as an experiment and tries to find naturally occurring comparison groups that can mimic the properties of the control group in the properly designed experimental context. This method is also often labelled 'difference-in-differences' since it is usually implemented by comparing the difference in average behaviour before and after the reform for the eligible group with the before and after difference for the comparison group. As we describe briefly below this removes unobservable individual effects and general macro effects. But, as is also discussed below, it does require strong assumptions and, again, cannot easily be used to assess policy reform proposals. However, the impact of the EITC reforms in the US have been studied extensively by this method. In particular, the important studies by Eissa and Liebman (1996) and Eissa and Hoynes (1998) show important impacts of the reforms on the labour market.

The aim of this chapter is to evaluate new reforms in Europe such as the WFTC in the UK. Although we can draw on the quasi-experimental and natural experiment findings, the evaluation of these 'in-work' benefit reform proposals requires a model that can simulate the behaviour of individuals as their earnings opportunities in work change. For this we draw on the recent simulation study by Blundell *et al.*, (2000) which builds a discrete model of labour supply behaviour and incorporates a complete description of each family's budget constraint and childcare availability.

To begin the discussion, in section 2 some of the recent social and economic trends are documented to place the agenda for reforms in a changing economic environment. Section 3 then provides a detailed summary of the three 'in-work' policy reforms. Section 4 discusses the method of quasi-experimental evaluation and draws from the SSP reforms in Canada. Section 5 considers the natural experiment approach and draws on the EITC policy reforms in the US. Section 6 details the structural approach and uses the evaluation of the recent WFTC reform in the UK as a basis for discussion. Finally, section 7 draws together some conclusions for policy reform in this area.

2   THE CHANGING STRUCTURE AND ECONOMIC ENVIRONMENT OF LOW WAGE WORKERS

Before discussing the particular types of reform, it is useful to place these reforms within the context of the current economic environment. Important changes have occurred in the low wage labour market in many countries and it is only within this new economic environment that one can begin to understand how this kind of welfare reform is going to operate.

There has been a remarkable shift in returns to education in many countries. For example, in the US real earnings for the lowest education groups has fallen yearly since the late 1970s. This is documented in Figure 6.1. This characteristic is quite exaggerated in the US, but it is none the less common to most developed countries. It is those with low skills and low education are exactly the types of people you find in the welfare system. For example, Figure 6.2 shows the relatively slow growth in real wages among those individuals in the UK who left school at the minimum leaving age.

Any analysis of wages in Europe has to be looked at alongside the growing level of non-employment especially among men and single parents. In Figure 6.3, the participation rates for the three groups of men corresponding to the education groups in Figure 6.2 are presented. The decline in participation among low educated men is a common characteristic of many European economies.

For women the picture is more complex. Figure 6.4 shows the relative fall in non-employment among women (all women and married women with children, MW-K) – contrasted with the increase for men. But as Figure 6.5 indicates, this is misleading and covers up the dramatic rise in non-employment of single women with children (SW-K). Moreover, the proportion of single women with children has risen threefold to 17 per cent in the UK over the last three decades.

It is these simple socio-economic facts that have focused policy attention on 'in-work' benefits for low wage families: the aim being to make work more attractive for families, with children, whose current labour market opportunities

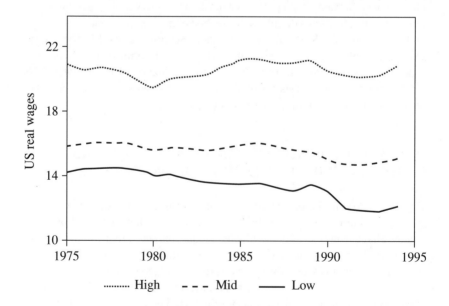

Figure 6.1   US male real wages by education level

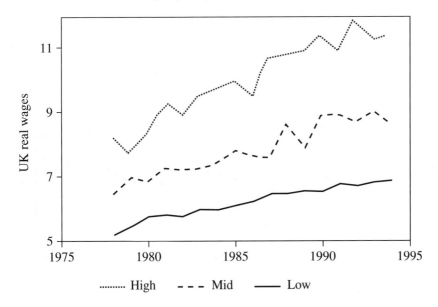

Figure 6.2   UK male real wages by education level

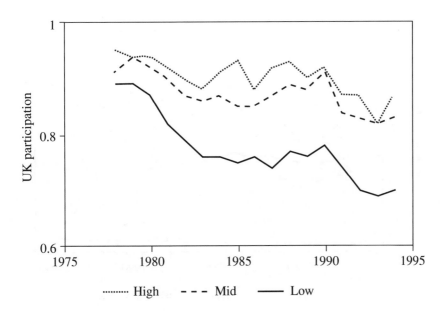

Figure 6.3   UK male participation rates by education level

Evaluation methods

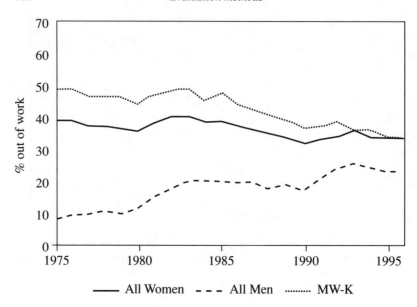

Figure 6.4   Non-employment in the UK

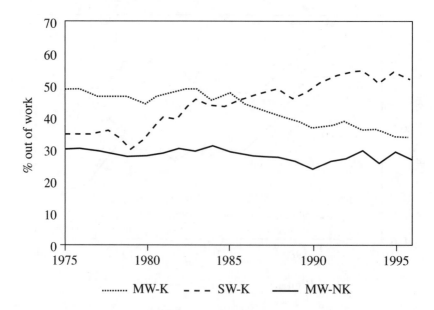

Figure 6.5   Non-employment by women with children in the UK

are not sufficient to induce work given the low real wages they can attract and the relatively high cost of childcare. Indeed, the Working Families Tax Credit reform in the UK is an attempt to directly address both these concerns.

3   THE EXISTING IN-WORK BENEFIT PROGRAMMES

In-work benefits are designed to counter the low wages and high implicit tax rates faced by those individuals on welfare. The idea is to modify the incentive structure so that a larger fraction of welfare recipients take jobs and leave welfare. The programmes discussed here all share very similar characteristics and aims. They are designed with slightly different labour markets and slightly different target groups in mind, but none the less they have very strong similarities.

These programmes are designed to stimulate work and remove families from the poverty trap; that is, the part of the welfare system that makes it difficult for individuals to take work because there is really no return and there could be losses of in-kind benefits from taking employment. Of course, individuals still do take employment, and there are good reasons for doing that. The stigma of being on welfare, for example, is enough for some people to take employment despite the loss of benefits. There may also be longer term payoffs to taking employment.

How do these systems work? A simple way of thinking about the welfare system is to consider all the income opportunities that an individual would have in and out of work, this set of opportunities is called the budget set. First we will take the example of the Earned Income Tax Credit (EITC) in the US.

3.1   The EITC in the US

The earned income tax credit began in 1975 as a modest programme aimed at offsetting the social security payroll tax for low income families with children. After major expansions in the tax acts of 1986, 1990 and 1993, federal spending on the EITC (including both tax expenditures and outlays) was 1.7 times as large as federal spending on Temporary Assistance for Needy Families (TANF) in 1996.

A taxpayer's eligibility for the earned income tax credit depends on the taxpayer's earned income (or, in some cases, adjusted gross income), and the number of qualifying children who meet certain age, relationship and residency tests. First, the taxpayer must have positive earned income, defined as wage and salary income, business self-employment and earned income below a specified amount (in 1996, maximum allowable income for a taxpayer with two or more children was $28 495). Second, a taxpayer must have a qualifying child, who must be under age 19 (or 24 if a full-time student).[2] The credit is refundable so that a taxpayer with no (federal) tax liability, for example, would receive a tax refund from the government for the full amount of the credit. Taxpayers may also receive the credit throughout the year with their paychecks.

The amount of the credit to which a taxpayer is entitled depends on the taxpayer's earned income, adjusted gross income and, since 1991, the number of EITC-eligible children in the household.[3] There are three regions in the credit schedule. These are presented in Figure 6.6, which provides a description of the EITC in 1984. The initial phase-in region transfers an amount equal to the subsidy rate times their earnings. In the flat region, the family receives the maximum credit. In the phase-out region, the credit is phased out at some phase-out rate.

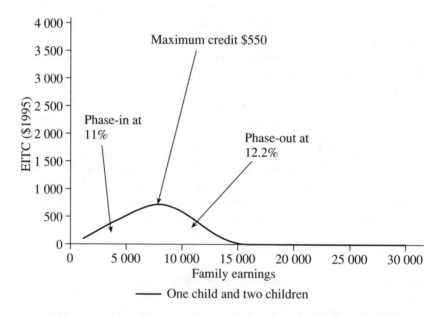

Figure 6.6   The US EITC in 1984

Table 6.1 summarizes the parameters of the EITC over the history of the programme. The real value of the credit increased only modestly in the early years and this was mostly due to inflation.[4] The 1987 expansion of the EITC, passed as part of the Tax Reform Act of 1986 (TRA86), represents the first major expansion of the EITC. The TRA86 increased the subsidy rate for the phase-in of the credit from 11 per cent to 14 per cent and increased the maximum income to which the subsidy rate was applied resulting in an increase in the maximum credit. The phase-out rate was reduced from 12.22 per cent to 10 per cent. The higher maximum credit and the lower phase-out rate combined to expand the phase-out region. The constant or flat region was lengthened in 1988.

Table 6.1   US EITC parameters

Year	Phase-in rate %	Phase-in range	Maximum credit	Phase-out rate %	Phase-out range
1975–78	10.0	$0–$54 000	$400	10.0	$4 000–$8 000
1979–84	10.0	$0–$55 000	$500	12.5	$6 000–$8 000
1985–86	11.0	$0–$55 000	$550	12.22	$6 500–$11 000
TRA86					
1987	14.0	$0–$6 080	$851	10.0	$6 920–$15 432
1988	14.0	$0–$6 240	$874	10.0	$9 840–$18 576
1989	14.0	$0–$6 500	$910	10.0	$10 240–$19 340
1990	14.0	$0–$6 810	$953	10.0	$10 730–$20 264
OBRA90					
1991	16.7[1]	$0–$7 140	$1 192	11.93	$11 250–$21 250
	17.3[2]		$1 235	12.36	
1992[3]	17.6[1]	$0–$7 520	$1 324	12.57	$11 840–$22 370
	18.4[2]		$1 384	13.14	
1993	18.5[1]	$0–$7 750	$1 434	13.21	$12 200–$23 030
	19.5[2]		$1 511	13.93	
OBRA93					
1994	26.3[1]	$0–$7 750	$2 038	15.93	$11 000–$23 755
	30.0[2]	$0–$8 425	$2 528	17.68	$11 000–$25 296
	7.65[3]	$0–$4 000	$306	7.65	$5 000–$9 000
1995					
	34.0[1]	$0–$6 160	$2 094	15.98	$11 290–$24 396
	36.0[2]	$0–$58 640	$3 110	20.22	$11 290–$26 673
	7.65[3]	$0–$4 100	$314	7.65	$5 130–$9 230
1996					
	34.0[1]	$0–$6 330	$2 152	15.8	$11 650–$25 078
	40.9[2]	$0–$8 890	$3 556	21.06	$11 650–$28 495
	7.65[3]	$0–$4 220	$323	7.65	$5 280–$9 500

Notes:
(1) Families with one qualifying child.
(2) Families with two or more qualifying children.
(3) Taxpayers with no qualifying children.

Source: Eissa and Hoynes (1998).

The 1991 expansion increased the maximum credit and introduced separate credit rates for families with two or more children. By 1993, a family with two or more children could receive a maximum credit of $1 511, $777 more than a family with one child.

The largest single expansion over this period was contained in the 1993 legislation. The 1993 expansion of the EITC, phased in between 1994 and 1996, led to an increase in the subsidy rate from 19.5 per cent to 40 per cent (18.5 to 34 per cent) and an increase in the maximum credit from $1 511 to $3 556 ($1 434 to $2 152) for taxpayers with two or more children (taxpayers with one child). This expansion was substantially larger for those with two or more children.

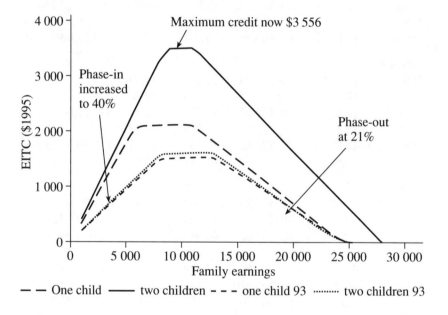

Figure 6.7   The US EITC in 1996

A picture of these changes is presented in Figure 6.7. The phase-out rate was also raised, from 14 per cent to 21 per cent (13 to 16 per cent) for taxpayers with two or more children (taxpayers with one child). Overall, the range of the phase-out was expanded dramatically, so that in 1996 a couple with two children would still be eligible with income levels of almost $30 000. The distribution of families by credit range is presented in Table 6.2.

Table 6.2   Distribution of families in the US by EITC credit range

	Married couples	Single parents
Percentage distribution of EITC recipients with children, tax year 1994[1]		
Phase-in or flat	27%	47%
Phase-out	73%	53%
Total	100%	100%
Percentage distribution of low educated families with children, tax year 1996[2]		
Phase-in	9%	–
Flat	6%	–
Phase-out	43%	–
Above phase-out	42%	–
Total	100%	

Notes:
(1) US General Accounting Office (1996).
(2) March 1997 Current Population Survey. Sample includes married couples with children where the wife has fewer than 12 years of schooling.

Source: Eissa and Hoynes (1998).

3.2   The Canadian Self-Sufficiency Programme

Another programme that is interesting to look at and which has many similarities with the EITC is the Self-Sufficiency Programme in Canada. This programme is thoroughly discussed and analysed in the Card and Robins (1998) study.

Figure 6.8 shows a budget constraint for a Canadian welfare recipient. It gives the budget set that an individual would face if they were earning the minimum wage in British Columbia, which was $6 an hour in 1996. Taking a job at a few hours a week attracts an earnings disregard of around $200; thereafter, all earned income is effectively lost in a dollar-for-dollar transfer back to the income assistance programme. So, until they have exhausted their income assistance – that is, working nearly 50 hours a week – they would get no return, with an implicit tax rate of 100 per cent on their earnings. Clearly, there are not going to be many individuals who choose to be in employment if that is the kind of schedule they face.

Of course, there are other programmes in British Colombia, such as an enhanced credit and enhanced earnings disregard system, that raise this line a little. So the example in Figure 6.8 is an exaggeration, but it tells the story. Most of the welfare recipients that are in this particular randomized trial seem to face a constraint something like this.

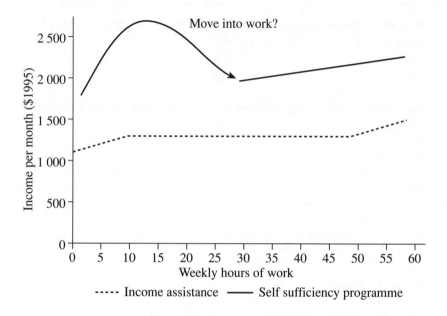

Figure 6.8   The Canadian SSP experiment (monthly income for a single parent with one child in BC)

The SSP is available to a single parent with twelve months' welfare history and who finds a job averaging 30 hours a week over a period of a month. This is calculated on a monthly rolling period. The minimum hours criterion is interesting as the UK system also has a minimum hours eligibility rule. It is a generous system and does not change the income assistance level; so it is not, for example, causing more individuals who do not find employment to be on lower incomes. It is giving a supplement to those who move into work.

3.3   The UK Family Credit and the Working Families Tax Credit

Introduced in the mid-1980s, Family Credit shares many of the features of the EITC. The 1998 Working Tax Credit Reform was designed to further align the UK system with the EITC. An unusual feature of the Family Credit system is the minimum weekly hours eligibility criterion. A family with children needs to have one adult working 16 hours or more per week to qualify for FC. At its introduction this was set at 24 hours but then reduced to encourage part-time work by lone parents with young children. In this system each eligible family is paid a credit up to a maximum amount which depends on the number of children. There is also a small addition if work is full time. Eligibility depends on family net income being lower than some threshold (£79.00 per week in 1998–9). As incomes rise the credit is withdrawn at a rate of 70 per cent. In 1996 average payments were around £57 a week and take-up rates stand at 69 per cent of eligible individuals and 82 per cent of the potential expenditure.

The recently implemented replacement of FC – the WFTC – is substantially more generous. It increases the generosity of in-work support relative to the FC system in four ways: it increases the credit for younger children; it increases the threshold; it reduces the benefit reduction rate or phase-out rate from 70 per cent to 55 per cent; finally, it incorporates a childcare credit of 70 per cent of actual childcare costs up to £150 per week. The effects of these changes relative to Family Credit are shown in Figure 6.9. The largest cash gains go to those people who are currently just at the end of the benefit reduction taper. The childcare credit increases the maximum amount of WFTC by 70 per cent of childcare costs up to a maximum of £100 per week for those with one child or £150 per week for those with two or more children. The credit is available to lone parents and couples where both partners work more than 16 hours per week. The distribution of childcare usage is provided in Table 6.3. The effect of the credit is also illustrated in Figure 6.9.

Table 6.3   Type of childcare usage in the UK, youngest child under five

Type of care	Couples	Lone parents	All
No care reported	35.4%	9.3%	32.9%
Relatives only	28.7%	44.0%	30.1%
Relatives and friends combined	1.1%	4.4%	1.4%
Friends only	3.0%	9.8%	3.6%
Childminders only	11.2%	11.1%	11.2%
Nursery care only	7.1%	6.7%	7.1%
Childminders & informal combined	2.5%	3.4%	2.6%
Nursery care & informal combined	4.3%	7.5%	4.6%
Multiple formal care	3.4%	1.0%	3.1%
Other forms of care	3.3%	2.6%	3.3%

Note: Data from the UK Family Resources Survey, 1994/5 and 1995/96.

Source: Blundell *et al.* (2000).

The central issue for this chapter is how family labour supply, labour market participation in particular, responds to these kinds of welfare reforms. This is

Evaluation methods

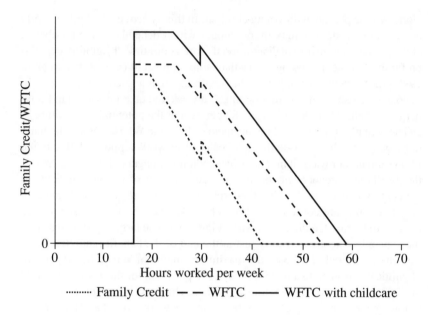

Figure 6.9   The UK WFTC reform

an empirical issue. We would like to know if such a reform is likely to get people moving off the welfare roles into work. But if we do put these credits in place, what are the responses of those already working, particularly in the phase-out region? Are they likely to cut back their work effort so that, in fact, the two effects counteract each other? It is possible that could happen. And if it does, then is there really any benefit to the system whatsoever? You could have some people moving in, but others working less who are already in.

The next three sections consider three alternative evaluation approaches and, in doing so, build up a picture of the likely labour supply impact of 'in-work' benefit reforms.

4   THE QUASI-EXPERIMENTAL APPROACH: EVALUATING THE CANADIAN SELF SUFFICIENCY PROGRAMME

The Canadian Self Sufficiency experiment entailed following 6 000 single mothers for five years starting in 1993. One-half of the group of 6 000 eligible individuals on welfare were offered the programme and the others were not – they are the controls. The individuals on the programme are the treatments – and we can compare those two groups.

This is a very well designed social experiment. The control and the treatment groups look very similar before the experiment takes place. That means that, effectively, the controls are really quite a good match for the treatment group. What we are looking for, then, is this self-sufficiency programme increasing labour market attachment.

There is almost a doubling in employment for the treatment group. This is displayed in Figure 6.10, which also shows the close relationship between employment rates across the control and treatment group before the experiment began. Card and Robins (1998) report many more results. The impact on hours and earnings is very similar. The treatment group increased its hours of work, more or less, twofold over the control group. So it has quite an effect on the hours of work chosen by these individuals.

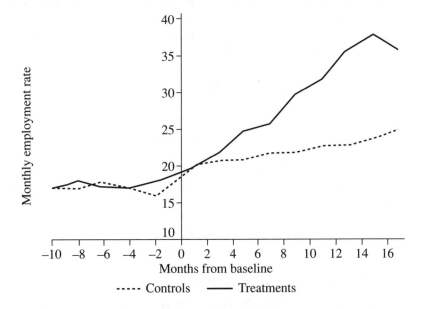

Figure 6.10 The Canadian SSP experiment (monthly employment rate)

Although this is a very specific target group and a programme with many individual idiosyncrasies, these are all single parents on welfare and it may be considered somewhat of a surprise that there is such an effect of financial incentives for those individuals. This type of experimental evidence certainly suggests that in-work benefits can have quite significant effects on employment and hours even among lone parents – one of the central target groups for the UK and US reforms.

5 THE NATURAL EXPERIMENT APPROACH: EVALUATING THE REFORMS TO THE US EITC

We have already documented the very dramatic increase in generosity of the EITC in the US over the late 1980s and early 1990s. It might be expected that these policy reforms could form a natural experiment by providing a 'before and after' assessment of the effectiveness in changing labour market behaviour.

The idea of the natural experiment approach is to find a comparison group, not affected by the reform, which is likely to have experienced a similar macro environment during the course of the reform. To be more specific we could label individuals in the eligible or treatment group as T. Time periods are then defined as B for before the reform and A for after the reform. The labour market participation rate before the reform for the treatment group is given by $P\{T,B\}$. For the control group, labelled C, it is given by $P\{C,B\}$.

To evaluate the effect of the reform on participation we simply calculate the difference in differences

$$(P\{T,A\} - P\{T,B\}) - (P\{C,A\} - P\{C,B\}).$$

This contrast between treatment and comparison group removes any common time effects in participation across the groups. That is, it strips out the effect of any common macro shocks that would otherwise be attributed to the reform. By comparing participation before and after the reform for the same group, it also removes any group effects. Consequently, it relies on two important assumptions:

$$(AI)\text{ Common time effects}$$

and

$$(AII)\text{ No composition changes}$$

Choosing a comparison group that satisfies these two assumptions is difficult. In the evaluation of the EITC policy reforms in the US, Eissa and Liebman (1996) use two treatment and control groups from the repeated cross-sections of the Current Population Survey data. For the impact of the reform on single mothers, either the whole group of single women with children are used with single women without children as controls, or the group of low education single women with children are used with the low education single women without children as controls.

The former comparison can be criticized for not satisfying the common macro effects – assumption *AI*. In particular, using all single women as a control group may be inappropriate. This control group is already working to a very high level of participation in the US labour market (around 95 per cent) and therefore cannot be expected to increase its level of participation in response to the economy coming out of a recession. In this case all the expansion in labour market participation in the group of single women with children will be attributed to the reform itself. The later group is therefore more appropriate as it targets better those single parents who are likely to be eligible for EITC and the control group has a participation rate of about 70 per cent.

Even with these caveats in mind, there are some relatively strong results on participation effects that come from the Eissa and Liebman study. For single parents there is evidence of a reasonable movement in to work. There is also some evidence of negative effect on hours for those in work but this is rather small.

A more recent study, Eissa and Hoynes (1998), has considered the impact on married couples and finds some evidence of negative 'income' effect reducing the labour supply of married women. As we will show in more detail for the WFTC reform below, this is to be expected in a family income-based credit like EITC.

In sum, these studies of the EITC reforms in the US point to a reasonably strong positive effect on participation of single parents with offsetting effects on the labour supply of married women. However, simple difference-in-differences methods are unlikely to give us sufficient information to simulate new reforms. Moreover, we have seen that they are only valid under the strong assumptions *AI* and *AII* above. Nevertheless, they do provide a 'theory free' robustness check on standard empirical labour supply models of the type we need to develop for simulation purposes.

6   THE DISCRETE CHOICE STRUCTURAL APPROACH: EVALUATING THE UK WFTC REFORM

In this approach a careful modelling of each individual's budget constraint is put together with a discrete choice model of hours and participation choices. To implement this a detailed tax-benefit routine is required that can simulate the budget constraint for each individual in each family in the data. That is, for any set of hours of work choices made by individuals in the family the tax-benefit routine must recover the level of net income. For non-workers this also requires a wage prediction equation. Such an equation would typically include education, age, demographic and regional dummy variables.

Modelling Preferences for Work and Income

For each individual or couple in the sample, preferences are written in terms of
hours of work, net income, a set of observable demographic factors and unknown
preference parameters. A separate specification is required for couples and for
lone parents. For example, in the specification for UK lone parents below, taken
from the Blundell *et al.* (2000) (a study which follows the framework developed
by Keane and Moffitt (1998)) the following quadratic specification is chosen.

$$U(h, Y) = \alpha_{yy}Y^2 + \alpha_{hh}h^2 + \alpha_{yh}Yh + \beta_y Y + \beta_h h$$

where Y represents the net income available to a particular lone parent who
works h hours, including his/her earnings, the α and β parameters are preference
parameters.

The β parameters are allowed to depend on observable and unobservable
factors according to:

$$\beta_y = \beta_{y0} + \beta'_x x + v_y$$

$$\beta_h = \beta_{h0} + \beta'_x x + v_h$$

where the x represent a vector of observable demographic and other household
characteristics. The v represent unobservable random terms. These unobservable terms are allowed to be correlated but are assumed to be jointly normally
distributed.

For couples, the model would need to allow for two hours dimensions
otherwise the quadratic form for preferences can be maintained. In the UK
simulation model below, male hours of work are simply allowed to be at full-
time or zero, reflecting the very low incidence of part-time work for men in
couple households with children.

Modelling Discrete Hours Choices

Hours-of-work choices are summarized by a finite set of points, e.g. {0, 10, 20,
30, 40}. To allow for preferences to vary quite widely over these hours choices,
the utility level for each hours point must be allowed to vary stochastically over
individuals. Typically an extreme value distribution is chosen so that, conditional on the v terms in the specification of the β parameters above, choices
across discrete hours points can be written as a multinomial logit model:

$$\Pr\left[U_i \geq U_j \mid \text{all } j\right] = \frac{\exp U\left(H_i, Y_i : \alpha, \beta\right)}{\sum_k \exp U\left(H_k, Y_k : \alpha, \beta\right)}$$

where the subscript represents a discrete hours point.

If there were no unobserved heterogeneity terms represented by the *v* terms then these probabilities would be exactly analogous to the terms in a multinomial logit model. However, the additional unobservable variables imply that to calculate the probabilities we first have to integrate over the range of the *v* variables. In doing this we effectively relax the otherwise strong distributional assumption. The integration is done by simulation methods assuming a multivariate normal distribution for the *v*s in the estimation and simulation routine.

Childcare Costs and Fixed Costs of Work

The simple multinomial discrete choice preference model described so far is unlikely to be sufficient to adequately describe the observed outcomes in the data. For example, in modelling the WFTC reform in the UK two additional features turn out to be critical. First, a model of childcare costs and childcare usage and second, a model of additional fixed costs of work. For example, Blundell *et al.* (2000) compute the relationship between hourly childcare costs and various demographic characteristics so as to associate with each household type a probability of choosing the relevant type of childcare. They also find the regression relationship between the amount of childcare used and the level of hours worked. Hence for each possible hours choice and each household type they associate the probability of using each type of childcare. This forms an input into the construction of the likelihood function of the data for estimating the unknown preference parameters.

Fixed costs are the costs that an individual has to pay to get to work. For many families they are made up in part by the childcare costs already covered above. In particular, in our model, childcare induces both fixed and variable costs that effectively act as a marginal tax rate. However, there are additional costs, for example, transport, which will vary by household type and by region. These are modelled as a once-off weekly cost. In the model they are subtracted directly from net income for any choices that involve work. Fixed costs are typically modelled in a similar way to preferences, in terms of a set of observable factors and an unobservable heterogeneity variable.

These terms will now enter the utility comparisons for each individual in their $FC = \gamma' x + \omega$ work–non-work choice. Consequently, they will also enter the probability terms described above. To calculate the probability of any observed hours point, the heterogeneity term ω will be integrated out in estimation along with the *v* terms, and the parameters γ will add to the list of parameters, along with the α and β parameters, to be estimated.

The unknown γ, α and β parameters can now be estimated by maximum likelihood. For each observed family there is a probability term generated from the above model. This can be written in terms of the unobservable parameters to be estimated. Taking the whole data set together generates the sample likelihood. To evaluate the probabilities entering the likelihood, simulation methods have to be used to integrate out the unobservable terms described above. Consequently maximum likelihood estimation is by simulation.

Evaluating the WFTC Reform in the UK

There are two distinctive features of the new WFTC system noted above. First, there is a more generous childcare component. Second, the benefit reduction rate is significantly reduced from 70 per cent in the current system to 55 per cent.

There are two target groups: single parents and married couples with children. Results for both groups drawn from the Blundell *et al.* (2000) are presented here. Two samples from the 1994–5 and 1995–6 British Family Resources Surveys are selected; single parent households and married or *de facto* married couples. Excluding self-employed and retired households, together with students and those in HM forces, leaves samples of 1807 single parents and 4694 two-person households for use in estimation. Nearly 50 per cent of currently working single parents were found to be in receipt of some Family Credit. For married couples with children this proportion is smaller, at around 16 per cent. However, the latter group is more than two-and-a-half times the size of the former. The weekly hours of work for various family categories are shown in Figure 6.11.

The WFTC reform is designed to influence the work incentives of those with low potential returns in the labour market. It does this via the increased generosity of in-work means-tested benefits. For single parents the WFTC does unambiguously increase the incentive to work. For couples, however, the incentives created by the WFTC lead to *lower* participation in the labour market.

Figure 6.12 shows the effect of the WFTC reform on a single parent. The strong incentive to move into work for a non-participant is clear. There is also an incentive to reduce hours of work among those single parents working full time. The balance between these is purely an empirical matter although the EITC analysis, discussed in the previous section, suggested this would not dominate the positive participation effect.

Figure 6.13 presents an example man in a single-earner couple. Again the incentives are unambiguously to move into work. Indeed, the gains are far larger than for our lone parent example, as the largest cash gains from the WFTC reform accrue to those at the end of the current taper. The incentives to change hours of work are ambiguous. But one interesting point is the marked increase in the effective marginal tax rate for those who become eligible for WFTC as a result of the reform. This group face an increase in their marginal tax rates from 33 per cent, produced by income tax and National Insurance, to just under 70 per cent, produced by the interaction of the 55 per cent WFTC taper on post-tax income. In the example the marginal tax rate rises from 33 per cent to just under 70 per cent above 40 hours of work.

One point, highlighted in our discussion of the EITC reforms above, is the incentive for some workers in married couples to move out of work altogether. Figure 6.14 shows the budget constraint for the partner of the man in Figure 6.13. The figure is conditional on the man working 40 hours a week. Thus the family income of the woman when she does not work is that shown at the 40 hours point. This means that the income at zero hours has increased through the WFTC reform. In the example, anyone working more than 10 hours has an increased incentive to reduce their hours or move out of work altogether. The situation changes when we allow for childcare costs at 16 hours. Here there is an additional incentive to work just over 16 hours to take advantage of the childcare credit.

Policy Simulations

Blundell *et al.* (2000) use the discrete choice structural labour supply model estimates to simulate the work incentive impact of the WFTC reform. Tables 6.4 – 6.6 report the simulation results for single parent households; women with employed partners and women with unemployed partners under the assumption of 100 per cent take-up of the WFTC. These results are presented both in the form of a matrix of simulated transitions between no work, part-time work and full-time employment under the two systems, and using summary measures of changes in participation rates and average changes in hours among workers and among the full sample.

Lone parents
In Table 6.4 the simulated work responses to the WFTC among our sample of single parents is reported. The simulated transition takes around 2.2 per cent of the sample from no work to either part-time or full-time work, with no offsetting movements out of the labour market. To take account of sampling variability, a standard error of 0.42 per cent is placed around this figure, which would admit the possibility that the actual increase could be as much as 3 per cent. One can clearly see the reason for this shift in our earlier graphs of the potential impact of the WFTC on single parents' budget constraints. At or above 16 hours per week the single parent becomes eligible for WFTC (with any childcare credit addition to which she may be entitled). For some women this extra income makes a transition to part-time employment attractive. The 2.2 per cent of single parents who are simulated to move into the labour market would gross up to around 30 000 women in the population.

There is a minor reduction in labour supply through a simulated shift from full-time to part-time employment among 0.2 per cent of the sample. This is consistent with a small (negative) income effect among some full-time single

women, for whom the increase in income through the WFTC encourages a
reduction in labour supply. Nevertheless, this is more than offset by the positive
incentive effect to work for single parents induced by this reform.

(a)   Lone mothers

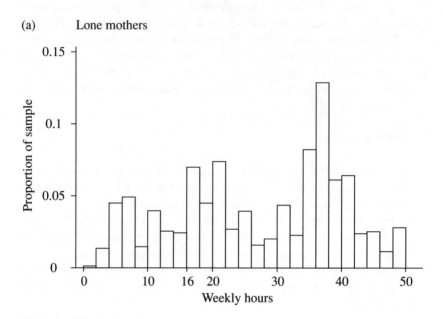

(b)   Married women

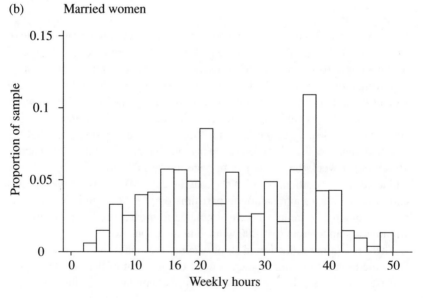

(c)   Men

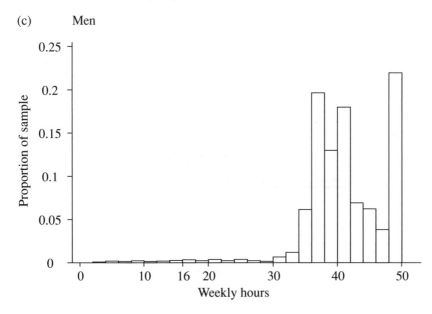

Figure 6.11   Weekly hours of work in the UK

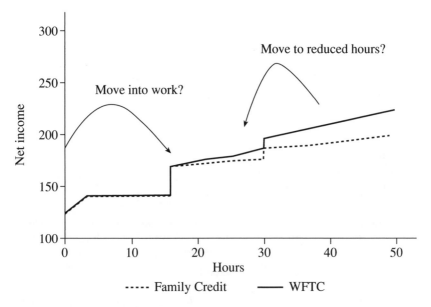

Figure 6.12   Lone parent on median wage (WFTC in the UK)

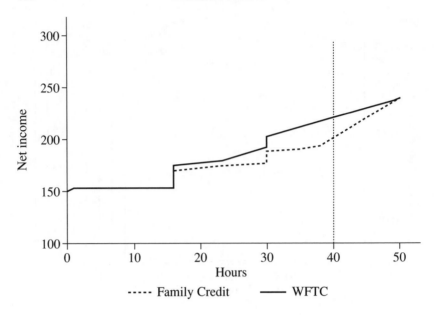

Figure 6.13   Single-earner male on 25th percentile wage (WFTC in the UK)

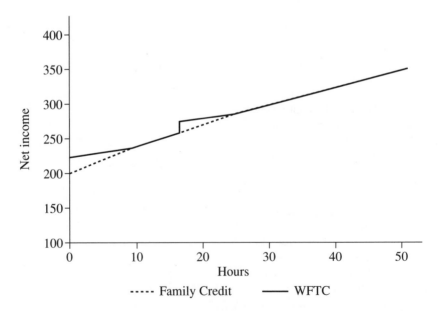

Figure 6.14   Partner in two-earner couple on 25th percentile wage (WFTC in the UK)

Table 6.4   WFTC simulation results: single parents

Transitions

		Post-reform		
Pre-reform	Out of work	Part-time	Full-time	Pre-reform %
Out of work	58.0	0.7	1.5	60.2
Part-time	0.0	18.6	0.5	19.1
Full-time	0.0	0.2	20.6	20.7
Post-reform %	58.0	19.4	22.6	100
Change (%)	–2.2	0.3	1.9	

Summary

	mean	*Std. dev.*
Change in participation	+2.20%	[0.42%]
Average change in hours (all)	+0.75	[0.16]
Average change in hours (workers only)	+0.22	[0.04]
Average hours before reform (all)	10.20	
Average hours before reform (workers)	25.70	

Notes: Transitions tables built by drawing 100 times from the distribution of unobserved heterogeneity and allocating each observation to the cell which yields maximum utility for each draw. Standard deviations for each transitions cell and summary measure are simulated by drawing 100 times from the estimated asymptotic distribution of the parameter estimates, and for each of those 100 parameter draws, applying the method described above to build transitions matrices.

Source: Blundell *et al.* (2000).

Women with employed partners

For married women the simulated incentive effect is quite different. Table 6.5 reports estimates of the transitions following WFTC among a sub-sample of women with employed partners. There is a significant overall *reduction* in the number of women in work of around 0.57 per cent, equating to a grossed-up figure of around 20 000 in the population. This overall reduction comprises around 0.2 per cent who move into the labour market following the reform, and 0.8 per cent who move from work to non-participation. The number of hours worked by women with employed partners is predicted to fall slightly, by 0.18 hours on average over the full sample.

Table 6.5   WFTC simulation results: married women with employed partners

Transitions

		Post-reform		
Pre-reform	Out of work	Part-time	Full-time	Pre-reform %
Out of work	32.2	0.1	0.1	32.4
Part-time	0.3	31.6	0.0	32.0
Full-time	0.4	0.1	35.0	35.6
Post-reform %	33.0	31.8	35.2	100
Change (%)	0.6	–0.1	–0.4	

Summary

	mean	*std.dev.*
Change in participation	–0.57%	[0.06%]
Average change in hours (all)	–0.18	[0.02]
Average change in hours (workers only)	–0.03	[0.005]
Average hours before reform (all)	17.34	
Average hours before reform (workers)	25.65	

Notes: As for Table 6.4.

Source: Blundell *et al*. (2000)

The predominant negative response is clearly not one that is intended, but from the earlier budget constraint analysis one can easily see why. There will be a proportion of non-working women whose low earning partners will be eligible for the WFTC. The greater generosity of the tax credit relative to the current system of Family Credit increases household income. This increase in income would be lost if the woman in the household were to work. And for those women currently in the labour market, the WFTC increases the income available to the household if she were to stop working.

Women with unemployed partners
In Table 6.6 the incentives for a sub-sample of women whose partners do not work are presented. For this group there is a significant overall increase of 1.32 per cent in the number of women who work, equating to a grossed-up figure of around 11 000 in the population. The reason for this shift is more straightforward, and stems from the increased generosity of the basic WFTC relative to the current Family Credit system for those women who choose to move into work. Note that for this group the generosity of the childcare credit component

of the WFTC is not an issue, since households only qualify for the childcare credit if both household members work 16 hours or more. There is, of course, potential for both members of an unemployed household to move into work in order to qualify for the WFTC including the childcare credit, but a joint simulation (not reported here) shows that such an outcome is virtually non-existent.

Table 6.6   WFTC simulation results: married women with partners out of work

Transitions

		Post-reform		
Pre-reform	Out of work	Part-time	Full-time	Pre-reform %
Out of work	56.8	0.4	0.9	58.1
Part-time	0.0	22.2	0.4	22.6
Full-time	0.0	0.1	19.2	19.3
Post-reform %	56.8	22.8	20.5	100
Change (%)	−1.3	0.2	1.1	

Summary

	mean	*Std. dev.*
Change in participation	+1.32%	[0.16%]
Average change in hours (all)	+0.46	[0.067]
Average change in hours (workers only)	+0.14	[0.017]
Average hours before reform (all)	10.04	
Average hours before reform (workers)	23.96	

Notes: As for Table 6.4.

Source: Blundell *et al.* (2000)

7   CONCLUSIONS

This chapter has considered three different reforms and three different methods for evaluating the labour market impact of in-work benefits for low-wage workers. Taking all these studies together, it has shown that a careful design of these programmes can induce a reasonably large and positive increase in labour market participation. These are reflected in studies for the US, Canada and the UK. It also appears that any offsetting negative effect on hours worked by those already in employment is not strong enough to counter this overall positive increase in labour supply. However, since these programmes are generally based on family income, there is evidence of a negative offsetting effect on the labour supply of married women in households with young children.

The chapter has considered evidence from quasi-experiments in Canada, from the before and after analysis of past reforms to the EITC in the US and to simulations of the new WFTC reform in the UK. All these different pieces of evidence tend to support this general conclusion. For the WFTC reform in the UK, the simulations suggest the participation rate for single mothers increases by 2.2 percentage points (5 per cent). The participation rate for married women with employed partners decreases because of an income effect arising from the improved benefit eligibility of their husbands. However the behavioural effects combined with those for men and women with non-working partners imply an increase in overall participation.

There are a number of specific issues relating to the precise design of these reforms. Probably the most important, although tied heavily to the level of the credit (or benefit given), is the choice of benefit reduction rate. As has been seen, the benefit reduction rate in the UK is 70 per cent for FC reducing to 55 per cent for WFTC. It is quite interesting that in the EITC programme it is quite low, at around 20 per cent. In the Canadian system, it is about 50 per cent. With the 70 per cent rate currently in the UK system, it is almost inevitable that some individuals working up above this limit are going to find it relatively attractive to move down into more part-time work. There is a trade-off between individuals moving in, and others moving down into part-time work. Exactly what phase-out rate to choose is an interesting and difficult question, because if it is too high, then there is a severe implicit tax rate. But if it is set too low, individuals on quite high incomes are made eligible for some supplement from this credit system. The latter is precisely what has happened in the redesigned in-work benefit Working Families Tax Credit (WFTC) in the UK. So the exact slope of the benefit reduction rate is critical, and it really all depends on how many people out there are likely to be affected.

Then there is whether a minimum hours limit should be set on eligibility. One interesting UK reform that took place in 1992, was to move the minimum hours limit from 24 work hours down to 16. This saw a pronounced increase in employment and a change in the distribution of hours worked by single parents with an increase in part-time work and a bunching at 16 hours.

Overall, how well do welfare to work benefits work? They are designed, as we have seen, to stimulate work for individuals in the welfare trap, typically poor families with children. Are individuals likely to respond to earning supplements of this type? And will those people who are already in work, but now are eligible for the supplement, choose to reduce their work effort because they can do just as well financially by working fewer hours over the year? The empirical evidence and simulations point to some quite positive increases in labour market attachment for single mothers with a possible reduction in participation for married mothers due to the family income based nature of the tax credits offered under these schemes.

Perhaps a more important question is whether there is a longer-run payoff to labour market attachment for low skilled workers? Eventually, one might hope, through the progression of wages, and becoming more attached to the labour market, workers get themselves out of a low income group and into a reasonable earnings level. This means, of course, they would be less likely to be drawing income assistance or any forms of tax credits. On the other hand, if this dynamic payoff is relatively low, then these individuals are likely to remain on these credits and may be stuck continuously in this part of the welfare system. This dynamic payoff for low skilled workers remains an open question.

NOTES

1. See Liebman (1996) for a detailed historical evaluation of the EITC.
2. Beginning in 1994, a small credit is available to low income workers without children.
3. See Eissa and Liebman (1996) for a more extensive discussion of EITC rules.
4. The EITC was first indexed to inflation in 1987.

BIBLIOGRAPHY

Blomquist, Soren (1983), 'The Effect of Income Taxation on the Labour Supply of Married Men in Sweden', *Journal of Public Economics*, **22**: 169–97.

Blomquist, Soren (1995), 'Estimation Methods for Male Labour Supply Functions: How to Take Account of Non-Linear Taxes', *Journal of Econometrics*, **70**: 383–405.

Blomquist, Soren and U. Hansson-Brusewitz (1990), 'The Effect of Taxes on Male and Female Labour Supply in Sweden', *Journal of Human Resources*, **25**: 317–57.

Blundell, Richard W. and Paul Johnson (1998), 'Labor Force Participation and the UK Pension System', *American Economic Review (papers and proceedings)*, May.

Blundell, Richard W. and Ian Walker (1986), 'A Life Cycle Consistent Empirical Model of Family Labour Supply using Cross Section Data', *Review of Economic Studies*, **53**: 539–58.

Blundell, Richard W., Alan Duncan and Costas Meghir (1992), 'Taxation and Empirical Labour Supply Models: Lone Parents in the UK', *Economic Journal*, **102**: 265–78.

Blundell, Richard W., Alan Duncan and Costas Meghir (1998), 'Estimating Labour Supply Responses using Tax Policy Reforms', *Econometrica*, **66**: 827–61.

Blundell, Richard W., John Ham and Costas Meghir (1987), 'Unemployment and Female Labour Supply', *Economic Journal*, **97**: 44–64.

Blundell, Richard W., John Ham and Costas Meghir (1998), 'Unemployment, Discouraged Workers and Female Labour Supply', *Research in Economics*, **52**: 103–31.

Blundell, Richard, Alan Duncan, Julian McCrae and Costas Meghir (2000), 'The Labour Market Impact of the Working Families Tax Credit', *Fiscal Studies*, **21**(1), March, 75–104, December.

Blundell, Richard W., Costas Meghir, Elizabeth Symons and Ian Walker (1986), 'A Labour Supply Model for the Simulation of Tax and Benefit Reforms', in R.W. Blundell and I. Walker (eds), *Unemployment, Search and Labour Supply*, Cambridge: Cambridge University Press.

Blundell, Richard W., Costas Meghir, Elizabeth Symons and Ian Walker (1988), 'Labour Supply Specification and the Evaluation of Tax Reforms', *Journal of Public Economics*, **36**: 23–52.

Bourguignon, François and Thierry Magnac (1990), 'Labour Supply and Taxation in France', *Journal of Human Resources*, **25**: 358–89.

Bosworth Greg and Gary Burtless (1992), 'Effects of Tax Reform on Labour Supply, Investment and Savings', *Journal of Economic Perspectives*, **6**(1): 3–25.

Browning, Edgar (1995), 'Effects of the Earned Income Tax Credit on Income and Welfare', *National Tax Journal*, **XLVIII**: 23–43.

Card, David and Philip K. Robins (1998), 'Do Financial Incentives Encourage Welfare Recipients to Work?', *Research in Labor Economics*, **17**: 1–56.

Council of Economic Advisors (1998), *Economic Report of the President*, United States Government Printing, Washington DC.

Dickert, Stacy and Scott Houser (1998), 'Taxes and Transfers: A New Look at the Marriage Penalty', *National Tax Journal*.

Dickert, Stacy, Scott Houser and John Karl Scholtz (1995), 'The Earned Income Tax Credit and Transfer Program: A Study of Labor Market and Program Participation', in J. Poterba, (ed.), *Tax Policy and the Economy*, Cambridge MIT Press.

Duncan, Alan and Andrew Dilnot (1992), 'Lone Mothers, Family Credit and Paid Work', *Fiscal Studies*, **13**: 1–21.

Eissa, Nada and Hilary Hoynes (1998), 'The Earned Income Tax Credit and the Labor Supply of Married Couples', National Bureau of Economic Research, Working Paper, 6856, December.

Eissa, Nada and Jeffrey Liebman (1996), 'Labor Supply Response to the Earned Income Tax Credit', *Quarterly Journal of Economics*, **CXI**: 605–37.

Flood, Lennart and Thomas MaCurdy (1991), 'Work Disincentive Effects of Taxes: An Empirical Analysis of Swedish Men', mimeo, Stanford University.

Hausman, Jerry and James Poterba (1987), 'Household Behaviour and the Tax Reform Act of 1986', *Journal of Economic Perspectives*, **1**(1): 101–19.

Hausman, Jerry and Paul Ruud (1986), 'Family Labor Supply with Taxes', *American Economic Review* (Papers and Proceedings), **74**: 242–8.

Heckman, James J., (1974), 'Effects of Child-Care Programs on Women's Work Effort', *Journal of Political Economy*, **82**(2): S136–63.

Hoffman, Saul and Laurence Seidman (1990), *The Earned Income Tax Credit: Antipoverty Effectiveness and Labor Market Effects*, Kalamazoo MI: Upjohn Institute for Employment Research.

Holtzblatt, Janet, Janet McCubbin and Robert Gilette (1994), 'Promoting Work through the EITC', mimeo, US Department of the Treasury, 4 June 1994.

Hoynes, Hilary Williamson (1996), 'Welfare Transfers in Two-parent Families: Labor Supply and Welfare Participation under the AFDC-UP Program', *Econometrica*, **64**(2): 295–332.

Keane, Michael P. and Robert Moffitt (1998), 'A Structural Model of Multiple Welfare Program Participation and Labor Supply', *International Economic Review*.

Kell, Michael and Jane Wright (1989), 'Benefits and the Labour Supply of Women Married to Unemployed Men', *Economic Journal*, Conference Supplement, 1195–265.

Liebman, Jeffrey (1996), 'The Impact of the Earned Income Tax Credit on Labor Supply and Taxpayer Compliance', Ph.D. Thesis, Harvard University, September.

MaCurdy Thomas, David Green and Harry Paarsch (1990), 'Accessing Empirical Approaches for Analysing Taxes and Labor Suppy', *Journal of Human Resources*, **25**(3): 415–90.

Meyer, Bruce and Daniel Rosenbaum (1998), 'Welfare, the Earned Income Tax Credit and the Labor Supply of Single Mothers', mimeo, Northwestern University.

Moffitt, Robert (1992), 'Incentive Effects of the US Welfare System: A Review', *Journal of Economic Literature*, **30**: 1–61.

Moffitt, Robert and Kenneth Kehrer (1981), 'The Effect of Tax and Transfer programs on Labor Supply: The Evidence from the Income Maintenance Experiments', in R.G. Ehrenberg (ed.), *Research in Labor Economics*, **4**: 103–50, Greenwich, Connecticut: JAI Press.

Mroz, Thomas A. (1987), 'The Sensitivity of an Empirical Model of Married Women's Hours of Work to Economic and Statistical Assumptions', *Econometrica*, **55**: 765–99.

Triest, Robert K. (1987), 'A Monte Carlo Test of the Robustness of Alternative Estimators of Labor Supply Functions', Working Paper, 198, Department of Economics, Johns Hopkins University.

US General Accounting Office (1996), *Earned Income Tax Credit: Profile of Tax Year 1994 Credit Recipients*, Washington DC: GAO.

Van Soest, Arthur (1995), 'Structural Models of Family Labor Supply: A Discrete Choice Approach', *Journal of Human Resources*, **30**: 63–88.

7. Tax reform and labour supply in Sweden: were low and high skill individuals affected differently?

Sören Blomquist and Matias Eklöf

1 INTRODUCTION

Tax reform in Sweden has been a gradual process. In this chapter we describe and discuss the series of tax reforms that took place between 1980 and 1991. This period is of special interest since marginal tax rates reached a historical high in 1980 and a low in 1991. Several motivations have been given for implementing the tax reforms. The old tax system had become quite complicated with many special rules and deductions. This made it possible for knowledgeable and resourceful persons to partly avoid paying taxes. Hence, although the tax system formally looked quite progressive it was, in many cases, possible to avoid the progressivity. An intention with the reform was to make the tax rules simpler and more transparent. It was hoped that this also would make the tax system horizontally more equal. A second important reason was a need to reduce the negative incentive effects of high marginal tax rates on household behaviour such as savings and labour supply. It would be too ambitious a task to assess the total effects of the reforms. In this chapter we focus on *the effects on married men's desired hours of work* and, in particular, to what extent low skill and high skill workers were affected differently by the reforms.

There have been several earlier attempts to evaluate the Swedish tax reform. A complicating fact is that the Swedish economy in the early 1990s were hit by a severe economic downturn and a dramatic rise in the unemployment rate. This meant that changes in individuals' actual hours of work were affected both by changes in the tax system and quantity constraints. Owing to difficulties in separating these confounding effects, most studies of the tax reform have only used data from before 1991. The calculations have been done in terms of changes in individuals' desired hours of work. We follow this line of study. Aronsson and Palme (1998) use the maximum likelihood method to estimate a household model on data from 1980. In simulations with the estimated model they focus on welfare measures and on how inequality was affected by the tax reform. They find that the reforms have led to a considerable reduction in the excess burden. Blomquist and Newey (1999) use data from three points in time to estimate a non-parametric labour supply function. Blomquist *et al.* (1998) use this function to evaluate the effect of tax reform on desired hours of work, tax revenue and the income distribution. They also compare the results with those obtained from a parametric model. Ackum-Agell and Meghir (1995) do not make any explicit calculations of how 'hours of work' was affected by the tax reform. However, their study is still of interest since, using other data and estimation methods, their estimated wage and income elasticities are similar to those found in several other Swedish studies. Klevmarken (1997) is the only study using data from after the 1991 reform. He uses data from 1986 and 1993 and a difference-in-difference approach to estimate the effect of tax reform on hours of work. Agell *et al.* (1996) give a broad evaluation of the tax reform drawing on results from several more specialized studies.

The remainder of this chapter is organized as follows. We give a stylized description of the Swedish tax reform in section 2. To evaluate the tax reform we use a non-parametric labour supply function. In section 3 we briefly describe the estimation procedure used. In section 4 we describe how the tax reform is decomposed and present our calculations of the effect of the tax reform on hours of work. We pay special attention to how the incentives differ between high and low skill groups. Section 5 concludes.

2 A SERIES OF TAX REFORMS

Following Blomquist *et al.* (1998) we describe the changes in labour income taxation, capital income taxation and real estate taxation during the period 1980 to 1991. Further, we analyse the transfer systems and indirect taxes as separate components of the reforms. In the interest of brevity this section only presents the main features of the tax and transfer systems. A more extensive presentation of the 1991 tax and transfer system can be found in appendix A of Blomquist *et al.* (1998). Blomquist and Hansson-Brusewitz (1990) contains a presentation of the 1980 tax system.

Personal Income Taxation

The proportional local income tax has increased by about two percentage points; the average local income tax rate was 29.1 per cent in 1980 and 31 per cent in 1991. The progressive federal income tax has undergone substantial change. The change in the federal income tax consists of two important parts. First, the marginal tax rates have fallen significantly. In 1980 the highest marginal tax rate for the federal income tax was 58 per cent. In 1991 it was 20 per cent.

Secondly, in 1980 capital income and imputed income of owner occupied homes were taxed simultaneously with labour income. If net capital income was negative, this amount was fully deductible against labour incomes. In 1991 capital and labour incomes were taxed separately; capital income being taxed at a uniform rate of 30 per cent. If the net capital income was negative then the overall tax liability was reduced by 30 per cent of the deficit. Hence, in contrast to the 1980 system of capital taxation, the 1991 construction, in practice, eliminated the link between the income of capital and the marginal tax rate on labour income. Finally, in 1991 individuals who owned their homes paid a real estate tax of 1.2 per cent of the rateable value of the house.

Transfer System

The income tax reform was predicted to benefit high income households more than low income households. In order to avoid this unwanted redistributional effect the transfer system was redesigned to improve the economic conditions of households with low income and/or many children. The child allowance, which was independent of income, increased from SEK 2 850 per child to SEK 3 963 per child plus an additional amount increasing with the number of children in the household.[1] Further, the part of the unreduced housing allowance which was dependent on family composition increased from SEK 1 500 per year and child to a fixed amount of SEK 5 300 per year if the household included children. On the other hand, the allowance associated with housing costs decreased from a proportional rate of 80 per cent of costs exceeding SEK 450 per month to an average rate of about 65 per cent of costs exceeding approximately SEK 600. The allowance was then reduced depending on the household composition, income and wealth. The construction of the reduction was not changed in the reform although the rates and limits were redefined. The reformed transfer system also made more households eligible for allowances.

Indirect Taxation

The government's net tax revenues, were predicted to be reduced by the income tax and transfer reforms. To compensate for this the VAT and payroll taxes were increased. Simultaneous with a broadening of the VAT base, the VAT rate increased from 21.34 per cent in 1980 to 25 per cent in 1991, measured as percentage of net price. The base broadening gives us reason to use an average VAT on a consumption bundle as an approximation of the aggregate effects of the increased VAT and base broadening. The average VAT equalled 12.8 per cent and 16.5 per cent in 1980 and 1991, respectively. Further, the payroll tax, measured as percentage of net wage payments, increased from 35.25 per cent to 37.47 per cent. Although a part of the payroll tax sometimes is considered as an insurance fee, we have chosen to treat it as a proportional tax. We neglect general equilibrium effects and assume that the pre-tax wages paid by employers are constant throughout all reforms. We also assume that all disposable income is consumed.

Effect on Budget Sets

To calculate the effect of tax reform on individuals' budget sets and labour supply we will make use of a representative sample from 1980 of 864 married or cohabiting men. For many of our calculations of the effect of tax reform we will use the joint distribution of gross wage rates, non-labour income and socio-demographic variables in this sample.[2]

To illustrate the effect of the tax reform on individuals' budget sets, we first describe how total marginal effects changed and how the level of the budget sets were affected. To accomplish this we will focus on three (fictitious) typical individuals. The individuals are assumed to be low, average and high skilled and the assigned gross wage rates are 20, 40 and 80 SEK/h, respectively. However, the marginal effects and levels also depend on capital income and socio-demographics. We can choose the level of the capital income and the socio-demographics in several different ways. One alternative would be to assign the same value of the capital income and the socio-demographics to each one of the three typical cases. A second alternative is to account for the observed covariation between gross wage rate and other sources of income and socio-demographic characteristics. The most important covariation is that between the gross wage rate and capital income. We have therefore chosen to let capital income vary and keep the socio-demographics constant at sample averages across the three types. This implies that the three types are representative w.r.t. gross wage rate and capital income, but not necessarily w.r.t. socio-demographics. The imputed capital incomes are calculated as averages of observed capital incomes for individuals with wage rates close to SEK 20, SEK 40 and SEK 80 per hour, respectively.[3]

In Figures 7.1–7.3 we illustrate how the total marginal effects of the tax and transfer systems vary with hours of work for these typical individuals. The figures illustrate the *total marginal effects*, that is, they include the effects of the income taxes, the indirect taxes and the transfer system. Hours of work (0–3 000 annual hours) is presented on the horizontal axis and the total marginal effects on the vertical axis. The broken line represents the 1980 tax system and the solid line illustrates the 1991 tax system. The budget sets are based on the wage rates and imputed capital incomes as stated in the headers.

The high marginal effects at low hours originate from the transfer systems, or more specifically, the income-dependent housing allowances. Figure 7.1 reveals that a low skilled person may actually face a higher total marginal effect

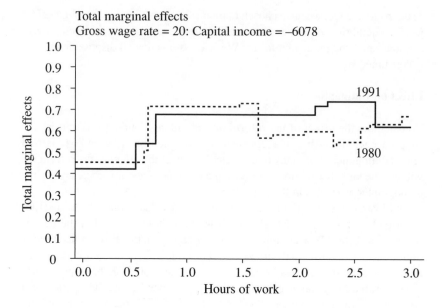

Figure 7.1   Total marginal effects, low skilled, wage rate 20 SEK/h

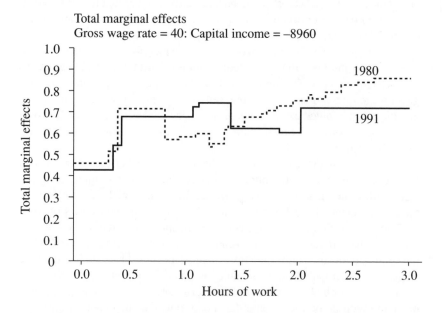

Figure 7.2   Total marginal effects, average skilled, wage rate 40 SEK/h

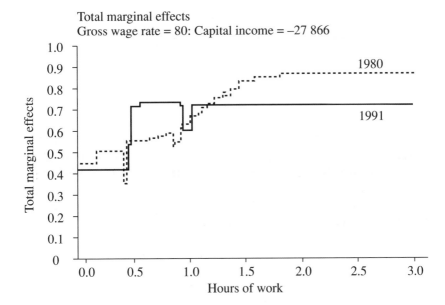

Figure 7.3   Total marginal effects, high skilled, wage rate 80 SEK/h

in the 1991 tax and transfer system than in the 1980 system. The figures also indicate that the widespread conception that the tax reform implied significantly lower marginal effects may be incorrect, at least for plausible hours and low or average skilled individuals.

In Table 7.1 we tabulate the observed total marginal effects at 1 040 and 2 080 annual hours of work, which represents part-time (50 per cent) and full-time working hours. Note that the marginal effects in some intervals vary significantly with hours of work. The 'point estimates' given in Table 7.1 should therefore be interpreted with care. Evaluating the marginal effect at a few hours more, or less, can give a different picture of the change in marginal effects. At part-time hours the marginal effects are, to a large extent, determined by the transfer system. The variations across individuals are thus determined by the family composition and housing situation rather than the capital and labour income.

The reform implied that the marginal effect for low paid men decreased by four percentage points at part-time hours. For average wage rates the marginal effect increased by 10 percentage points and for high paid men it increased by 5 percentage points. At full-time hours the total marginal effect for men with low wage rate has increased by about eight percentage points. This, however, is due to the transfer system, not the income tax system. For average wage rates the marginal effect has decreased by about four percentage points while for persons with high wage rates it has decreased by about 15 percentage points.

Table 7.1   Aggregate marginal effects at part and full time

Wage rate	Part time (1040 h/year)		Full time (2080 h/year)	
	1980	1991	1980	1991
20 SEK/h	0.71	0.67	0.59	0.67
40 SEK/h	0.58	0.68	0.76	0.72
80 SEK/h	0.67	0.72	0.87	0.72

The analysis of the marginal effects ignores the effect on the *level* of the budget sets, that is, the disposable income. In Table 7.2 we present the disposable income for the three typical individuals at part and full time working hours under the two tax systems. We also present the nominal differences and the percentage increase in disposable income.

Table 7.2   Disposable incomes at part- and full-time hours (in 1980 price level)

Wage rate	Part time (1040 h/year)				Full time (2080 h/year)			
	1980	1991	Δ	%Δ	1980	1991	Δ	%Δ
20 SEK/h	56 868	65 528	8660	15	68 039	76 640	8601	13
40 SEK/h	66 205	75 080	8874	13	88 391	95 756	7365	8
80 SEK/h	80 130	81 228	1098	1	104 311	119 465	15 153	15

The table indicates that, as a result of the tax reform, all three types experienced an increase in disposable income at full-time hours.[4] This is most pronounced for the high skilled type whose budget set shifted upwards by more than SEK 15 000 (about 15 per cent) at full time. The disposable income of the low and average skilled types also increased by a substantial amount. The low skilled individual received an additional SEK 8 601 because of the reform (mainly the transfer reform).

We conclude that the decrease in the total marginal effects were most pronounced for high skilled individuals and that the level of the budget sets increased for all types considered here.

3   THE NON-PARAMETRIC LABOUR SUPPLY FUNCTION

Parametric estimation methods impose further restrictions than those implied by economic theory. To overcome these restrictions non-parametric estimation methods have been developed and have become increasingly popular during the last decade. As argued in Blomquist and Newey (1999) the restrictions imposed by parametric methods are particularly severe when estimating labour supply functions generated by piece-wise linear budget constraints. They therefore develop a non-parametric method to estimate labour supply functions generated by non-linear piece-wise linear budget constraints. The method is based on the idea that labour supply can be viewed as a function of the entire budget set, so that one way to account non-parametrically for a non-linear budget set is to estimate a non-parametric regression where the variable in the regression is the budget set. In the special case of a linear budget constraint this estimator would be the same as non-parametric regression on wage and non-labour income, since these two numbers characterize the budget set. The method would then be similar to the one used in Hausman and Newey (1995).

Non-linear budget sets will be characterized by more numbers than two, for example, for piece-wise linear budget sets by location of kink points and slopes in between. An important part of the development of an estimation procedure is to find a way to characterize a non-linear budget constraint with just a few numbers. Blomquist and Newey (1999) suggest two methods to reduce the dimensionality of the estimation problem. The first step is to approximate the budget constraints with continuous budget constraints consisting of three piece-wise linear segments. In this way they reduce the dimensionality of the estimation problem to a manageable size. Separability assumptions reduce the dimensionality of the estimation problem further.

In this paper we use the non-parametric labour supply function presented in Blomquist and Newey (1999). We present this function in the Appendix. The function was estimated on data from three waves of the Swedish 'Level of living survey'. The data pertains to the years 1973, 1980 and 1990. The 1973 and 1980 data are briefly described in Blomquist (1983) and Blomquist and Hansson-Brusewitz (1990). The 1990 data are described in Blomquist and Newey (1999).[5] In the estimation only married or cohabiting men in ages 20–60 are used. We refer to the article by Blomquist and Newey (1999) for those who are interested in further details of the estimation procedure.

4 EFFECTS ON LABOUR SUPPLY

Decomposition of Tax Reform

The Swedish 1980–91 tax reform consists of several different parts. If the policy-makers were to make further changes in the tax system it would be of value for them to know the effect of the various components of the tax reform. Which changes in the past have stimulated labour supply most. What changes work in the opposite direction?

The decomposition can be made in several different ways. One way would be to follow the exact chronological order in which the reform has taken place. However, if we follow this route we intertwine decreases in marginal tax rates, base broadening and restrictions in rules for deductions. We believe this will blur the picture. Instead we have chosen to use the sequence given in Table 7.3.

Table 7.3   Applied decomposition of tax reform

(i)   Change the marginal taxes from the 1980 to the 1991 level taking account of changes in the personal exemption rules.
(ii)   Change the value added and payroll taxes from the 1980 to the 1991 levels.
(iii) Change the capital income tax rules and the rules for taxation of homes.
(iv)   Change the housing allowance and child allowance rules.

We calculate the effect of a reform, given the previous changes. This implies that the picture we obtain of the effect of the various parts of the reform depends on the sequence in which we introduce the various parts of the reform.

The specific order in which the components are introduced is motivated by the following. The decrease in marginal taxes was one of the cornerstones in the tax reform and many perhaps regard this as the quintessence of tax reform. One can regard some of the other changes in the tax system being of interest and politically feasible only after or in combination with decreased marginal taxes. The changes in the housing and child allowance systems were designed so as to correct for unwanted distributional effects of other changes in the tax system, so it is natural to place this part of the reform last in the sequence.

In our calculations presented below we assume that the spouse does not adjust her labour supply to the tax reforms, that is, we take the gross capital and labour income of the spouse as exogenous.[6] However, we do allow the husband to react to the changes in the post-tax income of the spouse, that is, we recalculate the net income of the spouse under each separate tax regime.

Labour Supply Effects

We will use the non-parametric labour supply function to perform several types of calculations. Our focus will be to illustrate how individuals with different gross wage rates have been affected. We start by showing a figure with several 'mongrel' curves. The mongrel function, first defined in Blomquist (1988), gives desired hours of work as a function of the gross wage, non-taxable non-labour income and taxable non-labour income, given a specific income tax system. A change in the tax system will shift the mongrel function. Hence, the five tax transfer systems defined by the 1980 tax system and the four changes described in Table 7.3 above will generate five different mongrel functions. In

Figure 7.4 we show mongrel functions that have been calculated for a fictitious individual with average values for the capital income and socio-demographics.

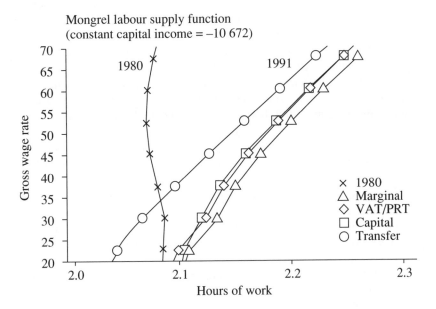

Figure 7.4   Mongrel supply function, constant capital income and socio-demographics[7]

The mongrel curve corresponding to the 1980 tax system is slightly backward bending in the range SEK 25–50 for the wage rate. For higher wage rates it is more or less vertical. The shape of a mongrel function depends both on the underlying preferences and the tax system. The shape of the mongrel function corresponding to the 1980 tax system is very much driven by the strong progressiveness of that tax system.

The right-most curve in the figure corresponds to a tax system where the 1980 tax system has been changed by the large decreases in the marginal taxes described in point (*i*) in Table 7.3. We see that this mongrel function has a positive slope throughout. Comparing this mongrel function with the one corresponding to the 1980 tax system, we find that the decrease in marginal tax rates work in the direction of increasing hours of work at all wage rates; only by a small amount at low wage rates, but by a substantial amount at high wage rates.

The other components of the tax reform all work in the direction of decreasing hours of work. Introducing the changes in the value-added and payroll taxes as described under (*ii*) in Table 7.3 shifts the mongrel curve to the left. The change in the indirect taxes decreases hours of work at all wage rates, more so for higher wage rates. Adding the changes in the rules for how capital income is taxed leads to a further small shift to the left of the mongrel curve, that is, the change in the rules for capital income taxation leads to a (small) decrease in hours of work at all gross wage rates. Finally, adding the changes in the transfer system leads to a further shift to the left of the mongrel function. At low gross wage rates there is a large shift, at high wage rates the shift is much smaller. That is, the change in the transfer system decreases hours of work at all wage rates. At low wage rates the decrease is substantial. Comparing the mongrel curves for the 1980 and 1991 tax systems, we see that at low wage rates the reform has led to a decrease in desired hours, at average hours there is a small increase whereas at high wage rates the increase is substantial.

In Figure 7.4 we set the capital income to the sample average. In reality, capital income varies with the gross wage rate in a systematic way. In 1980 individuals with large gross wage rates often had large negative capital incomes. This was often due to the fact that these individuals had owner-occupied homes with mortgages where interest payments were tax deductible. Of course, not all individuals with high gross wage rates had large negative capital incomes. In Figure 7.6 we have included the general pattern that the size of the deductions increases with the gross wage rate.

In order to impute capital income for different gross wage rates we have used the 1980 representative sample of married men described earlier and the following smoothing procedure. For a given gross wage rate W_i, the imputed capital income is calculated as an average of the observed capital incomes across individuals with a wage rate close to W_i. In Figure 7.5 we illustrate how the average capital income varies with the gross wage rate. In our calculation of the weighted average we can choose different 'bandwidths' within which we account for observed capital incomes. The broken line represents the imputed capital income as we include individuals with a gross wage plus minus 5 SEK from the desired wage rate. The solid line represents the imputed values as we use a window plus minus 10 SEK. In the following analysis we choose a bandwidth of plus minus 10 SEK.

Comparing Figures 7.4 and 7.6 we see that the general pattern of the effect of the different parts of the tax reform is the same in both figures. The most noteworthy difference is that the mongrel curve for the 1980 tax system is not backward bending at low wage rates. In fact, the desired hours of work has decreased for low wage rates and increased for high wage rates. There are at least two effects that influence this behaviour. First, and most important, is the income effect originating from the differences between sample means and imputed values for the capital income. For low wage rates we impute a capital income less negative in Figure 7.6 than in Figure 7.4. For high wage rates the opposite is true. The income effect thus implies that desired hours of work decrease for low wage

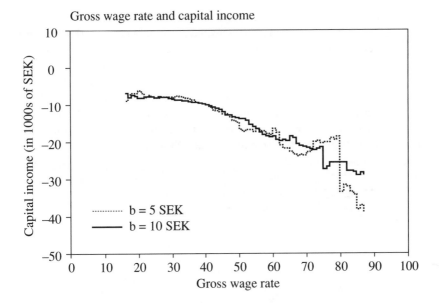

Figure 7.5   Smoothed average capital incomes vs gross wage rate

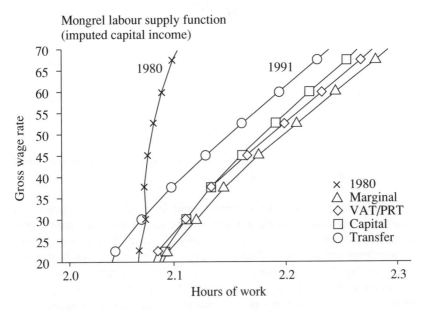

Figure 7.6   Mongrel supply function, imputed capital income varies with the gross wage rate, constant socio-demographics[8]

rates and increase for high wage rates. Second, in the 1980 tax system, the imputed capital income also influences the marginal tax rates. Here a more negative capital income reduces the marginal tax rates and thereby stimulates labour supply. This effect is less pronounced for low wage rates.

Finally, in Figure 7.7 we present calculations using the actual distribution of gross wage rates, capital income and socio-demographic variables of the 1980 representative sample. The number of observations at low and high wages are very few and therefore we have chosen to only illustrate the mongrel functions for observed wage rates between SEK 25 and SEK 65.

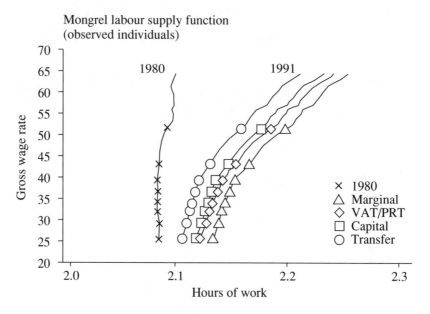

Figure 7.7   Mongrel supply function, observed distribution of capital incomes and socio-demographics[9]

The general pattern found in Figures 7.4 and 7.6 is valid also for Figure 7.7. However, there is one important difference. According to the mongrel curves in Figures 7.4 and 7.6 the changes in the transfer system reduced hours of work for low wage persons by a substantial amount. This feature is not as strongly suggested by Figure 7.7. Hence, taking account of the general covariance between the observed gross wage rate and the combination of the spouses' income and the socio-demographies we obtain a somewhat different picture of how low wage persons were affected by the reform in the transfer system. This shows that it is of value to complement calculations for 'typical' individuals with calculations building on an actual sample.

Three Typical Cases

Another way to illustrate how low and high skilled individuals were affected by the tax reform is to calculate the effect for three typical individuals defined in the same way as how we presented the marginal effects above. In Figure 7.8 and Table 7.4 we present such calculations. Figure 7.8 illustrates how desired hours of work vary as we implement the reforms stepwise. Above the point marked '1980' on the *x*-axis are hours of work for the low wage person (marked by a cross), the person with average wage (marked by a triangle) and the high wage person (marked by a diamond). Desired hours of work for the other tax systems are marked in a similar way. This presentation of the results is closely related to the mongrel functions previously analysed. The marks represent the points on the (original) mongrel functions presented in Figure 7.6 at the given gross wage rate and tax system. In Table 7.4 we tabulate the results.

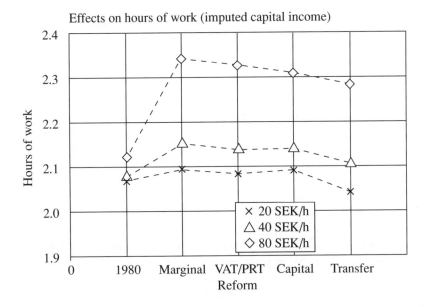

Figure 7.8   Effects of tax reform on hours of work for low, average and high skill individuals (imputed capital income varies with the gross wage rate; constant socio-demographics)

We see that under the 1980 tax system the desired hours of work were quite similar for low and high skilled individuals. Under the 1991 tax system this is no longer so. Desired hours for high skilled individuals are substantially higher than for low skill individuals. From Figure 7.8, and the corresponding table, we see that, to a large extent, it is the change in marginal tax rates that generates this result. The other parts of the tax reform decrease hours of work for all three typical individuals. However, although these decreases are not exactly the same for the three typical cases, they do not affect the relative magnitudes of hours of work for the three types.

Table 7.1 showed that the tax reform increased the total marginal effects at full hours of work for a low wage person, led to a small decrease in total marginal effects for a person with average wage rate, and implied a substantial decrease for a high wage person. Furthermore, Table 7.2 showed that the disposable income at plausible hours increased for all three types. These changes in marginal effects and levels are reflected in Table 7.4.

Table 7.4   Effects of tax reform on hours of work for low, average and high skilled individuals (imputed capital income varies with the gross wage rate)

Wage rate	1980	Marginal	VAT/PRT	Capital	Transfer
Low	2069	2091	2083	2091	2043
Average	2075	2151	2140	2139	2107
High	2121	2340	2325	2307	2284

The calculations shown in Table 7.4 imply that the effect of the overall tax reform was to *decrease* desired hours of work by 1.3 per cent for a typical low wage person, to increase desired hours by 1.5 per cent for a typical person with average wage rate and to increase it by 7.7 per cent for a person with a high wage rate.

Total Effects

Above we have focused on how the effect of the tax reform varies with the gross wage rate. It is also of great interest to calculate the total effects of the tax reform. To do this we have, for all individuals, in the 1980 sample, calculated desired hours for the five different tax systems. The distributions of hours of work obtained are shown in Figure 7.9 and Table 7.5. In Figure 7.9 we show a box plot of the distribution of hours of work for the five different tax systems.[10] In Table 7.5 we present the numeric values of the corresponding percentiles and the sample means in each tax-transfer system. Again, this figure is related to the mongrel function presented in Figure 7.7; the box plot simply represents the estimated distribution of desired hours of work under each separate tax system. Table 7.5 represents the box plot in numbers. The two bottom lines give the sample mean and the percentage differences between subsequent reforms.

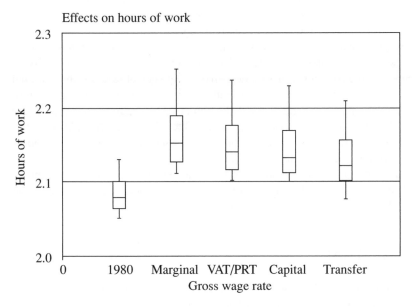

Figure 7.9   Box plot of the distribution of desired hours of work

Table 7.5   Distribution of hours of work

Percentiles	1980	Marginal	VAT/PRT	Capital	Transfer
90	2132	2256	2240	2233	2213
75	2102	2192	2179	2172	2159
50	2080	2154	2142	2135	2124
25	2065	2128	2118	2114	2102
10	2052	2113	2102	2100	2079
Sample means	2092	2172	2160	2154	2138
%Δ	–	3.8	–0.6	–0.3	–0.7

The figure indicates that, given the distribution of gross wages, capital incomes and socio-demographics of 1980, the marginal tax reform consider-

ably encourages labour supply, increasing the average hours of work from
2 092 to 2 172 (roughly 3.8 per cent). All other components of the reform reduce
the average hours of work. The rise in indirect taxes lowers the average about
12 hours per year ($\approx$–0.6 per cent). The reform of capital and property taxation
reduces the average about –0.3 per cent, where the disincentive effects are most
apparent for individuals associated with high hours of work (–0.3%). Finally,
the 1991 transfer system lowers the labour supply with approximately –0.7 per
cent. In particular, the lower decile reduce their supply by approximately 20
hours per year (more than –1 per cent). Considering the distribution of hours
of work, the dispersion increased by the aggregate reform, especially as
concerns the tails of the distribution. In our sequence of reforms, the marginal
tax reform and the change of the transfer system increase the dispersion of
hours. On the other hand, the introduction of increased indirect taxes and the
1991 system of capital taxation seems to tighten the distribution of hours. The
results from this section indicate that the marginal tax reform increases hours
of work while the other components reduce average labour supply for
married/cohabiting men. Considering the total reform the non-parametric model
predicts the average labour supply to increase by about 2.2 per cent and that
the distribution of hours becomes more dispersed.

5   SUMMARY

In this chapter we have studied how Swedish tax reform during 1980 to 1991
has affected married men's desired hours of work. In particular we have focused
on the extent to which low and high wage persons have been affected differently. To calculate changes in desired hours of work we have used a
non-parametric labour supply function. Part of our calculations have been done
for three fictitious typical persons. One low wage person, one person with
average wage rate and one person with a high wage rate. Our calculations show
that the effect of the changes in the tax and transfer systems on individuals'
budget constraints are: a) an increase in the total marginal effects and the
disposable income for a typical low wage person at full-time hours; b) a small
decrease in the marginal effects and an increase in the disposable income at
full-time hours for an individual with an average wage rate; and c) a decrease
in marginal effects and an increase in the disposable income at full-time hours
for a typical well paid individual. These changes in budget constraints imply
changes in desired hours of work for the three fictitious typical individuals; a
decrease of about 1.3 per cent in desired hours of work for the low wage person,
an increase of about 1.5 per cent for the average paid and a substantial increase,
about 7.7 per cent, for the high wage individual. Hence, low and high wage
persons have been affected differently by the tax and transfer reform.

We have also performed calculations using a representative sample from 1980. This sample consists of 864 married or cohabiting men aged 20–60. In our calculations we make use of the sample distribution of gross wage rates, capital income and socio-demographic variables. These results exhibit somewhat different features than the analysis based on typical low, average and high skilled individuals as a result of the covariation between observed socio-demographics and gross wage rate. Hence, these results intertwine the effects of the tax reform and the distribution of exogenous variables. As shown in Figure 7.7 above, given the 1980 tax and transfer system, there is practically no relation between the gross wage rate and desired hours of work. As the marginal tax rates decreased to the 1991 level, the estimated mongrel functions indicate that a strong positive correlation between gross wage rate and hours of work is induced. This positive relation, which is unaffected by the other components of the reform, is especially strong at high wage rates.

The mongrel functions based on the representative sample indicate that the decrease in marginal tax rates caused an increase in desired hours of work for individuals with low wage rates (around 20 SEK/h) of about 2 per cent, while for average (40 SEK/h and high wage rates (80 SEK/h) the increase equals 4.5 per cent and 9 per cent, respectively, and the sample average increased by 3.8 per cent. The other components of the tax reform counteract these effects and lower desired hours. Taking account of all parts of the tax reform we calculate that desired hours of work of low paid individuals increased by a small amount (less than 1 per cent), whereas the increase for average wage rates is almost 1.8 per cent and for high wage rates 7 per cent. In total the tax and transfer reform increased average desired hours of work by approximately 2 per cent.

NOTES

1. Henceforth all values are expressed in the 1980 price level.
2. This sample and the data source from which it originates is described in Blomquist and Hansson-Brusewitz (1990).
3. Exactly how these imputations are calculated is explained in section 4 below.
4. The tax reform was under-financed, which implies that public expenditures to a larger extent had to be financed by public debt. We do not account for how this structural tax deficit might have affected individuals and their labour supply.
5. Hours of work can be measured in several different ways. In this data source hours are measured as the number of paid-for hours. This implies that paid-for vacation hours are included in the measure of hours of work.
6. Aronsson and Palme (1998) estimate a parametric household model and use the estimated model to calculate the effect of tax reform. They find that the effect of the Swedish tax reform on married women's labour supply is quite small. This is because their labour supply is affected by two cancelling effects. The tax reform increases female net wage rates, which increases their labour supply. However, this is counteracted by a negative cross-effect from the increase in husbands' net wage rates. Aronsson and Palme also find that the cross-effect from women's wage rates to husbands' hours of work is quite small. The results of Aronsson and Palme

therefore suggest that the fact that we can not incorporate changes in women's hours of work might not be too serious.

7. In the approximation step of the estimator one needs to decide on the number of potential kinks. This implies that the mongrel functions are not continuous functions of the gross wage rate. To facilitate the analysis we have applied a smoothing procedure. In practice, a given point on the illustrated functions represents the average of the estimated desired hours for wage rates plus minus SEK 10 from the relevant wage rate.

8. See note 6.

9. See note 6.

10. Under each one of the tax-transfer systems we have ordered the observations w.r.t. desired hours of work. The box plot then illustrates the 10th and 90th percentiles by the whiskers, the 25th and 75 percentiles by the box and the median by the horizontal line inside the box.

11. The function presented in Table A7.1 might, to some readers, look like a parametric function. However, it is fully non-parametric. We refer the interested reader to Blomquist and Newey (1999) for a full account of this.

12. Ackum-Agell and Meghir (1995), using another data source and an instrumental variables estimation technique, present wage elasticities that are quite similar to those presented here.

REFERENCES

Ackum-Agell S. and C. Meghir (1995), 'Male Labour Supply in Sweden: Are Incentive Effects Important?', *Swedish Economic Policy Review* **2**: 391–418.

Agell J., P. Englund and J. Södersten (1996), 'Tax Reform of the Century – The Swedish Experiment', *National Tax Journal* **49**: 643–64.

Aronsson T. and M. Palme (1998), 'A Decade of Tax and Benefit Reforms in Sweden: Effects on Labor Supply, Welfare and Inequality', *Economica* **65**: 39–67.

Blomquist S. (1983), 'The Effect of Income Taxation on the Labor Supply of Married Men in Sweden', *Journal of Public Economics* **22**: 169–97.

Blomquist S. (1988), 'Nonlinear Taxes and Labor Supply', *European Economic Review* **32**: 1213–26.

Blomquist S. and U. Hansson-Brusewitz (1990), 'The Effect of Taxes on Male and Female Labor Supply in Sweden', *Journal of Human Resources* **25**: 317–57.

Blomquist S. and W. Newey (1999) 'Nonparametric Estimation with Nonlinear Budget Constraints', revised version of Working Paper 1997:24, Department of Economics, Uppsala University, Sweden.

Blomquist S., M. Eklöf and W. Newey (1998), 'Tax Reform Evaluation Using Non-parametric Methods: Sweden 1980–1991', NBER Working Paper, 6759.

Hausman J. and W. Newey (1995), 'Nonparametric Estimation of Exact Consumers Surplus and Deadweight Loss', *Econometrica* **63**: 1445–76.

Klevmarken N.A. (1997), 'Did the Tax Cuts Increase Hours of Work? A Pre-Post Analysis of Swedish Panel Data', Working Paper 1997:21, Department of Economics, Uppsala University, Sweden.

APPENDIX

In their estimation procedure Blomquist and Newey (1999) approximate actual budget constraints by constraints consisting of three piece-wise linear segments.

Denote the slopes of these segments by w_i, and the intercepts by y_i, $i = 1,2,3$, and define the variables $dy = \ell_1(y_1 - y_2) + \ell_2(y_2 - y_3)$ and $dw = \ell_1(w_1 - w_2) + \ell_2(w_2 - w_3)$. The estimated non-parametric function is then given in Table A7.1.[11]

Table A7.1 Non-parametric estimates using pooled data

Variables		
Const.	2.064	(49.85)
dy	−0.00210	(−4.37)
dw	−0.00145	(−1.16)
y_3	−0.0036	(−3.95)
w_3	0.00964	(6.61)
y_3^2	1.98×10^{-5}	(3.40)
wage elasticity	0.075	(6.61)
income elasticity	−0.038	(−4.31)
Cross validation	0.0373	

Note: t-values in parentheses. The delta method was used to calculate the t-values for the elasticities.

The wage and income elasticities are evaluated at the mean of the net wage rates and virtual incomes from the segments where individuals observed hours of work are located.[12]

PART IV

General Equilibrium Effects

8. The Dutch employment miracle and fiscal challenges of the twenty-first century

A. Lans Bovenberg, Johan J. Graafland and Ruud A. de Mooij[1]

1 INTRODUCTION

The Dutch economy has received a lot of acclaim recently because of its good economic performance, especially as far as employment is concerned. Twenty years ago, economists were discussing the Dutch disease. Now they talk about the Dutch miracle. However, the Netherlands still faces a number of serious problems on the labour market. In particular, as in other European countries, the Netherlands still suffers from a high level of inactivity, especially among the low skilled. Various reforms of labour-market institutions and the tax and social insurance systems have been put forward to fight this unemployment. These proposals include, in addition to reducing social benefits and minimum wages, cutting social insurance premiums and payroll taxes on low-skilled work, introducing wage subsidies for the long-term unemployed, and providing in-work benefits. The latter proposals aim to enhance low-skilled employment without seriously damaging the incomes of transfer recipients.

Another challenge for Dutch policy is related to the aging of the population. Aging implies that the increasing burden of social insurance benefits paid to the elderly must be financed by a relatively small number of workers. Indeed, the rising ratio between the number of inactive people collecting social insurance benefits and the labour force is a growing cause for concern. To mitigate this trend, the Dutch government aims at stimulating labour supply. Indeed, the low labour-force participation rates of women and the elderly leave substantial scope for raising labour supply. Proposals to boost labour supply include cutting marginal tax rates, reducing tax benefits to households with a non-participating partner, and decreasing early retirement benefits.

This paper employs an applied general equilibrium model for the Netherlands, the so-called MIMIC model, to explore various tax policies aimed at combating unemployment and raising the quality and quantity of labour supply.

MIMIC is designed so as to help Dutch policy-makers in investigating the structural labour-market implications of changes in the systems of taxation and social insurance. Hence, the model focuses on adequately describing wage formation, labour supply and demand, and the institutional details of taxation and social insurance. In doing so, the model combines a rich theoretical framework based on modem economic theories, a firm empirical foundation, and an elaborate description of the actual tax and social insurance systems in the Netherlands. The theoretical foundation of the model implies that one can interpret the model results rather easily in terms of rational microeconomic behaviour despite the disaggregated nature of the model and its rich institutional detail. This institutional detail makes the model especially relevant for policy making because actual policy proposals typically involve particular details of the tax and social insurance systems.

The chapter is organized as follows. The next section discusses the main factors behind the Dutch miracle as well as the remaining challenges facing Dutch policy makers. Section 3 provides a brief sketch of the MIMIC model. In section 4, this model is used to explore the effects of several tax policies on the labour market. Finally, section 5 concludes.

2   THE DUTCH EMPLOYMENT MIRACLE

Employment in persons in the Netherlands grew by about 1.6 per cent annually between 1983 and 1997. The corresponding figure for the EU-15 countries was only 0.4 per cent. If we express employment in terms of hours, the picture does not change fundamentally; in terms of employment growth, the Netherlands has been outperforming the rest of Europe by a considerable margin during the last fifteen years. This employment growth reflects rapid growth of labour supply during this period. Two main factors boosted Dutch labour supply, namely, first, relatively rapid population growth and, second, a gradual catching up of the female labour-force participation rate, which had been far lower than the European average. Despite the rapid expansion of labour supply, unemployment (measured as the number of persons who are actively looking for work) fell substantially. In 1983, the Dutch unemployment rate of 12 per cent exceeded the corresponding rate in the other EU countries by more than two percentage points. In 1997, in contrast, the Dutch rate of approximately 5 per cent was half the European average. The Dutch rate is now close to the unemployment rate in the United States.

2.1   The Role of Wage Moderation

Rapid employment growth in the Netherlands was facilitated by wage moderation. Whereas unit labour costs in Dutch manufacturing remained roughly constant over the last fifteen years, unit labour costs in other EU countries rose on average by about 2.5 per cent per year during this period. Wage moderation boosted employment through three main channels. First, it enhanced the profitability of businesses, thereby creating the room to increase investment. The share of labour income in enterprise income declined from 95 per cent in 1981 to around 81 per cent in recent years. Second, it improved the competitive position on world markets, thereby raising net exports. Third, it rendered growth more labour intensive. Indeed, the growth of labour productivity per hour worked lagged behind that in other EU countries.[2] Owing to the increase in employment in hours, however, growth of GDP *per capita* exceeded that in other EU countries.

The recent Dutch experience provides evidence for the effectiveness of wage moderation in stimulating employment. During the periods 1973–82 and 1983–94, growth of relevant world trade was similar. Dutch employment performance, however, was substantially better over the latter period. The main explanatory factor behind the improved performance of employment during 1983–94 is wage moderation. Also, an international comparison of employment growth and wage developments for the period 1983–94 confirms the importance of wage moderation. In particular, Dutch employment growth exceeded that in other countries while the wage share in national income declined more substantially.

2.2 Starting from the Dutch Disease

In the beginning of the 1980s, the Dutch economy was in dire straits: the fiscal deficit had widened to record levels, about two thirds of GDP was spent or redistributed by the government, taxation and social security contributions accounted for about half of GDP, business profitability and investment had plummeted dramatically, and for every ten employed persons there were more than eight persons on social benefits. Moreover, compared with other countries, GDP per head grew much more slowly than that in other EU countries.

In order to understand the origins of this crisis, we should go back to the 1960s when the welfare state expanded and rapid wage growth eroded profitability. Subsequently, the Netherlands, like the OECD countries, was hit by stagflation as a result of the abrupt increases in oil prices. Initially, the Dutch government attempted to address the economic downturn through expansionary policies and employment creation in the public sector. The rapid expansion of the public sector was financed by higher revenues from natural gas, higher taxes and premiums, and a widening fiscal deficit. At the same time, generous benefits in combination with lax administrative controls allowed employers and unions to put low-productive, redundant workers in social security schemes with open-ended benefits, such as the disability scheme.

When the second oil crisis hit at the end of the 1970s, Dutch policy-makers had lost all room for expansionary policies: the fiscal deficit was approaching 10 per cent of GDP, resulting in an explosion of the debt to GDP ratio. At that time, the Dutch economy was caught in a vicious circle of less employment and more claims on the welfare state. This vicious circle involved a lower level of employment boosting spending on open-ended social benefits. By raising labour costs, higher premiums depressed employment further. With the welfare state acting as a 'social hammock', the adverse macroeconomic shocks of the 1970s threatened the viability of the welfare state.

In the early 1980s, when unemployment was exploding, the need for drastic measures became increasingly apparent. The first Lubbers administration, which came to power in 1982, took decisive steps. In taking these measures, the government did not consult the social partners (i.e. the unions and employers). The character of the relationship between the government and social partners changed from bargaining over mutual concessions, like trading tax reductions for wage moderation, to the development of common policy orientations, like a strong employment performance. In this way, responsibilities of government and social partners were better delineated.

Social partners concluded a number of successful bilateral agreements in the 1980s and 1990s with non-binding qualitative recommendations on specific issues. These agreements contrast with the failed attempts to arrive at detailed 'social accords' of the 1970s. While the central organizations are issuing broad guidelines and agreements, these guidelines are implemented on a more decentralized, sectoral level. Actual wage negotiations, for example, are taking place at a sectoral level. This mix of centralized and decentralized negotiations has served the Netherlands quite well over the past fifteen years.

Wage moderation was facilitated by an agreement between social partners in 1982. Initially, the main factor behind wage moderation was the weak bargaining position of organized workers due to rapidly rising unemployment. Moreover, the easy option of reducing real wages by devaluating the currency was not available, as the guilder was closely linked to the Deutschmark. Later on, the positive results of wage moderation strengthened confidence in the revised consultation economy.

2.3   Reducing the Fiscal Burden

The government initially supported wage moderation by spending cuts, which resulted in lower replacement rates for social benefits. Among other things, the government broke the link between wages in the public sector and social benefits to wages in the private sector. Moreover, statutory social benefits were cut from 80 per cent to 70 per cent of gross wages. Finally, the minimum wage, to which the minimum social benefits are linked, was frozen in nominal terms. This reduced the after-tax minimum wage and the minimum social benefits in terms of the after-tax medium wage from 80 per cent in 1981 to 67 per cent in 1997.

The spending to GDP ratio fell from almost 67 per cent in 1983, which exceeded the EU average at the time by 10 percentage points, to 51 per cent in 1997, which is close to the EU average. Initially, the government used spending cuts to reduce the fiscal deficit rather than the tax burden. Fixed targets for deficit reduction became the main guiding post for fiscal policy in the 1980s. The Dutch experience thus shows that deficit reduction can be consistent with employment growth. When the deficit was reduced substantially in the beginning of the 1990s the government was in a position to support wage moderation through substantial reductions in the tax burden. The government has reduced the tax wedge on minimum incomes substantially in recent years: this in order to stimulate employment of low-skilled workers.

2.4 Restructuring of Social Insurance

It took a long time not only to get the public finances under control but also to turn the vicious circle of rising inactivity. The ratio of social security claimants to those employed stayed roughly constant between 1983 and 1995. Only by then could the number of social security recipients be stabilized and the ratio of social benefits to employment begin to fall. Cutting benefits had not been sufficient for reducing the number of recipients, in part because supplementary arrangements negotiated in collective labour agreements offset some of the cuts in disability and sickness benefits.

In the 1990s, eligibility criteria for social benefits were tightened. In 1993, the legal definition of the appropriate job was widened in the disability scheme. With residual earning power determining benefits, people who in the past would have received full benefits now receive only partial benefits. At the same time, the government reduced the discretion of the executive organizations by issuing specific criteria for determining disability and residual earning power. For existing claimants, a programme of reassessment was started in 1994.[3]

More recently, social security is being reformed more fundamentally by privatization of sickness insurance and introducing competition in disability insurance. These reforms have two primary aims (Besseling *et al.*, 1998). First, by introducing competition, efficiency gains are expected to be reaped in the implementation and administration of the insurance. Employers, private insurers, and administrators face more incentives to return the sick and disabled to work. Organizations that are most successful in preventing disability and encouraging revalidation and reintegration can exploit this as a comparative advantage.[4] Second, competition ensures that contributions closely match actuarial risks. Hence, employers are directly confronted with the costs and benefits of their actions on these risks; they can no longer shift the costs of their behaviour to a collective pool. This encourages employers to reduce risks by improving working conditions, and by cutting supplementary benefits.

2.5   Labour-market Flexibility

Another major factor behind the growth of employment is the growth of part-time and flexible jobs. These types of jobs account for most (three quarters) of the growth in employment since 1983. During the period 1983–93, most of the growth came from part-time work. More recently, flexible contracts started to grow faster. At the moment, about 40 per cent of workers has either a flexible contract (12 per cent) or a part-time contract (30 per cent).

A flexible contract features a limited duration (a fixed term) or a variable number of working hours. Especially, work through temporary work agencies has risen substantially in the last few years (to about 3.5 per cent of working hours). Dutch employers make more extensive use of temporary work agencies than any other EU country. More generally, employers increasingly use flexible contracts to avoid employment protection, to screen new employees, and to meet their need for flexibility.

Also, part-time work enhances working-time flexibility with respect to regular fluctuations in work loads. Moreover, it meets the needs of parents with young children who want to enter the labour market. Accordingly, by facilitating the access of women to the labour market (and exploiting their latent labour supply), part-time work has helped the participation rate of especially younger and middle-aged women to catch up with the European level. The job share of part-time work of 35 per cent is about twice as high as the EU average.

The match between the needs of employers and employees in the case of part-time work illustrates the win–win principle, namely, that enhanced flexibility can benefit not only the employer but also the employee; as tastes of employees become more heterogeneous and variable, market-oriented flexible working arrangements can be tailored to the individual needs of employees. To illustrate, rather than relying on uniform reduction of the work week, unions and employers are looking for solutions that allow individual employers and workers to find tailor-made solutions. Also, in the selection of the retirement age, unions and employers are looking for such tailor-made solutions that meet individual preferences on the basis of actuarially fair prices.

Flexible and part-time work contributes to a strong employment performance through other channels as well. First, it keeps more (especially young) people in touch with the labour market, thereby protecting their human capital and working skills. This, together with the improved access to the labour market, boosts effective labour supply and provides better insurance against human-capital risk. Second, a more flexible labour market is consistent with the need to tailor to technological and organizational innovations that demand more flexibility. For the same reasons, the Dutch government is currently also deregulating markets for goods and services.

2.6 Further Challenges

Now that we have looked at the impressive side of the Dutch model, it is time to turn the coin. The Dutch economy still faces a lengthy unfinished agenda.

2.6.1 Reducing unemployment

Most of the employment growth in recent years benefited those who did not draw on social benefits, like partners of bread-winners and young people lacking sufficient work history to be eligible for benefits. The recent reduction in the ratio between benefit recipients and employment has been attained mainly through an increase in employment rather than a decline in the number of benefit recipients.

Benefit recipients still seem to have very limited access to work. This is reflected in the high share of the long-term unemployed in overall unemployment. While the unemployment rates in the Netherlands and the United States are similar at the moment, the incidence of long-term unemployment is considerably higher in the Netherlands. Indeed, in terms of long-term unemployment and the low access to work of vulnerable workers without many marketable skills, the Dutch labour market is very much European rather than American. Thus, also, the Dutch have not yet been able to reconcile high benefit levels for needy groups with high levels of employment for these groups.

2.6.2 Raising labour supply

The current unemployment figure of 5 per cent substantially underestimates the overall level of inactivity in the Netherlands. Broadly defined unemployment, including hidden unemployment, may well amount to close on 20 per cent. In particular, the number of people collecting unemployment benefits is about 75 per cent higher than the number of unemployed who are actively searching for work. A large portion of those collecting benefits but not looking for work are older than 57.5 years old. This group is exempted from the obligation to actively look for work in order to be eligible for unemployment benefits. At the same time, in addition to discouraged workers and involuntary part-time workers, a large number of disability claimants are estimated to be hidden unemployed. Indeed, the share of people collecting disability benefits is still about twice the rate in neighbouring countries. Disability, unemployment, and early retirement schemes have reduced the participation rate of those aged 50–64 to very low levels. This low participation rate for older people is particularly worrying in light of the aging of the population. Inadequate labour supply may give rise to tensions on the labour market. These tensions may reduce profitability and investment, thereby bringing the Dutch miracle to an abrupt end and possibly setting in motion another vicious circle.

The low unemployment rate thus may be a sign of weakness rather than strength because it indicates that not many people on social security benefits are actively looking for work. Indeed, the success of the Dutch economy should not be judged on the basis of the unemployment rate but rather on the way it exploits the human capital of its population. On this latter score, the Dutch still have a long way to go.

2.7 Agenda for the Future

2.7.1 Social security reform

A first major challenge for the Dutch government in the coming decades will be to activate the latent labour supply locked in social security schemes and to increase the access of vulnerable groups to work. Technological and organization developments increasingly put vulnerable individuals with little marketable skills at risk. To prevent long-run dependency and social exclusion, the government should shift away from passive support towards active support that strengthens the earnings capacity, skills, adaptability, and employability of vulnerable individuals. Whereas social benefits were originally intended to carry people over relatively short unemployment spells, structural unemployment and long-term dependency require more active, interventionist policies with conditional and in-kind benefits (e.g. training) to avoid social exclusion.

Conditional transfers based on the transaction principle (i.e. balancing the carrot of the benefit with the stick of certain obligations) can be used to screen claimants, thereby alleviating moral hazard. Moreover, in-kind transfers can link support to activities (such as training, unpaid trial employment, community work) that encourage rather than discourage re-entry into employment. A shift towards more active policies involving conditional and in-kind benefits calls for tailor-made solutions implemented by a decentralized benefit administration that exploits its information advantage about individual circumstances. More generally, a more heterogeneous and diverse population requires more tailor-made and innovative solutions. Accordingly, social security administrations should be transformed from hierarchical bureaucratic organizations to more decentralized and customer-oriented bodies.

A channel through which labour supply can be increased is a higher average effective retirement age. This age is currently below 60 years in the Netherlands. Also this requires a mix of instruments at both the demand and supply sides. Moreover, life-long learning should increase employability of older workers by increasing their capability to learn and adapt. At the demand side, employers can be encouraged to employ older workers not only by increasing their skills but also by reducing wage costs. To achieve this, age-related pay schemes may have to be reconsidered so that wages can be better adjusted to individual productivity levels. At the supply side, early retirement schemes should be made actuarially fair to facilitate efficient retirement decisions. As people become more flexible, it is more important that they are confronted with proper incentive structures. Various routes for withdrawing from the labour force are substitutes. Accordingly, in confronting workers with the social costs of their labour-supply decisions, the government should pursue a comprehensive approach. Various conditional social security benefits, such as unemployment and disability benefits, are subject to moral hazard. As the workforce ages, these moral hazard problems become more serious as older workers are subject to higher disability and unemployment risk.

2.7.2 Fiscal policy
The number of hours worked per person is very low by international standards. Hence, the participation rate in terms of hours is still low. To encourage labour supply and broaden the tax base, a further reduction in the overall tax burden would be welcome. A lower aggregate tax burden would reconcile the need on the one hand, to increase the access to work of low-skilled labour by reducing tax rates on lower incomes and, on the other hand, to encourage workers to increase their working hours by reducing marginal tax rates. Indeed, as individuals become more flexible in selecting their own working hours, high marginal tax rates become more distortionary. In this connection, lower marginal tax rates could help facilitate a further expansion of female labour supply. There still is substantial room to raise the female participation rate, especially in number of hours. Survey information does indeed indicate that many women would like to work longer hours. Also better child-care facilities would facilitate this process.

Wage subsidies or vouchers for the long-term unemployed can be used as a particular form of in-kind benefits. In addition to stimulating and strengthening supply, lower taxes on low-skilled labour can help to boost demand. The rest of this chapter explores several of these fiscal policy measures aimed at raising labour-market participation in the Netherlands.

3   MIMIC

Policy-makers face several trade-offs in designing fiscal reform. For example, policies aimed at raising labour supply are typically not the most effective in reducing unemployment and *vice versa*. To illustrate the various trade-offs, we use an applied general equilibrium model for the Netherlands, called MIMIC.[5] The model draws on microeconomic theory to derive supply and demand from optimizing behaviour by decentralized agents. On the goods markets, firms set prices and supply goods, which are demanded by households and the public sector. In the open Dutch economy, the terms of trade on the commodity market is endogenous because domestically and foreign produced goods are imperfect substitutes. In modelling the labour market, the model departs from the traditional assumption in most applied general equilibrium models of market clearing. In modelling various labour-market imperfections that give rise to involuntary unemployment, MIMIC employs modern labour-market theories. In particular, it includes elements of wage bargaining, efficiency wages, and costly job matching. In this way, the model describes equilibrium unemployment in terms of the structure of the tax system, minimum wages, and the features of social insurance.

Another distinctive feature of MIMIC is a disaggregated household model aimed at adequately describing the impact of the statutory rates of taxation and social security premiums on labour supply and the income distribution. In particular, the model accounts for heterogeneity in household composition, labour-market status, educational level, wages, and preferences for leisure. Incorporating this heterogeneity allows the model to explore the various trade-offs facing policy-makers, including those between equity and efficiency.

MIMIC has a firm empirical basis. Various crucial relationships in the model, including contractual wage formation and the production function, have been estimated from time-series data. Furthermore, microeconometric estimates on Dutch labour supply have been used to calibrate the labour supply model. Moreover, income distributions have been calibrated by employing micro data. Finally, MIMIC pays close attention to the institutional details of the tax and social insurance systems. This makes the model especially suitable for exploring the implications of various detailed tax proposals for the labour market.[6]

This section is organized as follows. We first elaborate on the production sector of MIMIC which follows a more or less standard approach. Section 3.2 discusses the modelling of the household sector in MIMIC, which is characterized by a high degree of disaggregation. Section 3.3 discusses the model of wage formation in MIMIC while section 3.4 elaborates on the matching process between vacancies and the unemployed looking for a job. Section 3.5 discusses the modelling of public institutions while section 3.6 gives an overview of the model structure in a nutshell.[7]

3.1 Firm Behaviour

3.1.1 Commodity markets

MIMIC contains six firm sectors: the exposed sector, the sheltered sector, the construction sector, the non-market service sector, the mining sector (mainly natural gas), and the residential sector (i.e. the exploitation of real estate). The exposed and the sheltered sectors are the largest sectors. The sheltered sector supplies labour-intensive services facing little competition from abroad. It includes trade, banking and insurances and other private services. The exposed sector consists of capital-intensive industries subject to intense foreign competition. This sector includes manufacturing, agriculture, and transport.

The markets on which the firms in the exposed and sheltered sectors operate feature monopolistic competition. In particular, various market segments exist. Within each market segment, a large number of symmetric domestic firms compete. Each firm produces a unique good, which is a close, but imperfect, substitute for goods produced by other domestic firms competing on the same market segment. In the exposed sector, also foreign firms operate on these market segments. However, within any market segment, a commodity supplied by a domestic firm is a closer substitute for the output of another domestic firm than for the output of a foreign firm. This reconciles small observed profit margins of 5 to 10 per cent with relatively low price elasticities of import and export demands.[8] Figure 8.1 presents the nesting structure of the demands for the outputs of the firms in the sheltered and exposed sectors.

Using a CES function to describe this nesting structure of demand and assuming that the number of market segments is so large that the market share of a single market segment can be neglected, we arrive at the following expression for the inverse own-price elasticity of demand, ε:

$$\varepsilon = \frac{1}{\sigma_d + (\sigma_m - \sigma_d)S_d + (\sigma_s - \sigma_m)S_m} \tag{8.1}$$

where S_d denotes the market share of the individual firm in total domestic output on a particular market segment and S_m represents the market share of the individual firm in total output on a market segment. The substitution elasticity between outputs of domestic firms within a market segment is denoted by σ_d, that between outputs of domestic and foreign firms by σ_m, and that between various market segments by σ_s.

The own-price elasticity is an important determinant of pricing decisions. In particular, profit maximizing firms set prices as a mark-up on marginal costs:

$$P_y = \frac{1}{1 - \varepsilon} MC \tag{8.2}$$

where MC and P_y stand for the marginal costs per unit of output and the output price, respectively. The model is calibrated in such a way that the mark-ups are in line with empirical information on profit rates.

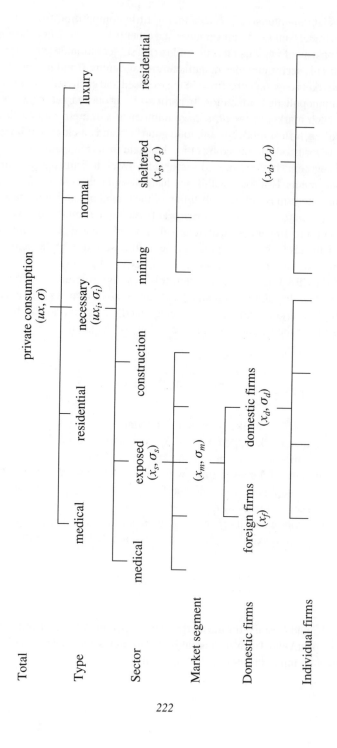

Figure 8.1 Output market structure in MIMIC

3.1.2 Input structure

Finns produce their firm-specific output by using five inputs: intermediaries, capital,[9] unskilled labour, low-skilled labour, and high-skilled labour. The transformation process is described by a constant elasticity of substitution (CES) neo-classical production function, which exhibits constant returns to scale. The substitution elasticities between the various inputs are based on recent empirical estimates by Draper and Manders (1996). In particular, the substitution elasticity between capital and the composite of labour inputs equals 0.15 in the exposed sector and 0 in the other sectors. The substitution elasticity between the three labour types is 1.1 in the exposed sector, 2.0 in the sheltered sector and the construction sector, and 1.5 in the non-market service sector.

Cost minimization yields input demands as a function of output and marginal input costs. In minimizing costs, firms take prices of non-labour inputs as given. Labour costs, C_l, are given by:

$$C_l = \sum_j W_j L_j + v\overline{W}_j Vl_j \qquad (8.3)$$

where W_j denotes the wage rate of a worker (with average labour productivity) of labour type j, L_j employment of labour type j, Vl_j the number of vacancies of labour type j, and $v\overline{W}_j$ search costs per vacancy of labour type j. A bar over a particular variable denotes the economy-wide average of that variable. Search costs are proportional to the average gross wage of the particular labour type, $\overline{W}_j$, which is exogenous to the firm, and the number of vacancies posted by the employer, Vl_j, which is given by:

$$Vl_j = (dL_j/dt + \omega_j L_j)/z_j \qquad (8.4)$$

where ω_j stands for the average quit rate of workers of type j and z_j denotes the rate at which vacancies for type j are filled. This specification implies that marginal labour costs, which are an important determinant of labour demand, increase if search costs rise because vacancies are open for a longer time. The rate at which vacancies are filled depends on the relative wage offered by the employer:

$$z_j = (W_j/\overline{W}_j)^\beta \bar{z}_j \qquad (8.5)$$

where W_j represents the wage offered by the firm and $\bar{z}_j \square Ml_j/Vl_j$ denotes the average rate at which vacancies for type j are filled, where Ml_j is the number of successful job matches.

3.1.3   Demand for black labour

For each skill type, firms in the sheltered sector and the construction sector can hire labour from the black market. This black labour combines with formal labour of the corresponding labour type in an additional nest of the CES-production function. The elasticity of substitution between black and formal labour is set at 2, which is based on empirical evidence in Baartmans *et al.* (1986).

Furthermore, firms may pay formal labour in part informally, that is, without reporting the wages to the tax authority. Firms determine this informal labour (L_c) by trading off lower taxes against a potential penalty for fraud. This yields the following optimal demand for informal labour (L_c):

$$L_c = \frac{(\tau_m)^\varepsilon}{\Delta} \tag{8.6}$$

where τ_m denotes the marginal burden of collective levies (i.e. taxes and social security premiums) on employers, and Δ depends on the potential penalty on tax evasion. In the absence of empirical evidence, the elasticity of informal labour with respect to the marginal tax is based on best-guess values and set at 1.0 for unskilled workers, 0.5 for low-skilled workers and 0.3 for high-skilled workers.[10]

3.2   Household Behaviour

3.2.1   Disaggregation

MIMIC distinguishes 40 types of households in order to adequately describe labour supply and explore the income distribution. In particular, MIMIC distinguishes couples, single persons, single parents, pensioners and students. To model the specific labour supply behaviour of those close to retirement, people aged between 55 and 65 years are represented by a separate household type. Couples consist of a so-called bread-winner (i.e. the individual with the higher personal income) and a partner (i.e. the adult with the lower personal income). Couples are subdivided into families with children and families without children. Individuals within each household may differ with respect to their skill level and their job status (i.e. holding a job in the formal sector or collecting a social benefit). Figure 8.2 presents an overview of the household types in MIMIC.

For each household type, MIMIC employs class-frequency income distributions based on micro data to describe the distribution of gross incomes. These income distributions are important determinants of the efficiency costs of high marginal tax rates: the more people are concentrated in a particular income range, the higher become the efficiency costs of high marginal rates in this income range. By applying the corresponding statutory tax and premium rates

Household type
- Single persons, younger than 55
- Families with children
- Families without children
- Families in which one partner receives a social benefit
- One-parent families
- Persons between 55 and 65
- Students
- Aged persons (over 65 years)

Skill type (for each household type)
- High skilled
- Low skilled
- Unskilled

Benefit type
- Unemployment insurance benefit
- Disability benefit
- Social assistance benefit

Per household type
Time participating on the formal labour market
- not participating (partners only)
- 30 per cent participation (partners only)
- 40 per cent participation (single persons only)
- 50 per cent participation (partners only)
- 80 per cent participation
- full-time participation (not for partners)
- 120 per cent participation (not for partners)

Figure 8.2   Household types in MIMIC

to gross incomes, MIMIC determines net incomes and the average and marginal tax rates that determine labour-supply decisions.[11]

3.2.2   Consumption demand
In optimizing utility, households first determine how to optimally allocate their income over various consumption commodities, while taking labour supply as given. Consumption consists of three categories: labour-intensive services from the formal market, labour-intensive services from the black market, and other consumption from the formal market.[12] In the CES utility structure, labour intensive services are first aggregated before combining with other consumption from the formal market to yield total consumption. The elasticity of substitution between labour-intensive consumption and other consumption equals 1.1 (see Eijgenraam and Verkade, 1988). The elasticity between labour-intensive services from the formal market and the black market is set at 2 (see e.g. Baartmans *et al.*, 1986).

3.2.3   Labour supply
In the second step of the optimization procedure, labour supply S is selected from a limited set of discrete options.[13] In particular, single persons can select

four options: a full-time job, a part-time job of 40 per cent or 80 per cent of a full-time equivalent, or a job that amounts to 120 per cent of a full-time equivalent. Bread-winners can choose between 80 per cent, 100 per cent and 120 per cent of a full-time equivalent. Partners of bread-winners may opt for non-participation and a part-time job of 30 per cent, 50 per cent or 80 per cent of a full-time equivalent. For each of the discrete choices an individual faces, utility is determined by:

$$G = U(Y, V) - \psi \mid S - \bar{S} \mid \tag{8.7}$$

where Y represents real household income that is allocated to consumption. Leisure V in the unconstrained optimum can be derived from the time constraint:

$$V = 1 - S \tag{8.8}$$

where the time endowment is normalized to unity. The autonomous preference for labour supply (_) varies between households and follows from a continuous probability density function. Optimal labour-supply behaviour of each household strikes a balance between, on the one hand, minimizing the loss associated with deviations from the autonomous preference (_) and, on the other hand, the highest possible utility from $U(.)$. The uniform probability density function of _ is determined such that the model reproduces micro data on Dutch labour supply. The calibration of the parameter ψ and the substitution elasticity between leisure and consumption ensure that the model reproduces labour-supply elasticities estimated in the empirical literature for the Netherlands. In particular, the uncompensated wage elasticity of labour supply by partners is set at 1.0, single persons feature a corresponding elasticity of 0.25 and most bread-winners of around 0.1. Older breadwinners, who may change their retirement decisions in response to changes in wages, feature a somewhat higher elasticity of 0.15. The income elasticities of labour supply are smaller than the wage elasticities, namely 0.2 for partners, 0.05 for single persons and almost zero for bread-winners.

3.2.4 Informal labour supply

In the next step of the optimization procedure, the following extended utility function determines the allocation of overall labour supply (S) across the formal labour market and the black labour market (S_z):

$$Z = G(.) - \delta^{\beta_z} S_z \tag{8.9}$$

The supply of black labour, S_z, is a discrete choice and amounts always to 20 per cent of a full-time equivalent. The optimal choice between formal and black labour trades off higher subutility $G(.)$ from the option with black labour (because black wages typically exceed after-tax wages in the formal labour market) against the moral cost associated with supplying black labour, measured by the parameters δ and β_z. The latter parameter is heterogeneous across households and is taken from a continuous uniform probability density function. Only households with a small β_z, that is, those who face low moral costs of supplying black labour, choose the option with 20 per cent black labour supply. The density function of β_z is such that the model reproduces the size of the black economy in the Netherlands, which is estimated at about 3 per cent of GDP. The parameter δ is set to reproduce an uncompensated wage elasticity of black labour supply of 0.75 found by Koopmans (1994).

Apart from labour in the underground sector, households can be involved also in a second type of informal labour, namely housekeeping activities. Time spent on housekeeping activities is modelled as a fixed fraction of leisure. We adopt the time allocation survey of SCP (1995) for the calibration of these fractions. Housekeeping yields household production, which is a perfect substitute for the consumption of labour-intensive services. Compared with the supply of black labour-intensive services, household production represents a larger part of the informal economy.

3.2.5 Training

A separate intertemporal optimization model (see de Mooij, 1999) endogenizes training enrolment. In this framework, higher future wages due to training are traded off against the effort cost of training. These effort costs are heterogeneous so that only part of the workers find it optimal to train. In particular, the number of workers that engages in training programmes depends on the replacement rate between the expected wage of a trained worker and the wage of an untrained worker. Training affects the distribution of workers across different skill types and determines the average productivity of workers within each skill type. The incentives for training depend importantly on the rate of return to training. This parameter is calibrated at 12 per cent, which is somewhat lower than suggested by most empirical estimates for the Netherlands (see Groot *et al.*, 1998).

3.3 Wage Formation

On the formal labour market, MIMIC distinguishes between contractual wages (sub-section 3.3.1), which are determined in collective negotiations between employers and unions, and incidental wages (sub-section 3.3.2), which are set by individual employers based on the tightness of the skill-specific labour markets. The distinction between contractual and incidental wages is important because social benefits are linked to contractual, rather than incidental, wages. Hence, higher incidental wages reduce the replacement rate.

3.3.1 Contractual wages

Wages are determined by a right-to-manage model in which an employers' organization and a trade union bargain over wages while employers determine employment. From this model, we arrive at the following wage equation:

$$W = \frac{\dfrac{\chi_1 \hat{W}}{1-TM} + \chi_2 Ph}{\dfrac{\chi_1(1-TA)}{1-TM} + \chi_2} \qquad (8.10)$$

where W represents the reservation wage, $\chi_1 = \alpha + \text{‰}(1 - \alpha)/(1 - \varepsilon)$, $\chi_2 = \text{‰}(1 - \alpha)$, α denotes the bargaining power of the employers' organization and h stands for labour productivity. Expression (8.10) reveals that the contractual wage (W) strikes a balance between the threat points of both bargaining parties. If the employers' organization dominates bargaining ($\alpha = 1$ so that $\chi_2 = 0$), the union is driven back to its threat point and the after-tax wage equals the reservation wage. The contractual wage increases if the union exerts more bargaining power, that is, if α becomes smaller. Since a wage contract will be concluded only if the maximum after-tax wage offer $((1 - TA)Ph)$ exceeds the minimum wage claim (_), (8.10) implies that the marginal tax rate unambiguously reduces the wage. At a given average tax rate (TA), a rise in the marginal tax rate implies that the government absorbs a larger share of a wage increase. Hence, increasing wages becomes less attractive for the bargaining parties (see also Hersoug *et al.*, 1986).

Instead of looking for another job on the official labour market, the employee may seek work in the informal sector. Accordingly, the reservation wage _ amounts to a weighted average of the opportunity wage in the official labour market and that in the informal sector. The opportunity wage in the official labour market depends on the expected wage in other jobs and on the unemployment benefit because a laid-off employee generally spends some time in unemployment before finding another job. The informal labour market, in which no taxes are levied, consists of home production and the black labour market. From these assumptions concerning the reservation wage, we arrive at the following wage equation:

$$\log W = \log h + \log P + \log\left[1 + \theta\left(\frac{P_c}{P(1-TM)}\right)\right]$$

$$- \log\left[1 + \frac{\chi_1}{\chi_2}\frac{1-TA}{1-TM}\left[1 - \beta_w\left(UR - (1-U)\right)\right]\right] \qquad (8.11)$$

where $\theta = (1 - \beta_w) \gamma \chi_1/\chi_2$ and $R \square B/(1 - TA)W$ stands for the replacement rate, defined as the net unemployment benefit as a ratio of the after-tax wage rate. Expression (8.11) implies that, at a given coefficient of progression $(1 - TM)/(1 - TA)$, a higher tax rate unambiguously increases the wage. Intuitively, taxes raise the relative attractiveness of working in the informal sector, thereby strengthening the bargaining position of the union in the formal sector.[14]

Equation (8.11) reveals that, at a constant coefficient of progression, the same effect on wages is exerted by the various components of the wedge between, on the one hand, the after-tax wage deflated by the consumer price and, on the other hand, the gross wage deflated by the producer price.

Another implication of equation (8.11) is that the wage effects of the replacement rate and unemployment rate are related. If unemployment is low, spells of unemployment are only short. Hence, the unemployment benefit level exerts only a small impact on the alternative wage in the official sector. At the same time, the influence of the unemployment rate on wages diminishes with the level of the replacement rate, becoming zero if the replacement rate equals one. A final implication of equation (8.11) is that labour productivity affects wages with a unitary elasticity.

Graafland and Huizinga (1996) estimated equation (8.11) in non-linear form and found that, on average for the sample period, the positive elasticity of the average tax is six times (0.6) as large in absolute value than the negative elasticity of the marginal tax rate (–0.1). The elasticity of the consumer price equals the sum of the elasticities of the marginal and average tax rates, that is, 0.5. Hence, at constant unemployment and replacement rates, the incidence of a higher tax wedge (by simultaneously increasing average and marginal tax rates) is split equally between employers and employees in terms of, respectively, higher gross wage costs and lower after-tax wages.

Contractual wages in the Netherlands are determined mainly through collective bargaining at the industry level. Since both skill-specific and macroeconomic factors play a role, the wage equation (8.11) is specified both on the macro-economic level and for the three skill types. The macro wage equation adopts macro-aggregates for the average tax rate, the marginal tax rate, the replacement rate and unemployment. Skill-specific aggregates are used in the skill-specific wage equations. Based on Graafland and Lever (1996),[15] the macro and skill-specific wage equations carry equal weights in determining the contractual wage for a specific skill.

3.3.2 Incidental wages

The wage structure among skills is further modified by a skill-specific, so-called incidental, wage component. The employer can use this incidental wage component, which is defined as the difference between the wage offered by the firm and the contractual wage determined by collective bargaining to minimize search costs. The incidental wage can be interpreted as an efficiency wage associated with hiring costs. In setting incidental wages, the employer thus exerts some monopsony power. Incidental wages are derived as a mark-up over the contractual wage. This mark-up rises with the tightness of the labour market as reflected in the ratio between vacancies and employment.

3.3.3 The black labour market
The black labour market is perfectly competitive. On this market, household demand for black labour-intensive services and firm demand for black labour are confronted with household supply of black labour.

3.4 Matching on the Labour Market

3.4.1 Heterogeneous matchings
On the formal labour market, unemployed workers of each skill meet firms that search for appropriate employees with those skills. A matching function describes the number of matches, Ml_j, for each type of labour:

$$Ml_j = Co_j fm_j \qquad (8.12)$$

where Co_j denotes the number of contacts between employers and the unemployed while fm_j stands for the share of these contacts resulting in successful matchings. The number of contacts follows from a Cobb–Douglas contact function, which features constant returns to scale:

$$Co_j = \gamma_j Vl_j^\rho (s_j U_j)^{1-\rho} \qquad (8.13)$$

where Vl_j represents the number of vacancies, s_j the search intensity of the unemployed, U_j unemployment, and γ_j a mismatch parameter, which reflects the mismatch due to differences between vacancies and unemployment in terms of skill, work experience and location.[16]

The share of contacts that results in an agreement depends on the acceptance rate of the employers and the unemployed. For a contact to result in a successful match, the productivity of the job match must exceed both the reservation wage of the unemployed and the minimum productivity standard of the employer (see below). The productivity of an individual job–worker combination is match-specific. In view of the heterogeneity of reservation wages and productivity, the average acceptance rate is modelled as a CES function of the shares of contacts acceptable to employers (fe_j) and the unemployed (fu_j):

$$fm_j = (fe_j^{-\lambda} + fu_j^{-\lambda})^{-1/\lambda} \qquad (8.14)$$

3.4.2 The minimum productivity standard

The search and selection strategy of employers involves the number of vacancies (discussed in sub-section 3.1.2 above) and a minimum productivity standard determining the fraction of matches that is acceptable to the employer. Under the assumption that individual workers of type j are perfect substitutes, the minimum productivity standard is derived from the condition that marginal labour costs per efficiency unit must be the same for workers with different labour productivities:

$$he_j = \frac{hn_jWm}{W_j\left[1+\dfrac{v}{z_j}\left(\omega_j+r-\dfrac{\dfrac{d}{dt}\left(\overline{W}_j/z_j\right)}{\overline{W}_j/z_j}\right)\right]} \qquad (8.15)$$

where he_j denotes the minimum productivity standard for labour type j while hn_j and $\overline{W}_j$ represent the average productivity index and wage level of all new employees of type j. Wm stands for the sector-specific effective minimum wage.[17] Marginal labour costs include wage and search costs (see expression (8.3)). Equation (8.15) implies that a higher effective minimum wage decreases the number of candidates whose productivity is acceptable to the employer. This raises vacancy duration, thereby boosting search costs for employers, and thus depressing labour demand.

The productivity of an individual job–worker combination of type j is match-specific. It follows from a log-normal distribution with standard deviation sd_j, which is based on micro data of the wage distribution for each type of labour, and an average productivity that is normalized at 1. The share of contacts that is acceptable to the employer can thus be defined as:

$$fe_j = 1 - G((\log he_j)/sd_j + 0.5sd_j) \qquad (8.16)$$

where G is the cumulative distribution function of the standard normal distribution.

3.4.3 The behaviour of the unemployed

Unemployed persons are drawn randomly from the pool of labour supply. A separate model akin to the search model of Pissarides (1990) is developed to model the behaviour of the unemployed in terms of two endogenous variables, namely the search intensity and the reservation wage.[18] This model applies to a representative unemployed worker of each skill and thus abstracts from heterogeneous preferences for leisure. In raising search intensity, the unemployed trade off the loss of leisure against the increased probability of moving into the employed state. The employed state yields more life-time utility than the unemployed state does because of higher income in work and because the unemployed may feel rejected and socially isolated. The optimal search intensity increases in the average transition rate into employment (because it raises the marginal return on search) and decreases in the replacement rate (which decreases the difference in life-time utility between the employed and unemployed states).

The second variable describing the behaviour of the unemployed is the reservation wage, which is the wage at which an unemployed job seeker is indifferent between the employed and unemployed states. The reservation wage rises with both the unemployment benefit and the average transition rate into employment. Together with the log-normal wage distribution of job offers, the reservation wage determines the acceptance rate of the unemployed (i.e. the share of contacts that is acceptable to unemployed job seekers).

A higher replacement rate thus exacerbates the mismatch on the labour market by lowering search intensity and raising the reservation wage. This pushes up incidental wages, thereby raising unemployment in equilibrium.

3.4.4   Short- and long-term unemployment

Long-term unemployed typically differ from short-term unemployed in their search behaviour, reservation wage and productivity. MIMIC therefore distinguishes between short- and long-term unemployment by using a steady-state flow model for job matches akin to Holmlund and Linden (1993).[19] In particular, the long-term unemployed are less productive than the short-term unemployed because of some lost human capital during their prolonged period of unemployment. If they find a job, the long-term unemployed face some (exogenous) probability to restore their human capital. The long-term unemployed take this benefit of entering work into account and hence feature a relatively low reservation wage. This is consistent with empirical evidence (see e.g. van den Berg (1990) and Devine and Kiever (1991)). Accordingly, rather than the reservation wage, the minimum effective productivity standard determining the acceptance rate of the employer mainly restricts the number of successful matches for the long-term unemployed. For the short-term unemployed, in contrast, a relatively high reservation wage is the most important barrier to successful job matches. As a relatively large number of long-term unemployed are unskilled, the minimum effective productivity standard amounts also to the most important restriction in the job-matching process of the unskilled.

Search intensity falls over the unemployment spell because the probability of finding a job declines as the unemployed lose some human capital during prolonged unemployment. Hence, the long-term unemployed search less intensively for a job than do the short-term unemployed. This is in accordance with empirical findings of Layard *et al.* (1991) and van de Aalst and Hermsen (1994). Hence, although the long-term unemployed feature a rather low reservation wage, their employment perspectives are worse than those of the short-term unemployed because of their relatively low productivity and the associated low search intensity. Hence, transition rates into employment are lower for long-term unemployed than for short-term unemployed. Also, this is in line with empirical studies, which typically report true duration effects (see e.g. Kerckhoffs et al. (1994), and Groot (1990)).[20] The model is calibrated so as to conform closely to the observed transition rates between the various states and to the main empirical findings on search intensity and the reservation wage.

3.5 Public Institutions

MIMIC contains several public institutions, including the Dutch personal income tax system in 1998. The personal income tax features a tax-free allowance of about DFL 8 600 and three tax brackets (see Figure 8.3). A partner whose labour income remains below the tax-free allowance can transfer the tax-free allowance to the bread-winner. The rate in the first bracket is about 36 per cent in 1998. The tax rate in the second tax bracket is 50 per cent and has to be paid on incomes above about DFL 55 000. The marginal rate in the third

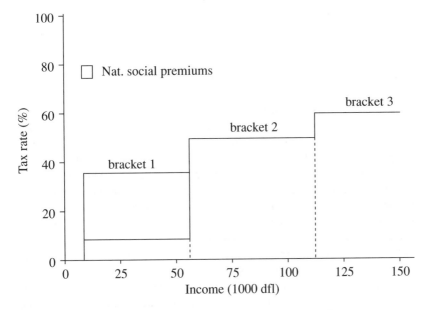

Figure 8.3   The income tax rates in 1998 in the Netherlands

tax bracket, which amounts to 60 per cent, is paid on incomes above DFL 115 000. Workers benefit from a special earned-income tax deduction, which amounts to 12 per cent of labour income with a maximum of around DFL 3 100. VAT in the Netherlands imposes a low rate on necessary goods (6 per cent) and a high rate for other goods (17.5 per cent). Other public institutions in MIMIC include employee and national social insurance schemes,[21] the employers' and employees' contributions to employee social insurances, the statutory minimum wage (which is linked to the average contractual wage rate), social assistance (which is linked to the statutory minimum wage), and a number of policy instruments targeted at specific groups, such as the long-term unemployed and the unskilled.

3.6   The Model as a Whole

Figure 8.4 provides an overview of the most important relationships between labour-market institutions and the functioning of the labour market in MIMIC. In particular, it summarizes how taxes and social benefits affect labour demand and supply, the process of wage formation and the job-matching process.

A number of parameters in MIMIC are calibrated so that the model reproduces Dutch data for the base year 1993. Elasticities in the wage equation and the production function are estimated. Most other elasticities are derived from the literature. For elasticities that suffer from a weak empirical basis, sensitivity analysis has been employed. This analysis suggests that most simulation results are quite robust (see Boone and Nieuwenhuis, 1998).

4   CUTTING TAXES IN MIMIC

This section employs the MIMIC model to investigate the long-run effects of a number of tax cuts.[22] The *ex-ante* (i.e. before behavioural responses have been taken into account) reduction in tax revenues is 0.5 per cent of GDP (3.5 billion guilders). A cut in public consumption balances the government budget *ex post*, that is, after the effects of the behavioural responses on the public budget have been taken into account. Hence, the required cut in public consumption reflects the impact of behavioural responses on the public budget. In particular, if the reduction in public consumption is less than the *ex-ante* cut in revenues of 0.5 per cent of GDP, behavioural responses help to mitigate the budgetary costs.

This section consists of three parts. The first part explores cuts in personal income taxes. The second part turns to cuts in social security contributions paid by employers. Finally, the third part investigates various forms of an Earned Income Tax Credit (EITC). These in-work benefits are aimed at increasing the reward of work in general and of low-skilled work in particular.

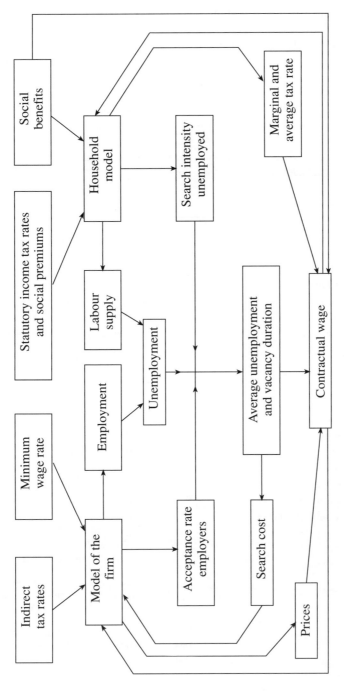

Figure 8.4 Main links in the MIMIC model

235

4.1 Personal Income Taxation

4.1.1 Cutting marginal tax rates

The detailed modelling of the personal tax system allows MIMIC to explore the labour-market effects of various parameters of the Dutch tax system. The first three columns of Table 8.1 contain the long-run effects of cuts in each of the three tax brackets of the Dutch personal income tax (see sub-section 3.5). These tax cuts reduce both marginal and average tax rates.

Table 8.1   Economic effects of cuts in the personal income tax according to MIMIC

	(1)	(2)	(3)	(4)
Prices	*percentage changes*			
Wage costs	–0.4	–0.3	–0.2	–0.1
unskilled	–0.6	–0.3	–0.2	–0.2
low skilled	–0.4	–0.2	0.0	–0.1
high skilled	–0.3	–0.3	–0.3	–0.1
Production price	–0.4	–0.4	–0.3	–0.1
Consumption price	–0.3	–0.3	–0.2	–0.1
Volumes				
Private consumption	1.3	1.3	1.3	0.9
Exports	0.6	0.6	0.5	0.2
Imports	0.5	0.6	0.5	0.2
Production	0.8	0.8	0.7	0.2
Employment	0.6	0.6	0.5	0.1
unskilled	0.8	0.5	0.3	0.1
low skilled	0.7	0.5	0.1	0.1
high skilled	0.6	0.7	0.6	0.1
Labour supply (persons)	0.1	0.1	0.0	–0.1
Labour supply (hours)	0.2	0.2	0.3	–0.1
bread-winners	0.0	0.2	0.4	0.0
partners	0.7	0.0	–0.3	–0.4
single persons	0.2	0.4	0.2	–0.2
55+	0.1	0.4	0.8	–0.1
Black labour (hours)	–0.2	–1.1	–1.9	0.4
Human capital index				
unskilled	0.0	0.0	0.0	0.0
low skilled	0.0	0.0	0.0	0.0
high skilled	0.0	0.1	0.1	0.0

Table 8.1   continued

	(1)	(2)	(3)	(4)
Ratios		*absolute changes*		
Unemployment	−0.3	−0.2	−0.1	−0.1
unskilled	−0.4	−0.3	−0.2	−0.2
low skilled	−0.3	−0.2	−0.1	−0.2
high skilled	−0.2	−0.2	−0.1	−0.1
Average replacement ratio	−0.1	−0.4	−0.1	0.3
unskilled	−0.2	0.0	0.3	0.3
low skilled	−0.1	−0.3	0.1	0.3
high skilled	0.0	−0.8	−0.4	0.3
Average tax burden[a]	−0.7	−0.7	−0.6	−0.4
Marginal tax burden[a]	−0.7	−1.9	−2.1	0.0
Government consumption[b]	−0.3	−0.3	−0.3	−0.5

Notes:
a   Weighted average of micro tax burdens of the employed.
b   Closure, in % of GDP.
(1) Reduction in the first tax bracket (by 1.2% points).
(2) Reduction in the second tax bracket (by 6.9% points).
(3) Reduction in the third tax bracket (by 24.6% points).
(4) Introduction of a general tax credit (of 255 guilders).

Table 8.2   Income effects of reductions in the personal income tax according to MIMIC

	(1)	(2)	(3)	(4)
Real disposable incomes		*percentage changes*		
Bread-winners employed	0.8	1.2	1.4	0.6
Bread-winners with benefit	0.7	0.1	0.1	1.0
Partners employed	2.2	0.3	−0.3	0.7
Partners with benefit	1.0	−0.4	−0.3	1.6
Single persons employed	1.2	1.2	0.3	0.6
Single persons with benefit	0.8	0.0	−0.2	1.4

Notes:
(1) Reduction in the first tax bracket (by 1.2% points).
(2) Reduction in the second tax bracket (by 6.9% points).
(3) Reduction in the third tax bracket (by 24.6% points).
(4) Introduction of a general tax credit (of 255 guilders).

Labour supply   All three tax cuts boost aggregate labour supply (in hours) because the substitution effect dominates the income effect. The composition of additional labour supply, however, differs. In particular, a lower tax rate in the first brackets raises especially labour supply of partners. This is because partners tend to work part-time jobs with relatively low (annual) labour incomes. Hence, their marginal labour income is typically subject to the tax rate in the first bracket. A cut in this tax rate therefore encourages partners to work longer hours, especially in view of the relatively large uncompensated wage elasticity of partners' labour supply.

Bread-winners and older workers tend to earn higher labour incomes than do partners. Indeed, the incomes of many of these workers fall in the second or third tax bracket. A lower tax rate in the first bracket reduces the average tax rate without affecting the marginal tax rate of those who fall in the second or third brackets. The infra-marginal character of the tax cut in the first bracket for many bread-winners explains why such a cut barely affects aggregate labour supply of bread-winners and older workers; the income effect is relevant for all bread-winners and older workers while the substitution effect applies only to those workers whose marginal labour income falls in the first bracket.

In contrast to tax cuts in the first bracket, tax cuts in the second and third brackets are effective in stimulating labour supply of bread-winners and older workers. Although these groups feature relatively low labour-supply elastici- ties, the impact of tax cuts in the higher tax brackets on aggregate labour supply (in hours) is substantial because bread-winners, single persons and the elderly account for a large share of aggregate labour supply (in hours). Compared to tax cuts in the first bracket, tax cuts in the second and third brackets reduce the average marginal tax rate (i.e. the marginal tax rate averaged over the various workers) substantially more (see Table 8.1).

Tax cuts in the higher brackets discourage partners from supplying labour because the income effect rather than the substitution effect mainly impacts on the labour supply of partners. In particular, by raising the incomes of bread- winners, the tax cuts in the higher brackets reduce partners' labour supply through the channel of higher household incomes. At the same time, the sub- stitution effect is not important because only few partners earn sufficiently high incomes to be marginally taxed in the second or third brackets.

Black labour supply and training   All three tax cuts reduce the size of the black economy. Supply of black labour declines because lower marginal income taxes make formal labour supply more attractive. Firm demand for black labour decreases because formal wage costs fall on account of a lower average tax burden. This encourages firms to hire formal rather than informal labour. Tax cuts in the higher brackets are most effective in combating the black economy because these tax cuts reduce the marginal tax rates most.

The lower marginal tax rate also raises the marginal return on training activities. Accordingly, human capital and labour productivity increase. The human capital index in Table 8.1 represents an index for the quality of either low-skilled labour or high-skilled labour by means of the share of workers that enrols in training programmes. As a result, the expansion of production exceeds the rise in employment.

Unemployment   The income tax cuts reduce equilibrium unemployment for two main reasons. The first is the drop in the average tax burden which moderates contractual wages (see wage equation (8.11)). The lower marginal tax wedge produces upward wage pressure. However, the positive elasticity of the average tax burden in wage equation (8.11) substantially exceeds the absolute value of the negative elasticity of the marginal tax burden. Hence, the overall effect of the tax cut is to moderate wages, thereby reducing equilibrium unemployment. Cutting taxes in the first bracket is most effective in reducing unemployment because it combines the decline in the average tax burden (the magnitude of which is similar for tax cuts in each of the three brackets) with the smallest decline in the marginal tax rate.

The second factor explaining the decline in unemployment is the lower replacement rate; workers tend to benefit more from lower marginal rates of personal income tax than do transfer recipients because the incomes of workers tend to exceed those of transfer recipients. This is especially so for tax reductions in the second bracket of the income tax. The tax rate in the third bracket exerts only a relatively small effect on the replacement rate because this income range is largely irrelevant for unemployed persons.

Employment   The three tax cuts raise aggregate employment through the channels of both lower unemployment and higher labour supply. In fact, all tax cuts generate a similar increase in aggregate employment. However, the composition of the employment gains differs. A tax cut in the first bracket is most effective in reducing unemployment and in raising employment for the unskilled, low skilled and partners. The other tax cuts are somewhat more effective in boosting aggregate labour supply (in hours) and high-skilled employment and in combating the black economy. These MIMIC simulations thus reveal a trade-off between cutting unemployment and raising formal labour supply.

Long-run income effects   Table 8.2 contains the long-run impact on average real disposable incomes of various types of households. Compared to tax cuts in the higher brackets, cutting taxes in the first bracket benefits transfer recipients and partners more. This is because these groups tend to earn lower incomes than do bread-winners and older workers. These latter groups benefit more from tax cuts in the higher brackets. These latter tax cuts may even reduce the incomes of benefit recipients because social benefits are linked to average contractual wages, which decline on account of wage moderation.

4.1.2 Introducing a tax credit

This sub-section explores the effects of introducing a tax credit (see the fourth column in Table 8.1). Partners who do not earn sufficient labour income to fully use the tax credit can transfer the tax credit to the bread-winner. The tax credit is thus in fact refundable for households with non-participating partners. Hence, this tax credit reduces the average tax burden but leaves the marginal tax burden unaffected, even for partners with small part-time jobs. The tax credit applies to both transfer recipients and workers.

Formal labour supply declines because the tax credit exerts only income effects on labour supply. The black economy expands although the marginal tax rate, and thus the allocation of labour between the formal and informal sectors, remains constant. Black consumption rises because the lower average tax burden raises the demand for consumption commodities from not only the formal, but also the informal sector. Hence, not only the formal private sector, but also the informal sector grows.

Unemployment declines despite an increase in the average replacement rate. The unemployed benefit relatively more from a tax credit than those in work because the unemployed typically collect lower incomes than the employed. The main reason for lower equilibrium unemployment is that the lower average tax burden together with the constant marginal tax burden moderates contractual wages (see equation (8.11)).

To summarize, a lower average tax rate at a constant marginal tax rate reduces both labour supply and unemployment. On balance, aggregate employment expands. The main difference with the cuts in tax brackets is thus that labour supply falls.

4.2 Lower Taxes for Employers

Table 8.3 explores three alternative ways to reduce the tax burden on employers. The first two columns analyse two ways to cut social security contributions (SSC) paid by employers, namely an across-the-board reduction in the rate of SSC and a targeted reduction of SSC for unskilled workers. A third experiment involves a two-year subsidy for firms that hire a long-term unemployed person.

4.2.1 Across-the-board reductions of employers' SSC

The first column of Table 8.3 shows the effects of an across-the-board cut in the rate of SSC paid by employers. Cuts in the rate of SSC reduce the average tax rate more than the marginal tax rate, thereby raising the coefficient of progression. This is because the contributions are paid only on labour incomes up to DFL 80 000. Indeed, the impact of the cut in the SSC rate on the marginal tax rate and hence on the labour market is quite similar to a weighted average of a reduction in the tax rate in the first bracket (explored in sub-section 4.1.1) and an across-the-board tax credit (explored in sub-section 4.1.2).

Table 8.3   Economic effects of reductions in the tax burden on employers according to MIMIC

	(1)	(2)	(3)
Prices	*percentage changes*		
Wage costs	−0.2	−0.8	0.2
unskilled	−0.4	−2.7	−1.5
low skilled	−0.2	−0.8	0.8
high skilled	−0.2	−0.4	0.6
Production price	−0.4	−0.4	−0.4
Consumption price	−0.2	−0.3	−0.3
Volumes			
Private consumption	1.1	0.7	0.9
Exports	0.5	0.6	0.6
Imports	0.4	0.3	0.4
Production	0.6	0.6	0.7
Employment	0.4	0.8	1.1
unskilled	0.6	3.2	6.1
low skilled	0.4	0.6	0.7
high skilled	0.4	0.5	0.4
Labour supply (pers.)	0.1	0.1	0.1
Labour supply (hours)	0.1	0.0	0.1
bread-winners	0.0	−0.1	0.0
partners	0.2	0.2	0.3
single persons	0.1	−0.1	0.1
55+	0.0	−0.1	0.0
Black labour (hours)	−0.1	2.3	0.0
Human capital index			
unskilled	0.0	−0.1	0.0
low skilled	0.0	−0.1	0.0
high skilled	0.0	0.0	0.0

Table 8.3   continued

	(1)	(2)	(3)
Ratios		*absolute changes*	
Unemployment	−0.2	−0.6	−0.6
unskilled	−0.4	−2.0	−4.1
low skilled	−0.2	−0.5	−0.4
high skilled	−0.2	−0.3	−0.2
Share long term unemployment	−1.2	−3.2	−6.5
Average replacement ratio	0.0	−0.3	−0.5
unskilled	0.0	−0.5	2.0
low skilled	0.0	0.2	−0.2
high skilled	0.0	0.0	−0.2
Average tax burden[a]	−0.5	−0.5	−1.0
Marginal tax burden[a]	−0.2	2.5	−0.3
Government consumption[b]	−0.3	−0.1	−0.2

Notes:
a   Weighted average of micro burdens of employees.
b   Closure, in % GDP.
(1)   Reducing the burden of social security contributions on employers.
(2)   Reducing the burden of social security contributions on employers of unskilled workers.
(3)   Introducing a subsidy for firms for hiring long-term unemployed.

Table 8.4   Income effects of reductions in the tax burden on employers according to MIMIC

	(1)	(2)	(3)
Real disposable incomes		*percentage changes*	
Bread-winners employed	0.8	0.2	0.6
Bread-winners with benefit	0.7	0.4	0.9
Partners employed	1.2	0.3	0.8
Partners with benefit	0.8	0.4	1.6
Single persons employed	0.9	0.4	0.6
Single persons with benefit	0.8	0.4	1.0

Notes:
(1)   Reducing the burden of SSC on employers.
(2)   Reducing the burden of SSC on employers of unskilled workers.
(3)   Introducing a subsidy for firms for hiring long-term unemployed.

The lower SSC burden directly reduces labour costs. Accordingly, employment for all types of labour expands while unemployment falls. Workers succeed in collecting part of the SSC cut in the form of higher net wages (see the income effects in Table 8.4). In particular, employees raise their wage claims in contractual wage formation as the higher profit margin raises the rents that are bargained over. Moreover, incidental wages rise as firms try to attract more applicants to fill the increasing number of vacancies. Also recipients of social security benefits gain (see Table 8.4) because of the institutional link between benefits and gross contractual wages. Higher wages mildly stimulate labour supply because the substitution effect dominates the income effect.

4.2.2   Targeted SSC cut

In order to enhance the employability of low productivity workers, the SSC cut can be targeted at unskilled labour. This sub-section investigates a targeted SSC cut for low-skilled labour, which amounts to DFL 2 500 for full-time workers who earn an hourly wage up to 120 per cent of the statutory minimum wage. The SSC cut is reduced proportionally for workers who work fewer than 36 hours a week.[23] It is phased out linearly between hourly wages of 120 per cent and 180 per cent of the statutory minimum wage. The phasing out of the cut raises the marginal tax rates on higher hourly wages in this range. However, it does not raise the marginal tax rate on hours worked because the SSC cut is based on hourly wages and hence increased proportionally for workers who work longer hours.

A comparison between the first and second columns of Table 8.3 reveals that a targeted SSC cut is more effective in raising employment than an across-the-board SSC cut, especially as far as unskilled employment is concerned. The cut in SSC for unskilled workers boosts the demand for these workers through substitution towards unskilled labour. Moreover, lower labour costs at the minimum wage level facilitate job matching. In particular, the lower wage costs reduce the minimum productivity standards due to minimum wage scales. Accordingly, an increasing number of unskilled unemployed, which often feature rather low productivities, meet the minimum productivity standards of employers. In this way, they become employable because the minimum productivity standard is the most restrictive factor in determining the overall acceptance rate for the unskilled (see sub-section 3.4).

The matching process is facilitated further by a reduction in the replacement rate for unskilled workers. This replacement rate drops because backward shifting of the tax cut boosts net wages collected by the unskilled; since social benefits are linked to average contractual wages in the economy as a whole, the higher relative wages of the unskilled widen the gap between income from unskilled work and unemployment benefits. The lower replacement rate moderates reservation wages and raises the search intensity of the unemployed.

The targeted SSC cut suffers from a number of drawbacks. First, by gradually reducing the tax allowance, the marginal tax rate on increases in hourly wages rises. Accordingly, increasing the net hourly wage is rather expensive because it substantially raises SSC. The high marginal tax burden on higher hourly wages harms the incentives for employers to train unskilled employees. Accordingly, the productivity level of unskilled workers drops. Indeed, Table 8.3 reveals that production rises less than employment, which reflects the loss in human capital of the unskilled. Moreover, private consumption rises less than under an across-the board cut in SSC. Furthermore, less on-the-job training hampers the upgrading of unskilled workers into low-skilled labour. Since unskilled workers face a higher replacement ratio than low-skilled workers do, this tends to mitigate the decline in the average replacement ratio, thereby moderating the employment gains.

Another disadvantage of a high marginal tax burden for employers is that it stimulates substitution between formal labour and informal labour. In particular, a high marginal tax burden encourages firms to pay additional wage income above the formal minimum wage in an informal fashion.[24]

4.2.3 Subsidies for hiring long-term unemployed

Snower (1994) proposes marginal labour subsidies for hiring the long-term unemployed. In this way, the funds currently used for paying passive unemployment benefits are diverted towards recruitment subsidies for the long-term unemployed. We analyse the impact of a hiring subsidy for an employer who hires a worker who has been unemployed for more than two years. The annual subsidy amounts to DFL 15 000, which corresponds to 100 per cent of the social assistance level in the Netherlands, and applies to the first two years of the employment contract.

The simulation results presented in the third column of Table 8.3 indicate that the hiring subsidy for long-term unemployed is more effective in fighting unskilled unemployment than the other policies analysed here.[25] Indeed, the cut in labour costs for long-term unemployed, which typically are unskilled and feature low productivity, is substantial during the first two years of employment. As a result, the minimum productivity standard for the long-term unemployed falls. This substantially raises the efficiency of the matching process because the minimum productivity standard (and thus the acceptance rate of the employer) is the most restrictive factor in determining the overall acceptance rate for the long-term unemployed (see sub-section 3.4).

In contrast to the targeted cut in SSC, the marginal labour subsidy does not raise the marginal tax rate for the employer. Accordingly, it neither stimulates the black economy nor harms the incentives to accumulate human capital. Instead, long-term unemployed who find a job are able to restore some of the human capital they lost during prolonged unemployment.

Despite the substantial decline in unskilled unemployment, the results are less favourable than Snower (1994) maintains. In particular, the fall in public consumption indicates that, in contrast to what Snower suggests, the hiring subsidy does not pay for itself. A major reason is the large dispersion in the productivity distribution for the long-term unemployed, implying that only a relatively small part of the long-term unemployed becomes employable. Moreover, the average productivity of the long-term unemployed is rather low. Hence, enhancing the employability of the long-term unemployed is rather expensive. Another factor limiting the employment impact is that part of the subsidy is shifted backwards to the employees, thereby containing the decline in wage costs. Finally, the higher transition rate of long-term unemployment into employment crowds out opportunities of short-term unemployed to find a job, thereby moderating the impact on the overall unemployment rate.

4.3 Earned Income Tax Credit

Table 8.5 contains the long-term effects of introducing various forms of a tax credit that applies only to workers — the so-called Earned Income Tax Credit (EITC). In several EU countries, this instrument is increasingly perceived as an attractive instrument to combat unemployment by raising the return to low-skilled work.

Table 8.5   Economic effects of in-work tax cuts according to MIMIC

	(1)	(2)	(3)	(4)	(5)
Prices		*percentage changes*			
Wage rate	–0.5	–0.7	–1.0	–1.0	–1.0
unskilled	–1.0	–1.7	–2.8	–3.8	–5.4
low skilled	–0.5	–1.0	–1.2	–1.0	–0.7
high skilled	–0.3	–0.4	–0.6	–0.6	–0.5
Production price	–0.5	–0.3	–0.6	–0.7	–0.6
Consumption price	–0.4	–0.2	–0.4	–0.5	–0.4
Volumes					
Private consumption	1.2	0.7	0.8	0.9	0.8
Exports	0.8	0.4	0.8	0.9	0.8
Imports	0.6	0.2	0.4	0.4	0.3
Production	0.9	0.4	0.9	1.0	0.9

General equilibrium effects

Table 8.5 continued

	(1)	(2)	(3)	(4)	(5)
Employment	0.8	0.7	1.2	1.3	1.2
unskilled	1.4	2.4	3.9	5.1	5.7
low skilled	0.9	1.0	1.1	0.8	0.5
high skilled	0.6	0.3	0.8	0.8	0.8
Labour supply (pers.)	0.5	1.6	0.2	0.2	0.2
Labour supply (hours)	0.0	−0.3	0.0	0.0	0.0
bread-winners	−0.1	−0.2	−0.2	−0.2	−0.2
partners	0.7	0.9	0.7	0.9	1.1
single persons	−0.2	−1.2	−0.1	0.0	0.0
55+	−0.1	−0.5	−0.1	−0.2	−0.2
Black labour (hours)	0.2	0.6	2.0	2.6	2.8
Human capital index					
unskilled	0.0	−0.1	−0.2	−0.2	−0.3
low skilled	0.0	−0.1	−0.2	−0.2	−0.2
high skilled	0.0	0.0	0.0	0.0	0.0
Ratios		*absolute changes*			
Unemployment	−0.5	−0.7	−0.8	−0.9	−0.8
unskilled	−0.8	−1.3	−1.7	−2.0	−2.1
low skilled	−0.5	−0.8	−0.9	−0.9	−0.8
high skilled	−0.4	−0.6	−0.7	−0.7	−0.6
Replacement ratio	−0.7	−0.5	−1.3	−1.6	−1.3
unskilled	−1.2	−2.7	−5.0	−7.0	−5.4
low skilled	−0.7	0.0	−0.5	−0.3	0.0
high skilled	−0.6	0.0	−0.5	−0.6	−0.5
Average burden[a]	−0.9	−1.1	−0.9	−0.9	−0.9
Marginal burden[a]	−0.2	1.2	1.8	1.6	1.6
Government consumption[b]	−0.2	−0.2	−0.1	−0.1	−0.1

Notes:
a   Weighted average of micro burdens on hours worked of employees.
b   Closure, in % of GDP.
(1) A uniform tax credit for workers.
(2) An EITC for low annual wage incomes, phased out between 120%–180% of minimum wage.
(3) An EITC for low hourly wage rates, phased out between 120%–180% of the minimum wage.
(4) An EITC for low hourly wage rates, phased out between 115%–150% of the minimum wage.
(5) An EITC for low hourly wage rates, phased out between 100%–130% of the minimum wage.

Table 8.6   Income effects of in-work tax cuts according to MIMIC

	(1)	(2)	(3)	(4)	(5)
Real disposable incomes		*percentage changes*			
Bread-winners employed	0.8	−0.2	0.5	0.5	0.5
Bread-winners with benefit	−0.2	−0.7	−0.6	−0.6	−0.6
Partners employed	3.7 ·	6.4	0.5	0.5	0.8
Partners with benefit	−1.1	−4.3	−1.0	−0.9	−0.9
Single persons employed	1.2	0.2	1.4	1.4	1.5
Single persons with benefit	−0.2	−0.9	−0.5	−0.4	−0.5

Notes:
(1)   Uniform tax credit for workers.
(2)   EITC for low annual incomes, phased out between 120%–180% of the minimum wage.
(3)   EITC for low hourly wages, phased out between 120%–180% of the minimum wage.
(4)   EITC for low hourly wages, phased out between 115%–150% of the minimum wage.
(5)   EITC for low hourly wages, phased out between 100%–130% of the minimum wage.

4.3.1   A flat EITC

The first column of Table 8.5 contains the impact of a flat EITC of 500 guilders per year (corresponding to about 1 per cent of the median gross wage). This non-refundable EITC reduces the marginal tax rate on small part-time jobs so that partners find it more attractive to enter the labour force. Accordingly, the participation rate (i.e. labour supply in persons) increases. The income effect reduces labour supply of other groups, thereby offsetting higher labour supply of partners. As a result, aggregate labour supply (in hours) remains constant.

Unemployment declines substantially. The reason is that the EITC accrues only to those in work and hence reduces the replacement rate. The lower replacement rate enhances job matching by reducing the reservation wage and by encouraging the unemployed to search more intensively for a job. Moreover, it moderates contractual wages. This wage moderation reduces the incomes from transfers recipients (see Table 8.6) because social benefits are linked to gross wages.

The comparison between the across-the-board tax credit (explored in subsection 4.1.2) and an EITC identifies a trade-off between cutting unemployment and raising transfer incomes. Whereas the EITC succeeds in cutting unemployment more than an across-the-board credit, it is less effective than an across-the-board tax credit in protecting the incomes of the unemployed. The probability of finding a job rises, however, so that a number of previously unemployed will experience a substantial rise in their income.

In MIMIC, the decline in the replacement rate, which results from targeting tax cuts at workers only instead of at both workers and transfer recipients, exerts a large effect on equilibrium unemployment. This is because the replacement rate affects both wage formation and job matching through the reservation wage and the search intensity of the unemployed.

4.3.2   A targeted EITC based on annual labour incomes

The second column of Table 8.5 explores the impact of an EITC that focuses on raising the reward to low-skilled work. The EITC analysed here depends on annual labour income of an individual.[26] It amounts to 4 per cent of annual labour income of the individual in a phase-in range up to the statutory minimum wage (DFL 30 000) and stays at DFL 1 200 in a flat range up to incomes of about DFL 36 000 (120 per cent of the minimum wage). Subsequently, the EITC is phased out linearly between annual labour incomes of DFL 36 000 and DFL 54 000 (i.e. 180 per cent of the minimum wage).

The EITC reduces the marginal tax burden on small part-time jobs, thereby encouraging partners to join the labour force. Accordingly, the participation rate increases. However, the average length of the work week falls. Only partners raise their average labour supply (in hours) because many partners fall in the phase-in range of the EITC. Bread-winners and singles, in contrast, reduce their labour supply because of a positive income effect and, to the extent that they fall in the phase-out range, a negative substitution effect associated with a higher marginal tax rate. On balance, the reduction in labour supply on account of the substitution effect in the phase-out range and the income effect dominates the positive effect on the participation rate. Hence, aggregate labour supply (in hours) drops.

The high marginal tax rate in the phase-out range reduces the incentives for training. Indeed, the human capital index falls because a larger part of wage increases due to productivity gains accrues to the government in the form of a lower EITC. Accordingly, compared to the flat EITC, the targeted EITC exerts smaller positive effects on production and consumption. The higher marginal tax rate in the phase-out range also boosts informal activities.

Compared to the fixed EITC, the targeted EITC is more effective in reducing the replacement rate for low-paid work. Accordingly, unemployed search more intensely for a job and reduce their reservation wage, thereby facilitating job matching. Furthermore, the lower replacement rate weakens the bargaining position of the unions in collective bargaining. Hence, contractual wages fall. Through all these channels, unemployment declines. Unemployment for the unskilled falls by 1.3 percentage points, which compares to a drop of 0.8 percentage points with a flat EITC.

The comparison between the flat and targeted EITC reveals once again a trade-off between, on the one hand, raising labour supply and, on the other hand, fighting unemployment. In particular, by widening the income gap between low labour incomes and social benefits, a targeted EITC is more effective in fighting unemployment. However, by reducing the income gap between low and high labour incomes, this EITC yields lower labour supply than does a flat EITC.

4.3.3 A targeted EITC based on hourly wages

If the objective is to reduce the number of unskilled who collect unemployment benefits, the targeted EITC explored above suffers from the disadvantage that it accrues also to part-time workers with high hourly wages but low annual incomes. This is relevant especially in the Netherlands, which features the highest share of part-time work of all OECD countries. Hence, in the Dutch policy discussion, a targeted EITC that depends on hourly wages rather than annual incomes has been proposed. Workers who earn the hourly minimum wage and hold a full-time job are eligible for the full EITC. The credit is reduced proportionally for workers who work less than a full-time job. It gradually drops also with the level of the hourly wage rate.

By reducing the credit for part-time workers, the EITC for full-time workers who earn an hourly wage up to 120 per cent of the statutory minimum wage can be more than doubled to DFL 2 500. The phase out range runs up to an hourly wage of 180 per cent of the minimum wage.[27] This EITC is thus phased out in the same way as the targeted SSC cut, which is also based on hourly wages. Just as the targeted SSC cut, this targeted EITC does not raise the marginal tax rate on hours worked in the phase-out range.

Labour supply   This EITC reduces the marginal tax burden only on part-time jobs with low hourly wages. Hence, the effect on the participation rate is smaller than in the previous experiment. The higher marginal tax rate in the phase-out range applies only to higher hourly wages and not to higher labour incomes on account of more hours worked. Accordingly, labour supply (in hours) drops only on account of the income effect. Both the effects on participation and labour supply (in hours) are thus smaller (in absolute value) than in the previous experiment. On balance, the positive effect on participation rate and the negative labour supply effect associated with the income effect cancel out. Consequently, aggregate labour supply (in hours) is unaffected.

Human capital   The marginal tax rate on higher hourly wages in the phase-out range is higher than in the previous experiment because the maximum credit is twice as large. This harms the incentives to accumulate human capital. Hence, compared to an EITC that depends on annual incomes, an EITC that depends on hourly wages does less harm to the quantity of labour supply but more harm to the quality of labour supply.

Unemployment   This EITC reduces the replacement rate for unskilled workers more substantially than the other EITCs explored above. Through skill-specific wage formation, this decline in the replacement rate for unskilled work reduces gross unskilled wages, thereby boosting demand for unskilled labour. Moreover, the lower replacement rate stimulates search and lowers the reservation wage, thereby facilitating the matching process for unskilled labour. Accordingly, the unemployment rate for the unskilled and the low skilled drops more substantially than under the EITCs analysed above.

Trade-offs   The comparison between an EITC that depends on annual incomes and an EITC that depends on hourly wages reveals a trade-off between two objectives of the Dutch government, namely between, on the one hand, increasing the participation rate of partners and, on the other hand, reducing the unemployment rate for the low skilled. An EITC that depends on annual incomes advances the first objective while an EITC that depends on hourly wages is more effective in cutting low-skilled unemployment.

Another trade-off involves the quality versus the quantity of labour supply. Compared to an EITC that depends on annual incomes, an EITC that depends on hourly wages enhances the quantity of labour supply (in hours) but harms its quality (in terms of human capital).

4.3.4   Targeting the EITC

The last two columns of Table 8.5 show the effects of two EITCs (based on hourly wages) that are phased out more rapidly than the previous experiment, namely, between 115 per cent of the minimum wage and 150 per cent of the minimum wage (the fourth column) or between the minimum wage and 130 per cent of the minimum wage (the fifth column). The advantage of more targeting is that the maximum credit for people who earn the minimum wage rate can be larger, thereby cutting the replacement rate of the unskilled more substantially. The disadvantage is that the marginal tax rate in the phase-out range increases more sharply and the (larger) decline in the replacement rate applies to fewer persons.

A moderately targeted version of the EITC (in the fourth column of Table 8.5) is slightly more effective in reducing the aggregate unemployment rate than the most targeted EITC (in the fifth column of Table 8.5). Also compared with the less targeted EITC (in the third column of Table 8.5), the moderately targeted EITC is more effective in reducing the aggregate unemployment rate. This suggests that an inverse U-shaped curve describes how the effectiveness of the EITC in cutting unemployment varies with the degree of targeting. Hence, moderately targeting the EITC seems the most effective way to reduce the overall unemployment rate.

4.3.5 Targeted SSC cut versus targeted EITC

A comparison between the targeted cut in SSC paid by employers (see sub-section 4.2.2) with a similar targeted EITC (see sub-section 4.3.3) reveals that the SSC cut is more effective in fighting unemployment among the unskilled but less effective in reducing aggregate unemployment. The SSC cut enhances the efficiency of the matching process primarily through lower minimum wage costs. This substantially reduces unskilled unemployment because the minimum productivity standard is the most restrictive factor in the matching process for the unskilled.

The EITC improves the matching process primarily through a lower replacement rate reducing the reservation rate of the unemployed. A lower reservation wage is less important for the matching process of the unskilled than a lower minimum productivity standard. However, a lower replacement rate also moderates wages in collective bargaining. This makes the targeted EITC more effective in reducing aggregate unemployment. The substantial decline in the replacement rate produced by the EITC is associated with a decline in the current incomes of transfer recipients. In case of a targeted SSC, in contrast, benefit recipients are better off because gross wages (to which benefits are linked) rise rather than fall.

5 CONCLUSIONS

The simulations with MIMIC reveal several trade-offs between various objectives. These objectives include cutting unemployment in general, and low-skilled unemployment in particular, stimulating the participation of women in the labour force, raising the quality and quantity of labour supply, and establishing an equitable income distribution, including a reasonable income level for those dependent on social benefits. Indeed, these objectives imply different priorities for how tax cuts should be structured. In particular, cutting unemployment primarily requires widening the gap between labour incomes and transfer incomes in unemployment. Raising the quantity and quality of labour supply in the formal economy calls for widening the income differentials between low formal labour incomes and high formal labour incomes.

The most effective way to fight economy-wide unemployment are in-work benefits. These benefits widen the gap between after-tax income from work and net transfer income, thereby raising the reward to work compared with relying on social benefits. This moderates wage costs, reduces reservation wages and encourages search of jobseekers. The wage moderation reduces social benefits because these benefits are linked to (gross) wages.

In-work benefits are particularly effective if targeted at the low-income groups. This is because the gap between labour income and transfer income is smallest for low-skilled workers. Hence, widening this small gap produces the largest pay-off in terms of reducing unemployment. However, by decreasing the gap between low and high labour incomes through a more progressive tax system for workers, a targeted EITC reduces the hours of labour supplied. This trade-off between cutting unemployment and raising labour supply (in hours) can be mitigated by linking the EITC to hourly wages rather than annual incomes and by reducing the EITC proportionally for small part-time jobs. Doing so, however, raises the marginal tax burden on hourly wage increases, thereby discouraging the accumulation of human capital and stimulating the black economy. Moreover, the lower benefits to small part-time jobs do not help to raise the labour-force participation of women. This is in contrast to an EITC targeted at low annual incomes which, together with tax cuts in the first tax bracket, exerts the strongest positive impact on female labour-force participation of all policies explored in this chapter. This points to a trade-off between targeting tax cuts at small part-time jobs of partners or at full-time jobs of breadwinners and singles earning low hourly wages.

Tax cuts in the higher tax brackets are most effective in raising the quantity and quality of formal labour supply (in hours). Indeed, these policies widen the after-tax income differentials between low and high labour incomes by reducing marginal tax rates. However, cuts in higher tax brackets are less effective in reducing unemployment, raising low-skilled employment, and stimulating female labour supply.

NOTES

1. CPB Netherlands Bureau for Economic Policy Analysis.
2. The level of GDP per hour worked is still high compared with other EU countries and matches that in the United States.
3. Don and Besseling (1996) discuss social security reform in the Netherlands in more detail.
4. Competition may, however, create selection problems. Therefore, supplementary measures have been introduced to avoid adverse selection; see Besseling *et al.*, 1998.
5. MIMIC stands for MIcro Macro model to analyse the Institutional Context.
6. Compared with an earlier version presented in Gelauff and Graafland (1994) MIMIC has been extended in several directions. These are theoretical extensions aimed at more adequately modelling the effects of high marginal tax rates on the quality and quantity of labour supply in the formal sector. In particular, labour supply of bread-winners and single persons as well as human capital accumulation, child-care and the incidence of disability were endogenized. Furthermore, the informal economy, which consists of the black economy and household production, was included in the model. The empirical foundation of the production function and contractual wage formation has been improved, while the model was calibrated on the basis of a more recent data set for 1993. Finally, to be able to explore specific policies targeted at combating long-term and unskilled unemployment, the new MIMIC model distinguishes between unskilled and low-skilled labour as well as between short-term and long-run unemployment.
7. Bovenberg *et al.* (1998) present a core version of the MIMIC model.
8. Most estimates for Dutch export and import elasticities are in the order of 2.

9. The cost of capital depends on the interest rate. The Netherlands is a small open economy in world capital markets. Hence, the interest rate is fixed.
10. Sensitivity analysis suggests that the outcomes for the formal sector are not sensitive to these parameters because the size of the informal sector is relatively small (see Boone and Nieuwenhuis, 1998).
11. For a more elaborate description, see chapter 3 in Gelauff and Graafland (1994).
12. This structure is similar to Frederiksen *et al.* (1995).
13. Empirical evidence for both the Netherlands and other countries suggests that hours worked do not exhibit smooth continuous patterns but rather are concentrated at discrete points (see, e.g., Woittiez, 1990 and Van Soest *et al.*, 1990).
14. If the informal sector does not impact the reservation wage, taxes affect the wage outcome only through the coefficient of progression $(1 - TM)/(1 - TA)$. Accordingly, at a constant replacement rate, proportional taxes are fully borne by the workers in terms of lower after-tax wages.
15. They find that sector-specific institutional variables account for 50 per cent of the total impact on wages while economy-wide factors account for the other 50 per cent.
16. The parameter ρ in the contact function is based on the estimation results in van Ours (1991), while the mismatch parameter is calibrated so as to reproduce data on average unemployment duration.
17. This wage may differ from the statutory minimum wage because the lowest wage scales in the Netherlands, which are agreed upon in collective wage agreements, generally exceed the official minimum wage.
18. Chapter 4 in Gelauff and Graafland (1994) and Jongen and Graafland (1998) discuss the modelling of the behaviour of the unemployed in more detail.
19. A detailed description of this model can be found in Jongen and Graafland (1998).
20. Part of the decline in the transition rate is explained by heterogeneity in the composition of the unemployed. MIMIC captures part of this effect through heterogeneity in skill types.
21. Employee insurances apply only to working people and cover employment risks, namely unemployment, disability, and sickness. Benefits depend on previously earned wages. All residents are entitled to national social insurance, which involves family allowances, disability benefits for the handicapped, special health costs, and a basic pension. In contrast to benefits from employee insurances, benefits from national social insurance are not related to previously earned wages.
22. A new long-run equilibrium is established after approximately 20 simulation periods.
23. The Dutch government recently introduced a reduction in employer's SSC that is structured similarly: the so-called SPAK (SPeciale AfdrachtsKorting). The maximum SSC cut is DFL 3 660 per year for a full-time worker earning the minimum wage.
24. In addition, firms face an incentive to overstate the number of hours worked. The MIMIC simulations abstract from this incentive.
25. Jongen and Graafland (1998) discuss these results in more detail.
26. Hence, this EITC differs from the EITC implemented in the US, which depends on family income and the number of children in a family.
27. The Dutch cabinet included a very similar EITC in its recent white paper on the future of the Dutch tax system.

REFERENCES

Aalst, M. van de and H. Hermsen (1994), 'Work after job search: behavior of the unemployed and their probability of finding a job (in Dutch)', Ministry of Social Affairs and Employment, Research Memorandum 333, The Hague.
Baartmans, K., F. Meyer and A. van Schaik (1986), *Houserepair and the informal sector* (in Dutch), University of Delft.

Berg, G.J. van den (1990), 'Search behavior, transitions to non-participation and the duration of unemployment', *Economic Journal*, **100**: 842–65.

Besseling, R, L. Bovenberg and R. de Mooij (1998), 'Premium differentiation in social insurance', *CPB Report* 1998/1: 19–22, The Hague.

Boone, J. and A. Nieuwenhuis (1998), 'Tax policy and the labor market: a sensitivity analysis with an AGE model', CPB Research Memorandum, The Hague.

Bovenberg, A.L., J.J. Graafland and R.A. de Mooij (1998), 'Tax reform and the Dutch labor market: an applied general equilibrium approach', NBER Working Paper, 6693, Cambridge MA.

Devine, T.J. and N.M. Kiever (1991), *Empirical Labor Economics*, Oxford University Press: Oxford.

Don, H. and P. Besseling (1996), 'Social security reforms: why and how?', CPB *Report* 1996/4: 14–16, The Hague.

Draper, D.A.G. and A.J.G. Manders (1996), 'Structural changes in the demand for labor', CPB Research Memorandum 128, The Hague.

Eijgenraam, C.J.J. and E.M. Verkade (1988), *Beta, a multisector model for the Dutch Economy*, Occasional Paper 44, CPB, The Hague.

Frederiksen, N.K., P.R. Hansen, H. Jacobsen and P.B. Sørensen (1995), 'Subsidising consumer services: effects on employment, welfare and the informal economy', *Fiscal Studies* **16**: 271–93.

Gelauff, G.M.M. and J.J. Graafland (1994), *Modelling Welfare State Reform,* North Holland.

Graafland, J.J. and F.H. Huizinga (1996), 'Taxes and benefits in a non-linear wage equation', CPB Research Memorandum 125, The Hague.

Graafland, J.J. and M.H.C. Lever (1996), 'Internal and external forces in sectoral wage formation: evidence from the Netherlands', *Oxford Bulletin of Economics and Statistics* **58**: 241–52.

Groot, W. (1990), 'The effects of benefits and duration dependence on re-employment probabilities', *Economics Letters* **32**: 371–76.

Groot, W. and H. Maassen van den Brink (1998), 'Bedrijfsopleidingen: wie neemt er aan deel en wat levert het op?', *Maandschrift Economie* pp. 28–40.

Hersoug, T., K.N. Kjaer and A. Rødseth (1986), 'Wages, taxes and the utility-maximizing trade union: a confrontation on Norwegian data', *Oxford Economic Papers* 38, pp. 37–51.

Holmlund, B. and J. Linden (1993), 'Job Matching, Temporary Public Employment, and Equilibrium Unemployment', *Journal of Public Economics* 51, pp. 329–43, North-Holland.

Jongen, E.L.W. and J.J. Graafland (1998), 'Vouchers for the long-term unemployed: a simulation analysis with MIMIC', CPB Research Memorandum 139, The Hague.

Kerckhoffs, C., C. de Neuburg and F. Palm (1994), 'The determinants of unemployment and jobsearch duration in the Netherlands', *De Economist* 142, pp. 21–42.

Koopmans, C.C. (1994),' Direct measurement of hidden labour', *Applied Economics* 26, pp. 575–81.

Layard, R., S. Nickell and R. Jackman (1991), *Unemployment*, Oxford University Press, Oxford.

Mooij, R.A. de (1999), 'Endogenizing (employ)ability in MIMIC', Internal Note no. I/99/06, CPB, The Hague.

Ours, J.C. van (1991), 'The Efficiency of the Dutch Labour Market in Matching Unemployment and Vacancies', *De Economist* 139, pp. 358–78.

Pissarides, C.A. (1990), *Equilibrium Unemployment Theory*, Basil Blackwell, Oxford.

SCP (1995), 'Time allocation survey', Social and Cultural Studies 22, Social Cultural Planning Bureau, Rijswijk.

Snower, D.J. (1994), 'Converting unemployment benefits into employment subsidies', *AEA Papers and Proceedings*, **84**, pp. 65–70.

Soest, A. van, I. Woittiez and A. Kapteyn (1990), 'Labour supply, income taxes and hours restrictions in the Netherlands', *Journal of Human Resources*, **25**, pp. 517–88.

Woittiez, I. (1990), 'Modelling and empirical evaluation of labour supply behavior', dissertation.

9. Skill-biased technical change, sectoral heterogeneity and wage setting: unemployment or wage inequality?

Werner Roeger and Hans Wijkander[*]

1 INTRODUCTION

In the beginning of the 1970s unemployment in Europe started to increase and in the almost three decades since then it has reached levels where it undoubtedly is Europe's most pressing economic and social problem. The development in the US differs from that in Europe. In the US, unemployment is not on an increasing trend but, instead, wage inequality has increased significantly. The development of total employment is also an important difference between Europe and the US. These developments have rightfully attracted much attention. Numerous articles have been written on the European unemployment problem since the 1970s, see, for example, Lindbeck (1996), Nickell (1997) or Siebert (1997). The increased wage inequality in the US took somewhat longer time to get noticed but has recently gained considerable attention, see, for example, Juhn *et al.* (1993) and Gottschalk (1997).

There exist numerous macroeconomic attempts to explain these labour market phenomena. Among the most prominent explanations for European unemployment are the lack of aggregate wage flexibility, high adjustment costs, (Bentolila and Bertola (1990)), high non-wage labour costs and generous unemployment benefit systems. Also, sometimes the argument is advanced that technical progress has contributed to the rise in unemployment. This also serves as an explanation for the increased wage dispersion in the US. Each of these hypotheses may have some explanatory power, but they also face some difficulties, especially if one compares the US and Europe over longer time horizons.

The US labour market has always been more flexible than the European labour market and the European social security system has always been more generous than the US system. Nevertheless, there was less unemployment in

---

[*] The views expressed in this chapter are those of the authors and do not commit the European Commission or its services where they work.

west Europe than in the US in the 1960s and early 1970s. Also, technological explanations at an aggregate level do not seem to be entirely convincing, as one rather observes a slowdown of productivity growth at the aggregate level since the middle of the 1970s. Though this may, to some extent, be a statistical illusion, it is certainly hard to argue that the rate of technical progress has increased dramatically relative to the 1960s.

The problems posed by the aggregate view have led many economists to look for other factors which have changed sufficiently such as to be possible candidates for an explanation of labour market trends. Two hypotheses have attracted a lot of attention. The first one is based on the observation of increased openness of industrialized countries and the fact that they face more competition from low-wage developing economies, see Woods (1995) and Leamer (1996). The other is based on the observation of increased skill-related wage dispersion in the US.[1] This fact, together with the observation of relatively constant wage differentials in Europe suggests that skill-biased technical progress (SBTP), together with different relative wage-setting behaviour, explain the observed difference in labour-market trends between the US and Europe, Krugman (1995).[2]

The trade hypothesis is certainly plausible and increased trade with developing countries may indeed have contributed to a fall in the relative demand of low-skilled labour leading to the increased wage dispersion in the US and the increased unemployment in Europe. However, the potential contribution of increased trade with less-developed countries seems to be quite limited. US imports from less-developed countries have increased from 0.4 per cent of GNP in 1970 to a mere 2.5 per cent of GNP in 1990. The increase in import to the European union is even smaller, from 0.5 per cent of GNP in 1970 to 2.1 per cent of GNP in 1990, see Freeman (1995).[3] Hence, it seems unlikely that this factor could be a main explanation for the changes in wage dispersion and unemployment, see Krugman (1995). That would leave us with SBTP. However, that explanation is also problematic since SBTP cannot be directly observed.[4] (Probably, that is the reason why such technological development has so far largely appeared as a residual when the other explanations have not been considered satisfactory.)

Even if one were to accept that technological development has favoured skilled workers, the mechanism whereby it causes a fall in the real wage of the unskilled is still somewhat puzzling. Within a macroeconomic context where workers are remunerated in accordance with marginal productivity, falling real wages among the low skilled would imply that SBTP not only increases the productivity of the skilled but also decreases marginal productivity of the low skilled, (compare Gregg and Manning (1997 p. 1180)). One explanation for this phenomenon would be that SBTP makes low-skilled workers redundant in their current jobs and forces them to perform tasks with lower skill requirements. This argument does, however, need a fall in the average efficiency of low-skilled workers.

This chapter looks at the relevance of the SBTP hypothesis from an explicit sectoral perspective. This means, we are not just calibrating the model, that is, selecting a set of parameters which fit a benchmark year, but we characterize more fully the observationally equivalent specifications within the class of constant elasticity of substitution (CES) production technologies. We find that SBTP is consistent with the major sectoral output, price, wage and employment trends in the US and France and, although technological parameters cannot be specified with a high degree of precision, there is no parameter constellation within the class of CES technologies which would be consistent with neutral (and possibly sector specific) technical progress.

It will also become evident from our results that, by adopting an explicit sectoral view, a fall in real wages can be understood without a fall in average efficiency of the low skilled. The reason is that, in such a framework, a decrease in the real wage may not only come from decreased productivity and wage but also from increased commodity prices. Another appealing feature of a multi-sector model is that it also captures other important observed empirical developments, such as different productivity trends in manufacturing and services and the movement into the service society (output trends).

Our theoretical analysis does, however, lead us to qualify statements based on the SBTP hypothesis. It is shown in the chapter that differences in technologies (especially elasticities of substitution) between sectors are crucial for the economic effects of SBTP. Not only quantitatively, but also qualitatively, different outcomes can emerge with different elasticities of substitution. Although it is not fully explored as yet, SBTP effects can be highly non-linear with trend changes in sector shares and elasticities of substitution (which could emerge from composition effects). A sectoral approach as conducted in this chapter may therefore be a suitable instrument for looking more closely at trend breaks like those that happened at the beginning of the 1970s.

In the final part of the chapter, the model is used to look at the effects of removing relative wage rigidity and to look at the effects of tax policies in the presence of relative wage rigidities with given rigidities. Tax policy should be a powerful instrument since the institutionalized wage setting in France and many other European countries provides a means for trade unions to increase the real wage of their members above the level that would be established in a competitive market. This may lead to smaller differences in real wages than in a competitive situation, but also to unemployment which is a highly undesired side effect. Such side effects can be regarded as a dead-weight cost of improving the incomes of the trade union members and, as in other cases of distortionary measures, it may be possible to improve the allocation by means of fiscal policy such as taxes and subsidies (compare Sørensen (1997)). Our objective is to trace out consequences of wage rigidities and therefore we only assume rigid relative wages. The first experiment, removing relative wage rigidity, represents a very drastic – and currently certainly not politically feasible – policy but has its interest as a reference point. In the current situation, such a change would lead to an efficiency gain but at the price of a welfare loss to the unskilled workers. We explore how the size of the loss to the unskilled and the gain to the skilled workers depend on the elasticities of substitution between skilled and unskilled workers in the two sectors. This experiment is, however, also useful from an empirical perspective since it allows us to study whether the French economy would behave more like the US economy if wage setting in France were to have been more like that in the US.

Two other, less controversial, policies are considered. Both aim at reducing unemployment by one percentage point and are budget neutral. The first policy is commodity taxation, that is, subsidization of consumption of services and taxation of consumption of manufacturing. Skilled workers would benefit from such a policy and the unskilled would lose from it. The reason for the difference in the welfare effects between the two groups is the difference in consumption mix between the two groups. The second policy is taxation that affects input prices. Hence, the tax policy is an increase in the progressivity of the income tax. Such a policy seems to hurt the skilled workers but will in fact, in the model, lead to a Pareto-improvement. The relative utility increase is in fact somewhat larger for skilled workers than for unskilled workers. The explanation for this result lies in how commodity prices are affected. Since our empirical analysis suggests that many different specifications of sector technologies can be consistent with the observed sector trends, we provide results for various specifications.

The chapter is organized as follows. In section 2 we describe the basic model and derive some analytical results. Section 3 contains stylized facts on developments in the US and France from the early 1970s to the early 1990s. Section 4 is about calibration and testing of the model. In section 5, we undertake a number of computational experiments in order to demonstrate the validity of the SBTP hypothesis and also to explore tax policies to reduce unemployment in France. Concluding comments are in section 6.

2   THE MODEL

a   Technology and Demand

We consider a model where labour is the only factor of production and where there are two types of workers, unskilled and skilled workers. Labour supply is exogenously given. Each worker supplies one unit of labour. The numbers of unskilled and skilled workers are L_u and L_h, respectively. The two commodities produced are manufactured goods and services, denoted M and S, respectively. The production functions in the two sectors are assumed to be CES. Technological development is assumed to be labour augmenting.

The production functions are as follows.

$$M = \left[a\left(q_{um} L_{um}\right)^{\rho} + b\left(q_{hm} L_{hm}\right)^{\rho} \right]^{\frac{1}{\rho}}, \quad \rho < 1, \quad \text{and} \tag{9.1}$$

$$S = \left[c\left(q_{us} L_{us}\right)^{\nu} + d\left(q_{hs} L_{hs}\right)^{\nu} \right]^{\frac{1}{\nu}}, \quad \nu < 1, \tag{9.2}$$

where L_{ij} is labour of type i, skilled or unskilled, in sector j, manufacturing or services. a, b, c and d are the distribution parameters in the production functions. ρ and ν are the parameters for the elasticity of substitution. Hence, the elasticity of substitution between unskilled and skilled labour in manufacturing is $\sigma_M = 1/(1 - \rho)$ and in services, $\sigma_S = 1/(1 - \nu)$. The augmentation factor of labour of type i in sector j is q_{ij}.

The corresponding cost functions are:

$$c_m\left(w_u, w_s, q_{um}, q_{hm}\right)M = M\left[a^{\frac{1}{1-\rho}}\left(\frac{w_u}{q_{um}}\right)^{\frac{\rho}{\rho-1}} + b^{\frac{1}{1-\rho}}\left(\frac{w_s}{q_{hm}}\right)^{\frac{\rho}{\rho-1}} \right]^{\frac{\rho-1}{\rho}} \quad \text{and}$$
$$\tag{9.3}$$

$$c_s\left(w_u, w_s, q_{us}, q_{hs}\right)S = S\left[c^{\frac{1}{1-\nu}}\left(\frac{w_u}{q_{us}}\right)^{\frac{\nu}{\nu-1}} + d^{\frac{1}{1-\nu}}\left(\frac{w_s}{q_{hs}}\right)^{\frac{\nu}{\nu-1}} \right]^{\frac{\nu-1}{\nu}} \tag{9.4}$$

where w_u and w_s are the wages of unskilled and skilled workers, respectively.

Workers have identical preferences, represented by a utility function of CES type, with Stone–Geary components which we write as follows.

$$U = \left[\alpha\left(m - m_b\right)^{\eta} + (1 - \alpha)\left(s - s_b\right)^{\eta} \right]^{\frac{1}{\eta}} \tag{9.5}$$

where α is the share parameter, m is the consumption of manufacturing goods, m_b is the minimum consumption of manufactured goods, s is the consumption of services and s_b is the minimum consumption of services. The elasticity of substitution between manufacturing and services is $\sigma_c = 1/(1-\eta)$.

Each worker maximizes utility subject to his or her respective budget constraints. The demand functions for manufacturing, m, and services, s are:

$$m_k = m_b + \frac{\alpha^{\frac{1}{1-\eta}} p_m^{\frac{\eta}{\eta-1}-1}\left(I_k - p_m m_b - p_s s_b\right)}{(1-\alpha)^{\frac{1}{1-\eta}} p_s^{\frac{\eta}{\eta-1}} + \alpha^{\frac{1}{1-\eta}} p_m^{\frac{\eta}{\eta-1}}} \quad \text{and} \qquad (9.6)$$

$$s_k = s_b + \frac{(1-\alpha)^{\frac{1}{1-\eta}} p_s^{\frac{\eta}{\eta-1}-1}\left(I_k - p_m m_b - p_s s_b\right)}{\alpha^{\frac{1}{1-\eta}} p_m^{\frac{\eta}{\eta-1}} + (1-\alpha)^{\frac{1}{1-\eta}} p_s^{\frac{\eta}{\eta-1}}}, \qquad (9.7)$$

where the subscript k indicates skilled, unskilled or unemployed worker. Commodity prices are p_m and p_s. I_k represents incomes of skilled, unskilled and unemployed workers. It takes on values $w_s (1 - t_s)$, $w_u (1 - t_u)$ and *ben*, where *ben* is the unemployment benefit (the only source of income for the unemployed). Income tax rates are denoted t_s and t_u.

We assume that the wage for skilled labour adjusts so as to bring the market for skilled labour into equilibrium. When the relative wage is rigid unskilled workers can become unemployed. Given our focus on wage compression, that seems to be a reasonable assumption since SBTP will make skilled workers more attractive.

The government budget constraint is

$$w_s t_s L_s + w_u t_u L_u (1 - un) + p_m t_m M + p_s t_s S = ben \times L_u \times un$$

where t_m and t_s are commodity tax rates on manufacturing and services, respectively. Hence, the government budget is balanced.

b   Equilibrium

Assuming that firms take commodity and factor prices as given, we have the following equilibrium relationship between commodity and factor prices.

$$p_m = c_m(w_u, w_s, q_{um}, q_{hm}) \qquad (9.8)$$

$$p_s = c_s(w_u, w_s, q_{us}, q_{hs}).$$ (9.9)

That is, commodity prices equal marginal costs.

Through Shephard's lemma we obtain the following equilibrium conditions for the two labour markets. First, the unskilled labour:

$$\frac{\partial c_m(w_u, w_s, q_{um}, q_{hm})}{\partial w_u} M + \frac{\partial c_s(w_u, w_s, q_{us}, q_{hs})}{\partial w_u} S = L_u(1 - un).$$ (9.10)

Second, the skilled labour:

$$\frac{\partial c_m(w_u, w_s, q_{um}, q_{hm})}{\partial w_s} M + \frac{\partial c_s(w_u, w_s, q_{us}, q_{hs})}{\partial w_s} S = L_s.$$ (9.11)

Equilibrium on commodity markets implies the following:

$$M = m_s + m_u + m_{un}, \text{ and}$$ (9.12)

$$S = s_s + s_u + s_{un}.$$ (9.13)

We explore two types of equilibria in this model. The first is where wages and prices are allowed to adjust without restrictions. Such an equilibrium will be characterized by full employment. The second is where relative wages are constrained. Such an equilibrium may not be market-clearing. We assume that there may be unemployment among unskilled workers.

c   Analytical Results

A central issue in the analysis is how technology in the two sectors will interact with SBTP in manufacturing to change wages and unemployment when wages are flexible or rigid. However, since the model in full generality seems somewhat too complex to lend itself conveniently to comparative static analysis we limit such analysis to deviations from a simple benchmark case.

The benchmark case is where consumer preferences and the production function in the service sector are Cobb–Douglas.[5] We assume that the share parameters in the utility function and the production function for services are ½, total factor productivity in services 2. The share parameters in manufacturing are 1. All the labour augmenting factors are 1, and the supply of skilled labour equals that of unskilled labour.[6] It is easy to see that, in this case, equilibrium with market determined wages entails the same wage for the two types of labour and that the price of manufactured goods will be twice that of services.

With the above simplifications, we write the market clearing conditions on the commodity markets as follows.

$$M = \frac{1}{2} \frac{\left[(1-un)L + wL\right]}{c_m} \qquad (9.14)$$

$$S = \frac{1}{2} \frac{\left[(1-un)L + wL\right]}{c_s} \qquad (9.15)$$

The market clearing condition for skilled labour is

$$\frac{\partial c_m}{\partial w} M + \frac{\partial c_s}{\partial w} S = L \qquad (9.16)$$

where w is the relative wage of the skilled workers (the wage of the unskilled workers is normalized to 1) and $L_u = L_s = L$. Inserting (9.14) and (9.15) into (9.16) and making use of the particular functional forms on production functions give us the following equation for the equilibrium w.

$$\frac{1}{2} \left(\frac{\left(\frac{w}{q}\right)^{\frac{\rho}{\rho-1}}}{w + w\left(\frac{w}{q}\right)^{\frac{\rho}{\rho-1}}} + \frac{1}{2}\frac{1}{w} \right)(1 - un + w) = 1 \qquad (9.17)$$

Denote the left-hand side of (9.16) $D(w, un, q, \rho)$. In the flexible wage case we have $un = 0$. The equilibrium wage is $w = w(q, \rho) = 1$ when $q = 1$. The change in the relative wage of the skilled workers due to a skill-biased productivity shock, from $q = 1$, in manufacturing is given by the following equation.[7]

$$\left.\frac{dw}{dq}\right|_{q=1} = -\left.\frac{\frac{\partial D}{\partial q}}{\frac{\partial D}{\partial w}}\right|_{q=1} = \frac{-2(1+w)\rho w^{1+\frac{\rho}{\rho-1}}}{(\rho-1) + (2\rho-4)w^{\frac{\rho}{\rho-1}} + (3\rho-3)w^{\frac{2\rho}{\rho-1}} - 2\rho w^{1+\frac{\rho}{\rho-1}}} \geq 0. \qquad (9.18)$$

And with $w = 1$, we have,

$$\frac{dw}{dq}\bigg|_{q=1} = \frac{-\rho}{\rho-2} = \frac{\sigma_M - 1}{1 + \sigma_M} \qquad (9.19)$$

Hence, for the case where $\rho \geq 0$, the wage of the skilled workers increases as a result of the productivity shock, except for the case where the production function in manufacturing is Cobb–Douglas. In that case the wage of the skilled workers is unaffected. The reason is that the case represents the limit where SBTP cannot be distinguished from (skill) neutral change. The implication of (9.19) is that SBTP leads to (increased) wage dispersion when the elasticity of substitution is larger in manufacturing than in services. To examine how the wage response to a technological shock is affected by the elasticity of substitution, we differentiate (9.18) with respect to ρ and evaluated in $w = 1$.[8]

$$\frac{d}{d\rho}\left(\frac{dw}{dq}\bigg|_{q=1}\right) = \frac{32}{(4\rho - 8)^2} = \frac{2\sigma_M^2}{(1 + \sigma_M)^2} > 0 \qquad (9.19a)$$

Hence, this derivative takes on its smallest value in the Cobb–Douglas case, ½, and its largest value, 2, for infinite elasticity of substitution in manufacturing. This result suggests that the change in the wage distribution owing to a skill-biased technology shock in manufacturing gets stronger, the larger the difference in elasticity of substitution between the two sectors. The intuition for this result is that when the elasticity of substitution is large in manufacturing, the productivity shock will create a large excess demand for skilled labour, which will be eliminated through an increase in the relative wage. If the elasticity of substitution is small in the service sector, a large wage increase is needed since demand for skilled labour from the service sector is unresponsive to the wage increases. In the case where the elasticity of substitution is high in the service sector the wage increase can be smaller since the demand for skilled labour from that sector would be responsive to wage increases. We return to this result in the simulation section.

How individual utility responds to technological development depends on how commodity prices and income changes. For any indirect utility function, $V = V(p_m(q), p_s(q), w(q))$, we can write the change in utility as follows.

$$\frac{dV}{dq} = -\frac{\partial V}{\partial w} w\left[\theta_m \frac{\frac{dp_m}{dq}}{p_m} + \theta_s \frac{\frac{dp_s}{dq}}{p_s} - \frac{\frac{dw}{dq}}{w}\right], \qquad (9.20)$$

where θ_m and θ_s are the budget shares. By making use of the equilibrium value of w and evaluating at $q = 1$, we have that the sign of the utility change of the low skilled is determined by the following condition:

$$sign\left(\frac{dV^u}{dq}\right) = -sign\left(2\frac{dw}{dq} - 1\right) = -sign\left(2\frac{-\rho}{\rho-2} - 1\right) \qquad (9.21)$$

and for the skilled workers:

$$sign\left(\frac{dV^s}{dq}\right) = -sign\left(2\frac{dw}{dq} - 1 - \frac{dw}{dq}\right) = -sign\left(2\frac{-\rho}{\rho-2} - 1 + \frac{\rho}{\rho-2}\right). \qquad (9.22)$$

The implications of (9.21) and (9.22) are that the utility of the unskilled will be positively affected by SBTP for $\rho < 2/3$ and negatively affected whenever $\rho > 2/3$. In terms of elasticities of substitution, the utility effect is positive where $\sigma_s = 1$ and $\sigma_M < 3$ and negative where $\sigma_s = 1$ and $\sigma_M > 3$. The utility effect on the skilled workers of the SBTP is always positive.

Suppose now that we lock the relative wage of the skilled workers at its equilibrium value with $q = 1$, and study the effect on unemployment of a SBTP in manufacturing. Hence, we compute the following derivative.

$$\left.\frac{dun}{dq}\right|_{q=1} = -\frac{\dfrac{\partial D}{\partial q}}{\dfrac{\partial D}{\partial un}} = \frac{-\rho}{2(\rho-1)} = \frac{1}{2}(\sigma_M - 1) > 0 \quad \text{for } \sigma_M > 1. \qquad (9.23)$$

We have that when wages are not allowed to respond to SBTP, such a shock would lead to (increased) unemployment. It is easy to see that the response of unemployment to SBTP is stronger, the larger is the elasticity of substitution in manufacturing. We get back to this result in the simulation section.

3   SOME STYLIZED FACTS

This section reports the major stylized facts on sector and wage trends over the period 1972–6 to 1992 for both France and the US. Table 9.1 lists the corresponding ratios for both countries. The figures in Table 9.1 clearly indicate that the two economies underwent significant sectoral adjustments over the last decades. Hence, the ratio of manufacturing to service output was around 0.5

in France and below 0.4 in the US in the 1970s and declined to levels below 0.4 in France and around 0.3 in the US in the beginning of the 1990s. This process was accompanied by an increase in the price of services relative to that of manufacturing products. The sectoral change also involved a sizeable re-allocation of employment from the manufacturing sector to the service sector. In fact, employment share in manufacturing decreased more strongly than the manufacturing output share. This development, together with the evolution of relative output prices, suggests sizeable differences in productivity growth in the two sectors.

The sector output, employment and price trends show remarkable similarities between the two countries. The difference in the trend growth of high-skilled wages relative to that of low-skilled workers is also remarkable. Differences can also be observed for the trend movement of the unemployment rate. Relative manufacturing output has declined by about 0.6–0.7 per cent per year. Relative manufacturing prices have declined between 0.5 and 0.6 per cent per year and the share of total employment in manufacturing has fallen in both countries. However, the fall has been more pronounced in France than in the US.

The differences in relative wage trends have been reported extensively in recent years. Many studies of the US suggest that the difference of average wages for workers above the 50th percentile and those below that percentile has increased between 20–25 per cent in the last two decades, see for example Gottschalk (1997). (In the sequel we refer to workers above the 50th percentile as high skilled or simply skilled workers and those below the 50th percentile as low- or unskilled workers.) Some empirical analyses even suggest that real wages of low-skilled workers have actually declined. This seems especially to be the case for very low-skilled men. The data reported in Gottschalk suggest that average real earnings (men and women) below the 50th percentile have stayed roughly constant. In Europe the wage trends have been different. In France relative wages have stayed roughly constant, see for example, Nickell and Bell (1995).

In contrast to the US, unemployment in France has a rising trend. This holds especially for the unemployment rate of the low skilled, see for example Nickell and Bell (1995). Their data suggest that the unemployment rate of the low skilled in France has risen from 5 per cent to 13.6 per cent over the relevant time period.[9] It seems likely that these reported figures are biased downwards. In particular, some of the increased high-skilled unemployment in official statistics is probably related to skills that have become obsolete owing to new technological developments and changes in tastes. It is therefore questionable whether they should not, instead, have been reported as unskilled unemployment. Also not counted in these data is the rise in early retirement, which hides some unemployment and may also, to some extent, reflect the depreciation of human capital acquired in former years.

Table 9.1   Some stylized facts for France and the US

	France			US		
	1970	1990	1990–70	1970	1990	1990–70
Relative output (YM/YS)	0.5	0.37	–1.51	0.38	0.3	–1.48
Relative prices (PM/PS)	1	0.78	–1.24	1	0.8	–1.39
Relative employment (LM/LS)	0.49	0.25	–3.36	0.35	0.22	–2.90
Relative wages (WM/WS)	1.07	1.14	0.32	1.27	1.28	0.05
WH/WU	1.25	1.25	0.00	1.4	1.68	1.14
Man. productivity (YM/LM)	0.22	0.38	2.73	4970	6881	2.03
Serv. productivity (YS/LS)	0.24	0.3	1.12	4412	4757	0.47
Man. per capita output (YM/L)	1.35	1.67	1.06	0.53	0.52	–0.12
Serv. per capita output (YS/L)	2.68	4.51	2.60	1.41	1.71	1.21
Unemployment rate (low skilled)	5	13.6	8.6	6.5	6.5	0

Note: Figures in columns 3 and 6 are average annual percentage changes.

4   CALIBRATION AND TESTING

4.1   Data Issues

In order to make empirically relevant predictions with the model, its parameters must be selected so that it replicates important stylized facts of the US and the French economies. Unlike in conventional computable General Equilibrium modelling, where parameters are selected such that the model fits important ratios in a benchmark year, we go one step further and select parameters such that the model not only fits the ratios in a base year but also the observed trends. This seems to be a necessary step, given our focus on an explanation of significant changes in both the wage distribution and rates of unemployment that have taken place over the last two decades in both economies.

One major reason for the statistical problems in this field arises from the fact that employment by skill is, both for principal and for statistical reasons, not easily observable. Ideally one would like to divide employment into different skill categories and one would also like to observe wages for these skill categories. However, skill is likely to be too complex a variable for easy categorization since it has many dimensions, ranging from innate ability to human capital acquired in the work place and in formal education. In practice, at most it is possible to get employment/labour force data broken down into production/non-production workers, levels/years of education and into male and female. These categories are crude approximations for true skill differences, which imply severe difficulties for any econometric assessment of elasticities of substitution.

An alternative way to approach the problem and the one adopted in this chapter is to assume that all workers are paid according to their marginal product, that is, the wage distribution reflects the distribution of skills in the economy. This implies that we capture 'marketable' skills, not the general skill-level of a person. However, this approach is, of course, not without problems. One can, for example, argue that the income of certain professions may currently be high because they are temporarily in high demand and not because they require a particular skill. However, since we focus on long-term trends, such temporary effects should not be important. Nevertheless, it is important to notice that our definition of skill differences not only captures objective factors, such as the level of education, for example, but it also captures preferences.

The only information on the skill distribution we use for calibrating the model is information on the aggregate wage distribution; in particular, we look at the relative wages between the upper and the lower 50th percentile of employees in the economy at a particular date.[10] This has several implications to bear in mind when interpreting our results. First, we look at the lower and the upper 50th percentile in the two dates; that is, we standardize the level of skills at each date. It does therefore not make much sense with this approach to compare skills across time. This aggregate information, together with the assumption that these two skill categories are paid an identical wage in both sectors, and the observed trends of sector output, prices and employment is sufficient to determine the sectoral evolution of employment by skill categories in the two sectors.

Given the information on the sectoral trends in both countries (see Table 9.1) we can calculate the following ratios between high-skilled and low-skilled employees in the two sectors, countries and dates.

The results in Table 9.2 suggest the following interpretation. In both countries, there is a significant difference in the skill intensity between sectors. The skill intensity in services has stayed roughly constant over time in both countries. However, in manufacturing there are different trends in skill intensity. There is a strongly rising trend in France, while it is slightly declining in the US. This is in contrast to some other studies, which usually find rising skill intensities in both sectors and generally higher skill intensity in services. The results we obtain rest mainly on the observed higher wage per employee in manufacturing than in services. As explained above we interpret this as a higher marketable skill level of manufacturing employees.[11] Note that by definition we cannot observe a higher overall skill intensity in the second year.

Table 9.2 Skill intensities in manufacturing and services, US and France (1970s; 1990s)

	1970s		1990s	
	L_{hm}/L_{um}	L_{hs}/L_{us}	L_{hm}/L_{um}	L_{hs}/L_{us}
US	2.18	0.76	1.76	0.88
France	1.25	0.89	4.07	0.82

4.2 Calibration of Production Parameters[12]

We now turn to a discussion of parameter selection and identification problems. We observe sectoral aggregate data at two points in time 1970s and 1990s.[13] These data are real value added in manufacturing and services (M, S), price indices of manufacturing and services (p_m, p_s) employment in manufacturing and services (L_m, L_s), the average wage of the high skilled (above 50th percentile) and the low skilled (below 50th percentile) (w_s, w_u), and average wage per employee in manufacturing and services (w_m, w_s). How can production parameters (share parameters, elasticities of substitution) and technology constants (the efficiency levels of low- and high-skilled workers) be selected to fit these observations?

The sectoral production model provides eight equations, namely, a production function for manufacturing and services, two equations determining the skill intensity in both sectors, two zero profit constraints and two adding up constraints for high- and low-skilled workers. These relationships can be used to select eight parameters and/or unobservable variables. As already mentioned above, the zero profit constraint and the adding up constraint can be used to determine labour demand by skill in each sector. Since no production parameter enters these constraints, skill intensities are independent from production parameters. The four remaining equations can be used to select four additional parameters or variables. However, ten additional parameters remain to be determined, namely, the four share parameters, the four efficiency constants and the two elasticities of substitution. Note that since the efficiency constants and the share parameters cannot be separately identified, one can select the share parameters *a priori* (we set them equal to 0.5). This leaves six free parameters to be determined by four equations. This in turn leaves two degrees of freedom for parameter choice. In other words, for any theoretically feasible choice of the elasticity of substitution,[14] in the two sectors there exist four efficiency parameters, which make the model fit the data perfectly. This can be repeated for any data, thus, for any choice of ρ and v the calibration would trace out the corresponding evolution of the efficiency indices over time. This, in a sense, is a discouraging result since it means that there exist many *obser-vationally equivalent* specifications of production and, without adding further (*a priori*) restrictions to the model, it is not possible to determine the size for elasticities of substitutions.[15]

There are various ways to impose additional structure on the process of technological change. For example one can assume that the efficiency of the low skilled is not declining ($q_{um90} \geq q_{um70}$, $q_{us90} \geq q_{us70}$). Or, one can impose the somewhat stronger assumption that the efficiency of the low skilled do not change ($q_{um90} = q_{um70}$, $q_{us90} = q_{us70}$). Alternatively, one can impose neutral technical progress, this implies that (q_{um90}/q_{um70}, $= q_{hm90}/q_{hm70}$ and q_{us90}/q_{us70} $= q_{hs90}/q_{hs70}$). Under any of these assumptions it would be possible to determine values for ρ and v (in the case of equality constraints) or ranges for ρ and v (in the case of inequality constraints). However, imposing those restrictions on technical progress seems far too arbitrary. Therefore, we choose a different calibration strategy, namely, we calculate efficiency trends for the two types of labour in the two sectors for an entire range of elasticities of substitution in the interval (0.17, 5.0). This interval covers essentially the whole range values for the elasticity of substitution, which are regarded as plausible. This strategy allows us to see whether some robust patterns on the nature of technical progress emerge from such an analysis. In particular, we are interested to see whether there are parameter constellations, which are consistent with neutral and possibly sector specific technical progress, given the observations on sectoral trends. The results from this exercise are reported in the next section.

Results

The CES production function adopted in this chapter allows for elasticities of substitution between zero and infinity. In practice, elasticities of substitution exceeding 4 are hardly regarded as realistic. The Hamermesh estimate of 3.0 can be regarded as an upper bound. Therefore, in this section we look at values in the range between 0.17–5.0. This corresponds to values of ρ and v in the interval (–5.0, 0.8).

The results in Table 9.3 exhibit a number of interesting features. First of all, it is important to observe that for all feasible choices of the elasticities of substitution, the US data imply SBTP. However, the efficiency of low-skilled workers in manufacturing also rises strongly (average annual growth rate between 0.6 per cent and 1.6 per cent). The growth rate of the efficiency index of high skilled workers is larger, namely around 2.6 per cent and varies only slightly across alternative parameter choices. The results on the nature of technical progress in the service sector are less robust. They show a decline in the efficiency parameter for the low skilled and high efficiency growth of the high skilled for high values of the elasticity of substitution, and a high growth rate for low-skilled efficiency for low elasticities of substitution. This result can be explained from the fact that with low elasticity of substitution, an increase in the efficiency of low-skilled workers, at given wages, actually implies a shift of labour demand towards more skilled labour while an increase in the efficiency of low-skilled workers under high elasticity of substitution implies higher demand for low-skilled workers.

Table 9.3   Elasticity of substitution and efficiency, US

ρ	ν	Δq_{us}	Δq_{hs}	Δq_{um}	Δq_{hm}
0.8	0.8	0.96	1.24	1.26	1.49
0.5	0.5	0.84	1.38	1.30	1.48
−0.5	−0.5	1.7	0.78	1.14	1.54
−5.0	−5.0	1.24	1.01	1.21	1.52
0.8	−5.0	1.24	1.01	1.27	1.49
0.8	−0.5	1.7	0.78	1.26	1.49
0.8	0.5	0.84	1.38	1.26	1.49
−5.0	0.8	0.96	1.24	1.10	1.51
−5.0	0.5	0.84	1.38	1.21	1.52
−5.0	−0.5	1.70	0.78	1.21	1.52

Note: Numbers in columns 3–6 give the ratio of the factor efficiency indices between the 1990s and 1970s.

Note that the aggregate US price, wage and output trends imply an increase in the skill intensity in the service sector, from 0.76 to 0.88, and a decline of the skill intensity in the manufacturing sector, from 2.18 to 1.76.[16] The necessary reduction of low-skilled labour in services can either be the outcome of a declining efficiency of low-skilled workers in services and high elasticity of substitution or, alternatively, it is the outcome of an increase in the efficiency of low-skilled workers combined with a low elasticity of substitution.

These results also shed some light on the ongoing debate on the relative impact of SBTP versus trade effects for the observed pattern of low-skilled wages and wage distributions. The first view is mainly associated with Krugman, while some trade theorists (see, for example, Leamer (1996)), claim that this pattern is not the result of SBTP, but is rather the outcome of trade induced output price changes and can be consistent with neutral technical progress. However, it can be seen from our table that there is no way to explain the observed sectoral trends without assuming some form of SBTP. Thus the technological explanation seems to be an indispensable part for understanding of US wage developments. That observation, of course, does not necessarily

General equilibrium effects

imply that trade effects are not important. This question could only be addressed by calculating trade induced price changes of manufacturing products.

Table 9.4   Elasticity of substitution and efficiency, France

ρ	ν	Δq_{us}	Δq_{hs}	Δq_{um}	Δq_{hm}
0.7	0.7	1.51	1.45	1.29	2.14
0.5	0.5	1.55	1.42	0.77	2.51
−0.5	−0.5	1.27	1.66	28.1	0.81
−2.5	−2.5	1.38	1.56	6.67	1.27
0.6	−0.1	0.86	2.27	1.04	2.29
0.6	−0.2	1.10	2.02	1.04	2.32
0.6	−0.5	1.27	2.02	1.04	2.29
−2.5	0.5	1.55	1.42	6.67	1.27
−2.5	−0.1	0.86	2.27	6.67	1.27

Note: Numbers in columns 3–6 give the ratio of the factor efficiency indices between the 1990s and 1970s.

Results for France are somewhat different from those for the US (see Table 9.4). Note especially that we observe a very different evolution of skill intensities in manufacturing. This pattern can be generated by the production model under two alternative technological assumptions, implying very different efficiency trends. Under the assumption that elasticities of substitution in manufacturing exceed one, SBTP in manufacturing emerges. For low elasticities of substitution the observed trends could in principle be consistent with a very strong increase in the efficiency of the low skilled. In both cases, the result would have been a reduction in the demand for low-skilled labour. There are areas in the parameter space (especially for ρ around 0.6 and ν around −0.2,−0.5) which allow us to interpret the observed evolution of sectoral aggregates, wages and unemployment as being consistent with SBTP in favour of high-skilled workers. Finally, also in the French data set, an extensive search over the entire feasible parameter space shows that the sectoral patterns could not be explained from observed output price movements together with the assumption of neutral technical progress.

The results in this section indicate that, despite close similarities in aggregate price and output movements in both countries, the production structure in both regions has developed in quite different directions. Thus, it is possible that the two different patterns for relative wages may involve strong sector composition effects whereby low-skill intensive manufacturing has survived in the US but not in France where skill intensive manufacturing may instead have grown.

A more disaggregated analysis, that is, at the two-digit level, would therefore be an interesting extension of this work.

4.3 Calibration of Preference Parameters

In order to capture the trend increase in services over the last decades we assume CES Stone–Geary utility function (see equation 9.5). Besides selecting parameters for the elasticity of substitution and share parameters, we must select two additional constants to determine specific income elasticities for commodities and services. Selecting the corresponding parameters is, in principle, less problematic than selecting production parameters because the composition of consumption (goods and services) of different household types is, in principle, observable from household income and expenditure surveys. For the model to generate an increasing/falling service/commodity share in consumption expenditure with rising income, the parameter m_b should be positive and s_b should be negative. The value we have chosen for m_b is 0.24 and the value for s_b is –0.16. These values together with an elasticity of substitution of 0.8 allow us to replicate both the time series and the cross sectional consumption patterns.

5 SIMULATION RESULTS

The simulation experiments are calibrated in the model to describe the developments in France over the period 1975–94. The first experiments aim at exploring the hypotheses (*i*) that a large elasticity of substitution in manufacturing and a small elasticity of substitution are important for generating a large increase in wage inequality when wages are flexible, and (*ii*) that a large elasticity of substitution in manufacturing is needed to generate large unemployment when the relative wage is rigid. We also do two types of policy experiments. The first type relates to a large institutional change. Hence, we explore the development of wages, sector mix, commodity prices and factor intensities in France, should wages in France have been entirely market determined. The second type of experiment explores secondary effects of mitigating the unemployment problem by means of taxation. The government budget is balanced in these experiments. The first experiment of this type relates to commodity taxation and the other relates to changes in the degree of progressivity of the income tax. All experiments are carried out under two different assumptions on the combination of elasticities of substitution in the two sectors. The first combination is when the elasticity of substitution in manufacturing is 2.5 and in services 0.833. This is our main case. The second is when they are both 0.67. Our baseline simulation is shown in the Appendix.

General equilibrium effects

5.1 Productivity Increase under Alternative Elasticities

Table 9.5 shows the change in the relative wage and the increase in unemployment, relative to the base case, for different combinations of elasticities of substitution. The shock is in all cases a percentage point increase in the efficiency parameter on skilled labour in manufacturing.

Table 9.5 Productivity shock to skilled labour in manufacturing (percentage deviation from base case)

		1974	1975	1985	1990	1994
$\rho = 0.6, v = -0.5$	relative wage	0.00	1.08	9.00	10.43	10.20
	utility of unskilled	0.00	−0.14	−1.93	−2.51	−2.59
$\rho = 0.6, v = 0.6$	relative wage	0.00	0.01	0.04	0.03	0.01
	utility of unskilled	0.00	0.01	0.11	0.17	0.21
$\rho = 0.1, v = 0.6$	relative wage	0.00	0.00	−0.04	−0.06	−0.06
	utility of unskilled	0.00	0.02	0.21	0.26	0.26
$\rho = 0.1, v = 0.6$	unemployment	0.00	−0.07	−0.55	−0.97	−1.60
$\rho = 0.6, v = 0.6$	unemployment	0.00	1.53	0.99	0.61	0.21
$\rho = 0.6, v = -0.5$	unemployment	0.00	1.53	0.99	0.61	0.21

The upper three entries in Table 9.5 shows that the relative wage increases the most when the elasticity of substitution is large in manufacturing and low in services. They also show that the utility (real wage) of the unskilled decreases when the elasticity of substitution is large in manufacturing and low in services. Indeed, for the two other elasticity constellations, an increase in the efficiency of high-skilled workers in manufacturing does not lead to significant changes in relative wages and is even associated with an increase in the real wage of low-skilled workers. In these cases the marginal product of low-skilled workers increases as a result of efficiency improvements of the high skilled as would generally be expected from production theory. The lower three entries show that unemployment increases more when the elasticity of substitution is high in manufacturing than if it is low. An interesting feature of these results is that the size of the elasticity of substitution in services does not influence the effect on unemployment. This is the case because, unlike in the flexible wage case, relative wages do not change and therefore the optimal factor ratios in services are unaffected irrespective of the elasticity of substitution. These results illustrate in particular our theoretical point, namely, that SBTP will only have significant labour market consequences in an environment characterized by sufficient sectoral heterogeneity. Also the direction of the effect is *a priori* undetermined.

5.2   The Effects of Flexible Wages in France

Tables 9.6 and 9.7 are the result of the first type of experiment, that is, entirely market-determined wages. The results are shown as percentage deviations from the calibrated cases. The two calibrated cases differ with respect to the efficiency factors and elasticities of substitution. Table 9.6 contains the results for different elasticities of substitution while Table 9.7 illustrates the effects in the low elasticity case.

Table 9.6   Flexible wages in France (percentage deviation from base case,
$\rho = 0.6$, $v = -0.2$)

	1975	1985	1990	1994
Relative wage	0.97	7.88	9.01	8.73
Skilled wage	0.97	7.88	9.01	8.73
Unskilled wage	0.00	0.00	0.00	0.00
Net relative wage	0.97	7.88	9.01	8.73
Unskilled unemployment	−100.00	−100.00	−100.00	−100.00
Utility unemployment	0.09	−0.31	−0.77	−0.98
Utility unskilled	−0.09	−1.39	−1.86	−1.96
Utility skilled	0.80	5.68	6.17	5.80
Man. productivity	0.14	0.88	0.84	0.70
Serv. productivity	0.75	4.74	4.86	4.38
Factor intensity man.	−2.40	−17.27	−19.40	−18.87
Factor intensity serv.	−0.81	−6.12	−6.94	−6.73
Price man.	0.64	5.99	7.28	7.35
Price serv.	0.55	4.30	4.86	4.67
Rel. commodity price	0.09	1.62	2.31	2.56
Unskilled labour man.	1.75	16.66	20.20	20.22
Skilled labour man.	−0.69	−3.49	−3.12	−2.47
Unskilled labour serv.	1.21	8.48	9.09	8.42
Skilled labour serv.	0.39	1.83	1.52	1.12
Lumpsum tax (absolute)	0.00	−0.04	−0.05	−0.05

As could be expected, wage differences would increase and the utility of unskilled workers would decrease. The production of both commodities would increase, much more for services than for manufacturing. Hence, there would be a clear efficiency gain but at the price of a loss of equity. Considering the stylized facts, three other interesting empirical features emerge from these experiments. First, with differences in elasticity of substitution, the skill intensity would decrease significantly more in manufacturing than in services, while in the second case the relative change in factor intensity would be the same in the two sectors. In the first case the French economy would move more closely to US factor proportions. A second observation is that, increasing wage flexibility has little effect on relative sector output and price developments. This is again consistent with the empirical observations in the stylized facts. The third observation is that relative wages of skilled workers would increase strongly, which again resembles the US experience.

Table 9.7   Flexible wages in France (percentage deviation from base case,
$\rho = -0.5, v = -0.5$)

	1975	1985	1990	1994
Relative wage	1.65	11.23	13.12	13.88
Skilled wage	1.65	11.23	13.12	13.88
Unskilled wage	0.00	0.00	0.00	0.00
Net relative wage	1.65	11.23	13.12	13.88
Unskilled unemployment	−100.00	−100.00	−100.00	−100.00
Utility unemployment	−0.49	−3.26	−3.82	−4.07
Utility unskilled	−0.61	−3.97	−4.62	−4.90
Utility skilled	1.03	6.37	7.32	7.71
Man. productivity	0.10	0.44	0.35	0.24
Serv. productivity	0.63	3.74	4.25	4.45
Factor intensity man.	−1.09	−6.85	−7.89	−8.30
Factor intensity serv.	−1.09	−6.85	−7.89	−8.30
Price man.	1.09	8.65	10.72	11.80
Price serv.	0.93	6.12	7.05	7.39
Rel. commodity price	0.15	2.39	3.43	4.10
Unskilled labour man.	0.83	6.15	7.40	7.97
Skilled labour man.	−0.27	−1.12	−1.07	−0.99
Unskilled labour serv.	1.25	7.92	9.10	9.54
Skilled labour serv.	0.15	0.53	0.49	0.45

The relative wage response is, however, larger with low elasticities of substitution. This suggests that one should use a lower elasticity of substitution in services in the first case in order to produce a strong resemblance between the two economies. These experiments thus show that introducing relative wage flexibility in France could lead to sector patterns which resemble those of the US.

5.3 Taxation as a Means to Reduce Unemployment

(a) Commodity taxation

Tables 9.8 and 9.9 show the results of a reduction of the unemployment rate by one percentage point by means of commodity taxation. The main case is shown in Table 9.8.

Table 9.8 Commodity taxation (percentage deviation from base case, $\rho = 0.6$, $v = -0.2$)

	1975	1985	1990	1994
Relative wage	0.00	0.00	0.00	0.00
Skilled wage	0.00	0.00	0.00	0.00
Unskilled wage	0.00	0.00	0.00	0.00
Net relative wage	0.00	0.00	0.00	0.00
Unskilled unemployment	−3.73	−6.20	−8.57	−11.68
Utility unemployment	−0.09	−0.65	−0.74	−0.75
Utility unskilled	−0.01	−0.05	−0.06	−0.05
Utility skilled	0.06	0.47	0.55	0.58
Man. productivity	−0.14	−1.55	−2.36	−3.09
Serv. productivity	0.12	1.01	1.30	1.48
Factor intensity man.	0.00	0.00	0.00	0.00
Factor intensity serv.	0.00	0.00	0.00	0.00
Price man.	0.00	0.00	0.00	0.00
Price serv.	0.00	0.00	0.00	0.00
Rel. commodity price	0.00	0.00	0.00	0.00
Unskilled lab. man.	−0.14	−1.55	−2.36	−3.09
Skilled labour man.	−0.14	−1.55	−2.36	−3.09
Unskilled labour serv.	0.12	1.01	1.30	1.48
Skilled labour serv.	0.12	1.01	1.30	1.48
Tax man.	0.00	0.05	0.07	0.09
Tax serv.	0.00	−0.02	−0.03	−0.03

The commodity taxes do nothing to relative wages and consequently do not change the skill intensity in the two sectors. However, they change the demand and production towards more services and less manufacturing. The consumer price of services will decrease and that of manufacturing will increase. This turns out to increase the utility of the skilled and decrease it for the unskilled. The reason for the different outcomes for the two groups is that the skilled workers have a larger share of their budgets allocated to services than do the unskilled workers.

Table 9.9   Commodity taxation (percentage deviation from base case,
*   ρ = –0.5, v = –0.5)*

	1975	1985	1990	1994
Relative wage	0.00	0.00	0.00	0.00
Skilled wage	0.00	0.00	0.00	0.00
Unskilled wage	0.00	0.00	0.00	0.00
Net relative wage	0.00	0.00	0.00	0.00
Unskilled unemployment	–4.46	–7.74	–9.81	–11.68
Utility unemployment	–0.09	–0.58	–0.69	–0.75
Utility unskilled	–0.01	–0.05	–0.05	–0.05
Utility skilled	0.06	0.43	0.52	0.58
Man. productivity	–0.14	–1.75	–2.52	–3.09
Serv. productivity	0.12	0.99	1.28	1.48
Factor intensity man.	0.00	0.00	0.00	0.00
Factor intensity serv.	0.00	0.00	0.00	0.00
Price man.	0.00	0.00	0.00	0.00
Price serv.	0.00	0.00	0.00	0.00
Rel. commodity price	0.00	0.00	0.00	0.00
Unskilled labour man.	–0.14	–1.75	–2.52	–3.09
Skilled labour man.	–0.14	–1.75	–2.52	–3.09
Unskilled labour serv.	0.12	0.99	1.28	1.48
Skilled labour serv.	0.12	0.99	1.28	1.48
Tax man.	0.00	0.05	0.07	0.09
Tax serv.	0.00	–0.02	–0.03	–0.03
Lumpsum	0.00	0.03	0.04	0.05

Table 9.9 shows the results of commodity taxation with the low elasticities of substitution. The results of the commodity tax experiment are practically identical under the two parameterizations. Thus the policy conclusions one can draw are fairly robust with respect to technological assumptions.

(b) Progressive income tax/wage subsidy for low skilled
Tables 9.10 and 9.11 show the simulation results of a reduction of the unemployment by means of changes in the progressivity in the income tax. The main case is in Table 9.10.

This policy works through changing the relative cost to firms of employing different types of workers. The assumed relation between after tax wages keeps the ratio of high-skill worker utility to unskilled worker utility almost unaffected. Hence, the policy increases the pre tax wage of the skilled workers. That decreases the skill intensity in both sectors, more in the manufacturing sector

Table 9.10 Income taxation (percentage deviation from base case, ρ = 0.6,
        ν = –0.2)

	1975	1985	1990	1994
Relative wage	0.04	0.49	0.78	1.03
Skilled wage	0.04	0.49	0.78	1.03
Unskilled wage	0.00	0.00	0.00	0.00
Net relative wage	0.00	0.00	0.00	0.00
Unskilled unemployment	–3.73	–6.20	–8.57	–11.68
Utility unemployment	0.02	0.18	0.26	0.32
Utility unskilled	0.02	0.18	0.26	0.32
Utility skilled	0.02	0.18	0.26	0.32
Man. productivity	0.01	0.05	0.07	0.08
Serv. productivity	0.03	0.30	0.43	0.52
Factor intensity man.	–0.09	–1.22	–1.93	–2.53
Factor intensity serv.	–0.03	–0.41	–0.65	–0.85
Price man.	0.02	0.38	0.64	0.88
Price serv.	0.02	0.27	0.43	0.56
Rel. commodity price	0.00	0.11	0.21	0.32
Unskilled labour man.	0.07	1.02	1.69	2.29
Skilled labour man.	–0.03	–0.22	–0.27	–0.29
Unskilled labour serv.	0.05	0.53	0.78	0.99
Skilled labour serv.	0.01	0.12	0.13	0.13
Tax unskilled	0.00	0.00	–0.01	–0.01
Tax skilled	0.00	0.00	0.00	0.00

than in the service sector since the elasticity of substitution is larger in the former than in the latter. Since manufacturing is the skill-intensive production, the unit cost and the price of manufacturing increase more than the price of services. This leads to a shift in the demand towards services and some high-skill labour would be reallocated from manufacturing to the service sector. The policy would represent a Pareto improvement in this model where the increase in the marginal income tax has no disincentive effects on labour supply. The reason why unskilled workers gain from the policy is that they get increased net wages and the skilled workers gain more from the changes in commodity prices than they lose on increased income tax. The tax change partially corrects the distortion that comes from the limited wage dispersion, while the limited wage dispersion keeps the utility ratios virtually unchanged. These change only as a result of differences in budget shares but since relative prices change only marginally, utilities of different groups change in a similar fashion.

Table 9.11   Income taxation (percentage deviation from base case, ρ =
*   −0.5, v = −0.5)*

	1975	1985	1990	1994
Relative wage	0.07	0.86	1.26	1.59
Skilled wage	0.07	0.86	1.26	1.59
Unskilled wage	0.00	0.00	0.00	0.00
Net relative wage	0.00	0.00	0.00	0.00
Unskilled unemployment	−4.46	−7.74	−9.81	−11.68
Utility unemployment	0.02	0.17	0.25	0.31
Utility unskilled	0.02	0.18	0.25	0.32
Utility skilled	0.02	0.18	0.26	0.33
Man. productivity	0.00	0.04	0.04	0.03
Serv. productivity	0.03	0.30	0.43	0.54
Factor intensity man.	−0.05	−0.57	−0.83	−1.05
Factor intensity serv.	−0.05	−0.57	−0.83	−1.05
Price man.	0.05	0.66	1.04	1.36
Price serv.	0.04	0.47	0.69	0.86
Rel. commodity price	0.01	0.19	0.35	0.49
Unskilled labour man.	0.04	0.48	0.73	0.93
Skilled labour man.	−0.01	−0.09	−0.11	−0.12
Unskilled labour serv.	0.06	0.61	0.89	1.11
Skilled labour serv.	0.01	0.04	0.05	0.06
Income tax unskilled	0.00	−0.01	−0.01	−0.01
Income tax skilled	0.00	0.00	0.00	0.00

In the case with the low elasticities of substitution the change in the progressivity of the income tax has to be somewhat larger than in the former case.
That results in a larger increase in the relative price of manufacturing and
somewhat larger increase in the service production and smaller increase in the
production of manufacturing than in the former case. The skill intensity of manufacturing will decrease less and that in services more than in the former case.
The reallocation of high-skill labour from manufacturing to services will be
somewhat smaller than in the former case. Utilities will change in a somewhat
more uneven fashion than in the former case. The tax change is more favourable
to skilled labour in this case than in the former.

6   CONCLUDING COMMENTS

The analysis in this chapter shows the following results. First, it seems to be
the case that many sector trends, both in the US and in Europe, can be replicated

if one assumes SBTP both in the manufacturing and the service sector. Under the hypothesis of sufficient sectoral heterogeneity, quite drastic labour market outcomes can emerge from SBTP. Thus, from a sectoral perspective, SBTP and differences in the elasticity of substitution, between manufacturing and services, seems to be a plausible explanation for both the increased wage dispersion between skill groups in the US and, together with limited wage dispersion, to the increased unemployment in France. The second conclusion that can be drawn from this exercise is that taxation may be used as a means of reducing unemployment. In a rigid labour market, such tax policies may, in fact, lead to Pareto improvements.

Though the tax policy results are fairly robust to technological parameters, they nevertheless rest on several simplifying assumptions concerning wage behaviour, participation and hours decisions of skilled and unskilled workers. In our analysis the relation between the after-tax wages of skilled and unskilled workers is exogenously fixed. This is a reasonable assumption given the observed relative wage rigidity in Europe and our limited interest in tracing out the macroeconomic consequences of this labour market friction. Nevertheless, this leaves unexplained the economic mechanisms that have generated this outcome.

On the labour market for skilled workers, wages are assumed to adjust so that there is no unemployment among skilled workers. Given our approach on marketable skills as the basis for the distinction between skilled and unskilled workers, such an assumption seems somewhat natural since, if a skilled worker cannot get employment at the going rate, one may question whether or not the worker in fact is skilled. Such an argument disregards several potential labour market features, such as efficiency wage considerations, see for example, Shapiro and Stiglitz (1984) and Agénor and Aizenman (1997), and the possibility that also the labour market for skilled workers is characterized by considerable cartelization. However, we think that trade unions are much more important in the wage setting for unskilled workers than for skilled workers but, given that there is some evidence for increased unemployment among skilled workers, this issue deserves some additional attention. Notice, however, the observation of unemployment within the group of high-skilled workers (especially if it is defined as the upper 50th percentile) could be due to relative wage rigidity within this group. In this case, the same mechanisms as explored in the chapter could generate this observation among the high skilled.

Finally, labour supply in the model is exogenous. This implies that neither hours worked nor labour-market participation can be captured in the analysis. Important differences between the US with its more market-determined wages, and European countries with more institutionalized wage setting, could therefore not be explored. An example of such a difference is the development of total employment which has increased significantly in the US the last two or three decades and, in fact, decreased slightly in many European countries over the same period. Differences in the development of relative wages can probably not be excluded as main contributors to the difference in employment growth between the US and Europe. Extending our analysis in this direction may reveal so far unexplored effects of wage compression. Adding these features to the model would most certainly generate more interesting tax policy responses.

A lack of sufficiently long time series extending back to the early 1960s has precluded an analysis of longer term sectoral employment, price and output trends in this chapter. It would certainly be interesting to look into the question of whether sectoral developments (changes in sectoral composition and/or changes in the type of technical progress) may have triggered the break in labour market trends since the 1970s, and contrast this more closely to an explanation which stresses institutional features more strongly. A more disaggregated analysis may be helpful in this respect.[17] After completion of the necessary data work, such an exercise could be attempted.

Our analysis has so far only touched the issue to what extent trade effects may have played a role. The role of trade can only satisfactorily be dealt with by linking regional models for the EU, the US and emerging economies together because, only in this way, is it possible to trace the output and price effects of increased trade and competition.

NOTES

1. There has also been a significant increase in wage inequality within skill groups in the US.
2. See also Lawrence and Krugman (1994).
3. Freeman (1995) reports that standard factor content analysis leads to that 10–20 per cent of the fall in demand for unskilled labour.
4. It is theoretically uncontroversial that skill-biased technological development may increase wage dispersion, where wages are market determined, and increase unemployment, where wages are not allowed to adjust fully. However, the empirical relevance is not undisputed. Nickell and Bell (1995) as well as Card, Kramartz and Lemieux (1999) argue that the development of the unemployment or employment in different skill groups seems to contradict the hypothesis of skill-biased technological development. Hence, they note that the development of low-skilled unemployment, relative to that of the skilled, seems not to be significantly different in countries where wage dispersion has not increased and where it has increased, as might have been expected, there should have been skill-biased technological development. However, the generality of the analysis and the quality of data are potential problems with this counter evidence.
5. No Stone–Geary components in the utility function.
6. The production function in the service sector then is $S = 2L_{us}^{\frac{1}{2}}L_{hs}^{\frac{1}{2}}$. The cost function in the service sector then is $c_s = \sqrt{(w*S)}$.
7. We have used *Mathematica* to derive explicit solutions for the derivatives.
8. Note that in (9.18), $w = w(q,\rho)$.
9. The data refers to the period 1982–95.
10. In fact we can look at any point of the wage distribution and we could also look at more than two categories.
11. Another possible interpretation is that manufacturing industries have to pay a premium relative to service industries owing to differences in work conditions.

12. At the outset it should also be mentioned that we are making a number of simplifying assumptions. In particular, we are not distinguishing between the private and the public sector, that is, we implicitly assume that the government produces manufacturing commodities and services in the same mix and with the same technology as the private sector. It is, of course, an obvious next step to distinguish between market and non-market services.
13. In principle, we observe more but since we only want to fit the trend, only two data points can be used.
14. Theoretically, the elasticity of substitution can go from zero to infinity. Thus, theory does certainly not tightly restrict the parameter space. There is, however, an extensive debate on the appropriate size of the elasticity of substitution. Hamermesh (1993) reports estimates of around 3 for manufacturing. Woods (1995), on the other hand, believes that this estimate, which is based on aggregate data is biased upwards because it also captures product substitution within sectors, and he himself reports results which are around 0.5. The sensitivity analysis that is conducted below will be roughly confined within this range.
15. Before jumping to conclusions about the usefulness of calibration versus econometric estimation, one should clearly keep in mind that econometric estimation is confronted with exactly the same identification problem. Generally this problem is unnoticed because in econometric estimation one makes some (seemingly innocent) *a priori* choices on the functional form of the technology trend.
16. This may be a composition effect. There may have been a relative increase of low-tech manufacturing in the US.
17. As a first step, one could envisage a disaggregation of services into market and non-market services and manufacturing into high and low-tech sectors.
18. Looking at some more decimals on the unemployment figures, we find that it is not monotonic. It has a peak at 1990. The critical factor that gives rise to this pattern of unemployment probably is the relative size of sectors.

REFERENCES

Agénor P.R. and J. Aizenman (1997), 'Technological Change, Relative Wages, and Unemployment', *European Economic Review*, **41**: 187–205.
Bentolila, S. and G. Bertola (1990), 'Firing Costs and Labor Demand: How Bad is Eurosclerosis', *Review of Economic Studies*, **57**(3): 381–402.
Card, D., F. Kramartz and T. Lemieux (1999), 'Changes in the Structure of Wages and Employment: A Comparison of the United States, Canada and France', *Canadian Journal of Economics*, **32**:843–77.
Freeman, R. (1995), 'Are Your Wages Set in Beijing?', *Journal of Economic Perspectives*, **9**(3), 15–32.
Gottschalk, P. (1997), 'Inequality, Income Growth, and Mobility: The Basic Facts', *Journal of Economic Perspectives*, **11**(2): 21–40.
Gregg, P. and A. Manning (1997), 'Skill-biased Change, Unemployment and Wage Inequality', *European Economic Review* **41**: 1147–73.
Hamermesh, D. (1993), *Labour Demand*, Princeton, NJ: Princeton University Press.
Juhn, C., K.M. Murphy and B. Pierce (1993), 'Wage Inequality and the Rise in Returns to Skill', *Journal of Political Economy*, **101**(3): 410–42.
Krugman, P. (1995), 'Technology, Trade, and Factor Prices', *NBER Working Paper*, 5355.
Lawrence, R. and P. Krugman (1994), 'Trade, Jobs and Wages', *Scientific American*, April.
Leamer, E.E. (1996), 'In Search of Stolper–Samuelson Effects on US Wages', *NBER Working Paper*, 5427.
Lindbeck, A. (1996), 'The West European Employment Problem', *Weltwirtschaftliches Archiv*, **132**(4): 609–37.

Nickell, S. (1997), 'Unemployment and Labor Market Rigidities: Europe versus North America', *Journal of Economic Perspectives*, **11**(3): Summer.

Nickell, S. and B. Bell (1995), 'The Collapse in Demand for Unskilled and Unemployment in the OECD', *Oxford Review of Economic Policy*, **11**: 40–62.

Shapiro, C. and J.E. Stiglitz (1984), 'Unemployment as a Worker Discipline Device', *American Economic Review*, **74**: 433–49.

Siebert, H. (1997),' Labor Market Rigidities: At the Root of Unemployment in Europe', *Journal of Economic Perspectives*, **9**(3): Summer.

Sørensen, P.B. (1997), 'Public Finance Solutions to the European Unemployment Problem?', *Economic Policy*, October: 223–64.

Woods, A. (1995), 'How Trade Hurt Unskilled Workers', *Journal of Economic Perspectives*, **9**(3): Summer.

APPENDIX

Table A9.1 illustrates our baseline simulation for France in the main case. Observations from the 1970s and the 1990s were used to calibrate the model. Table A9.1 describes the paths from the initial period to the last period of

Table A9.1   Base case, absolute numbers

	1975	1985	1990	1994
Relative wage	1.45	1.45	1.45	1.45
Skilled wage	1.22	1.65	1.95	2.25
Unskilled wage	0.84	1.14	1.35	1.55
Net relative wage	1.45	1.45	1.45	1.45
Unskilled unemployment	0.01	0.09	0.09	0.09
Utility unemployment	0.06	0.08	0.09	0.10
Utility unskilled	0.09	0.11	0.13	0.14
Utility skilled	0.13	0.17	0.19	0.21
Man. productivity	0.34	0.37	0.39	0.41
Serv. productivity	0.68	0.87	0.99	1.11
Factor intensity man.	1.33	2.40	3.22	4.08
Factor intensity serv.	0.89	0.85	0.84	0.82
Price man.	1.00	1.00	1.00	1.00
Price serv.	1.01	1.12	1.20	1.28
Rel. commodity price	0.99	0.89	0.83	0.78
Unskilled labour man.	0.14	0.07	0.05	0.04
Skilled labour man.	0.18	0.17	0.16	0.16
Unskilled labour serv.	0.36	0.38	0.40	0.42
Skilled labour serv.	0.32	0.33	0.34	0.34

relative wages between high-skill and low-skill workers, commodity prices of manufacturing and services, output of manufacturing and services, utility by the different types of workers, employment patterns of skilled and unskilled workers in the two industries and unemployment.

The development of wages, output, commodity prices and employment are monotonic in the sense that they either increase from one period to another, or decrease from one period to another. Hence, (*i*) wages of both the unskilled and the skilled workers increase over time, more strongly for the skilled workers; (*ii*) the production of both manufacturing and services increase over time, services much more strongly; (*iii*) the commodity price of services increases over time while the price of manufacturing remains constant; (*iv*) the labour usage in the manufacturing sector decrease over time, more for unskilled labour; (*v*) the labour usage in the service sector increases over time, more for unskilled labour; and (*vi*) unemployment rises from the very low 1 per cent to the 9 per cent level.[18]

Index